The Amazing Adventures of
THE ESCAPIST™
VOLUME 2

Based on *The Amazing Adventures of Kavalier*
& Clay by Michael Chabon

Wraparound Cover Art by Matt Kindt

DARK HORSE BOOKS™

Editor
DIANA SCHUTZ

Editorial Assistant
KATIE MOODY

Book Design
AMY ARENDTS

Digital Production
DAN JACKSON
& RICH POWERS

Publisher
MIKE RICHARDSON

Master of Ceremonies
MICHAEL CHABON

MICHAEL CHABON PRESENTS THE AMAZING ADVENTURES OF THE ESCAPIST VOLUME 2

This volume collects issues 3 and 4 of the Dark Horse comic-book series *Michael Chabon Presents the Amazing Adventures of the Escapist.*

Published by
Dark Horse Books
A division of Dark Horse Comics, Inc.
10956 SE Main Street
Milwaukie, Oregon 97222

www.darkhorse.com
www.MichaelChabon.com

Representation for Michael Chabon
by Mary Evans, Inc. Literary Agency
and Law Offices of Harris M. Miller II, P.C.

First Edition: November 2004
ISBN: 1-59307-172-8

10 9 8 7 6 5 4 3 2 1

PRINTED IN CANADA

CONTENTS

by Bubbles LaTour

IN 1950, THREE YEARS AFTER WILLIAM GAINES INHERITED Educational Comics from his late father Max, he changed the name of the company to Entertaining Comics and began publishing some of the best comic books in the history of the medium. With titles like *Crime SuspenStories*, *The Vault of Horror*, *Weird Science*, and *Two-Fisted Tales*, among others, EC covered the gamut of popular '50s genres and filled the pages of its comics with many of the brightest artistic stars of the day, including Harvey Kurtzman, Bernie Krigstein, Wally Wood, Jack Davis, Al Williamson, and even Frank Frazetta.

Though the company won the hearts (and dimes) of its readers, its huge sales success provoked an entirely different reaction on the part of its competitors. In 1954, following U.S. Senate investigations into the purported relationship between comic books and juvenile delinquency, comics publishers — with the notable exception of EC publisher Gaines — banded together to create the Comics Code Authority. Ostensibly, the Code was set up as a self-policing (i.e., self-censoring) entity, despite the fact that comics had ultimately been exonerated by the Kefauver Committeee Hearings. However, in reality, the Code spelled the untimely demise of Entertaining Comics, with many of its prohibitions seemingly aimed directly at Gaines's titles and their content. Some comics historians *[Frank Miller and Steve Bissette, for instance — BLT]* have, in fact, argued that the establishment of the Code was nothing more than a cutthroat ploy on the part of the competing publishers to drive the successful Gaines right out of business.

The Escapist story that follows was written and drawn in 1955, just as the formation of the Comics Code Authority forced EC to abandon its horror titles. Looking for material to put in EC's "New Directions" line, Gaines acquired the Escapist license and decided to give costumed heroes a try. Unfortunately, the Code rejected the story because of its "gross anti-American insensitivity" as well as horrific elements unacceptable in the new political climate, including the visible display of the Nazi swastika — the latter a legacy of comics censorship that remains to this very day, especially for printed material sold in Germany and Russia.

Deciding that the superhero genre was perhaps not EC's forte, Gaines surrendered the Escapist license — also shelving his plan to create a character named Swastika Man — and focused his energy on converting one of the company's color comics, the brainchild of Harvey Kurtzman, into a new black-and-white magazine called *Mad*.

"Heil and Fear Well!" is the only EC Escapist story ever written and drawn. It has never been published until now.

HEIL and FEAR WELL

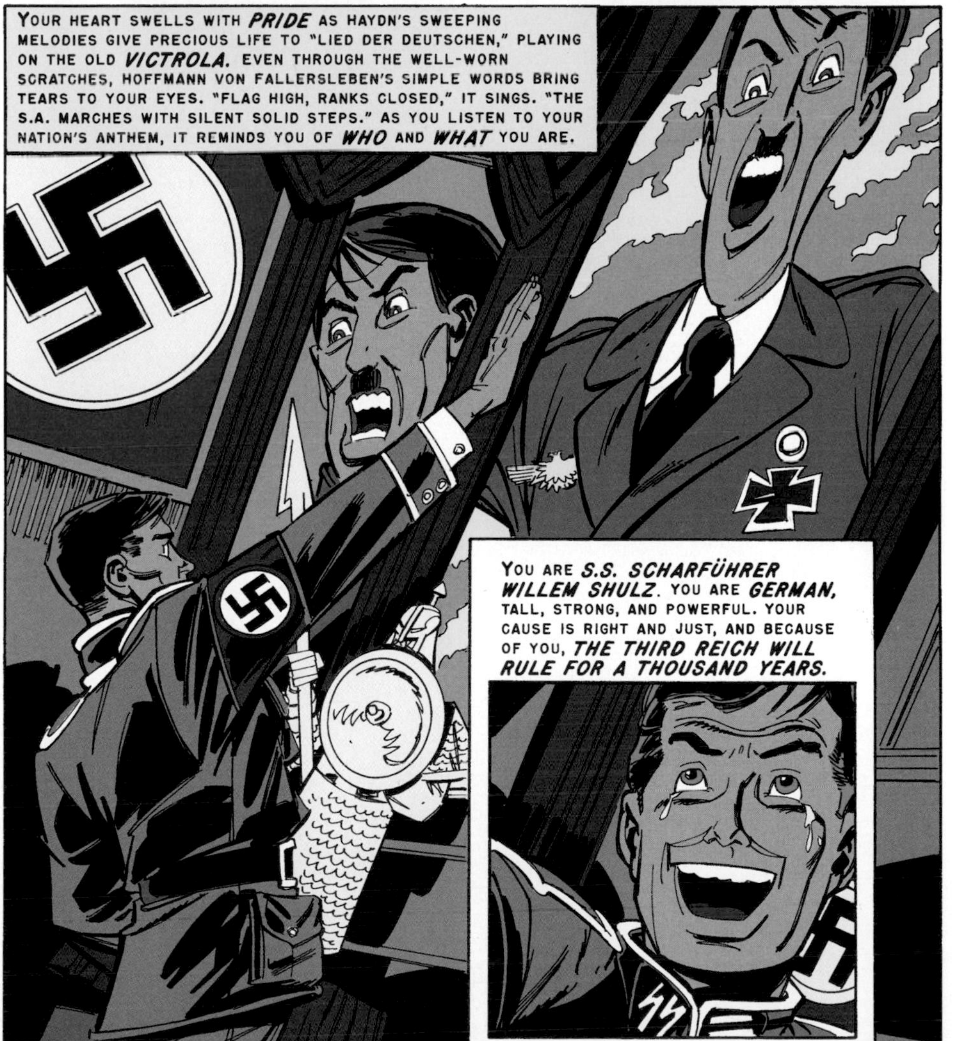
YOUR HEART SWELLS WITH PRIDE AS HAYDN'S SWEEPING MELODIES GIVE PRECIOUS LIFE TO "LIED DER DEUTSCHEN," PLAYING ON THE OLD VICTROLA. EVEN THROUGH THE WELL-WORN SCRATCHES, HOFFMANN VON FALLERSLEBEN'S SIMPLE WORDS BRING TEARS TO YOUR EYES. "FLAG HIGH, RANKS CLOSED," IT SINGS. "THE S.A. MARCHES WITH SILENT SOLID STEPS." AS YOU LISTEN TO YOUR NATION'S ANTHEM, IT REMINDS YOU OF WHO AND WHAT YOU ARE.
YOU ARE S.S. SCHARFÜHRER WILLEM SHULZ. YOU ARE GERMAN, TALL, STRONG, AND POWERFUL. YOUR CAUSE IS RIGHT AND JUST, AND BECAUSE OF YOU, THE THIRD REICH WILL RULE FOR A THOUSAND YEARS.

YOU HAVE ***POWER*** IN YOUR HANDS, WILLEM. POWER TO ***CRUSH*** YOUR ENEMIES. POWER TO ***DESTROY*** ANY WHO--

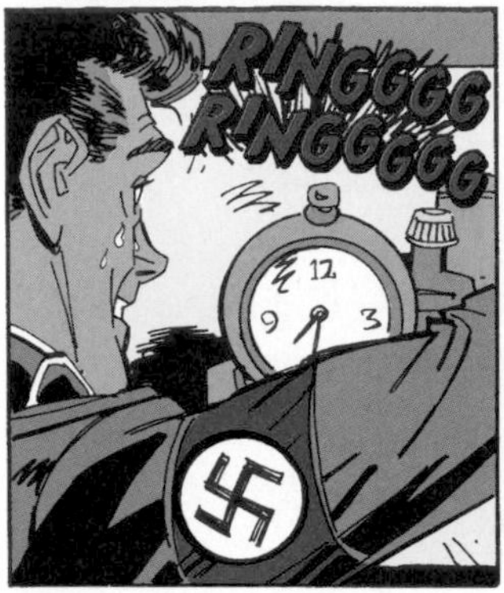
RINGGGG
RINGGGGGG

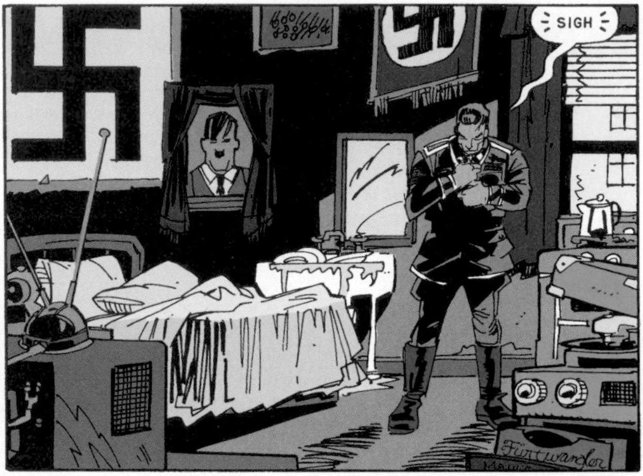
SIGH

THOSE NEAR-FORGOTTEN CHORDS ARE NOW ONLY MEMORIES OF A TIME ***TEN YEARS PAST,*** WHEN YOUR UNIFORM GAVE YOU ***POWER*** AND YOUR COUNTRY BROUGHT YOU ***JOY*** AND ***HOPE.***

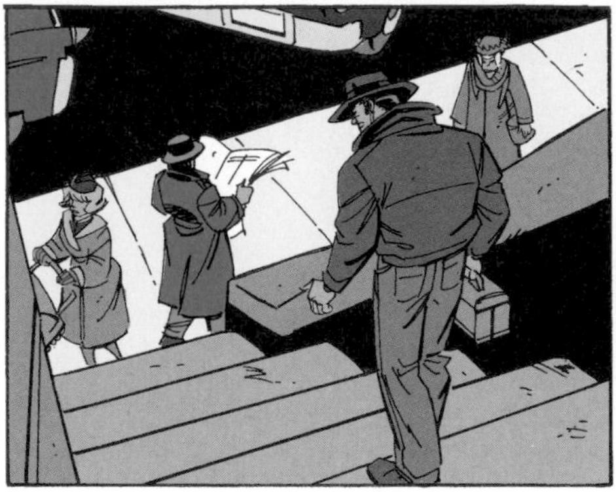

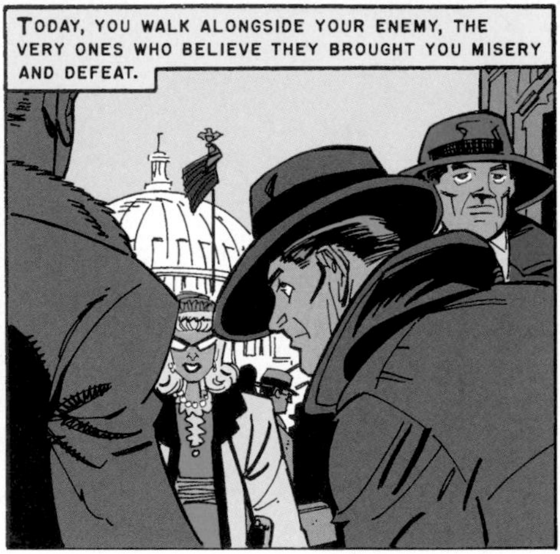
TODAY, YOU WALK ALONGSIDE YOUR ENEMY, THE VERY ONES WHO BELIEVE THEY BROUGHT YOU MISERY AND DEFEAT.

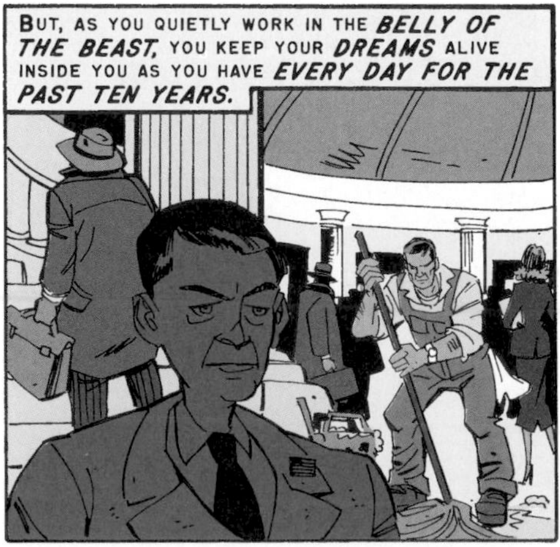
BUT, AS YOU QUIETLY WORK IN THE BELLY OF THE BEAST, YOU KEEP YOUR DREAMS ALIVE INSIDE YOU AS YOU HAVE EVERY DAY FOR THE PAST TEN YEARS.

THOSE GLORIOUS DAYS ROLL THROUGH YOUR THOUGHTS AS THOUGH STILL ALIVE, BUT THEY ALSO ***DISTRACT*** YOU FROM YOUR DUTIES TODAY.

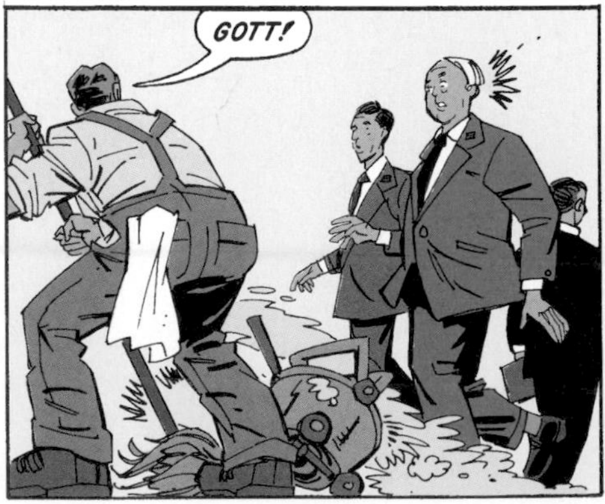
GOTT!

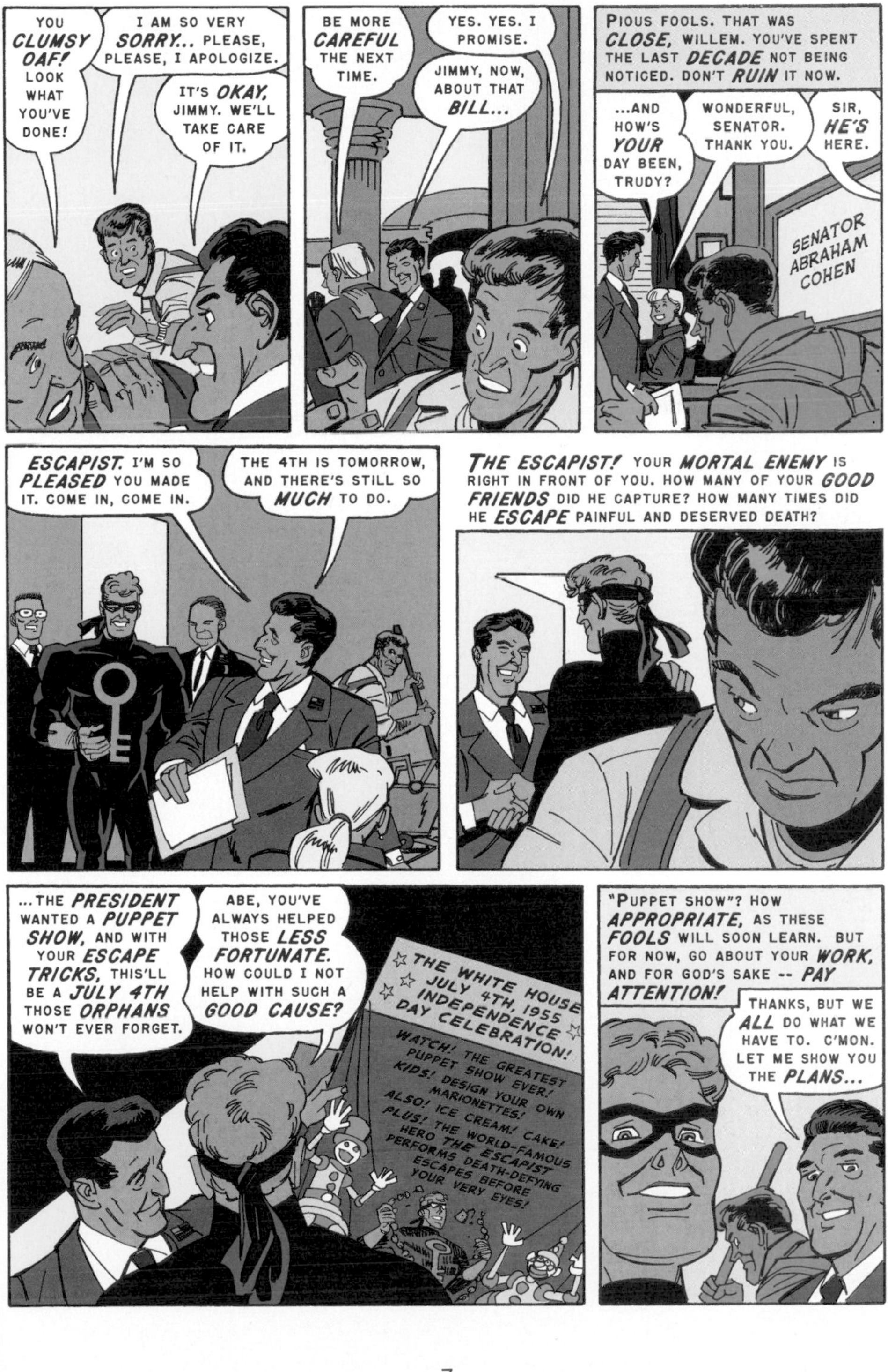

YOU CLUMSY OAF! LOOK WHAT YOU'VE DONE!
I AM SO VERY SORRY... PLEASE, PLEASE, I APOLOGIZE.
IT'S OKAY, JIMMY. WE'LL TAKE CARE OF IT.
BE MORE CAREFUL THE NEXT TIME.
YES. YES. I PROMISE.
JIMMY, NOW, ABOUT THAT BILL...
PIOUS FOOLS. THAT WAS CLOSE, WILLEM. YOU'VE SPENT THE LAST DECADE NOT BEING NOTICED. DON'T RUIN IT NOW.
...AND HOW'S YOUR DAY BEEN, TRUDY?
WONDERFUL, SENATOR. THANK YOU.
SIR, HE'S HERE.
SENATOR ABRAHAM COHEN
ESCAPIST. I'M SO PLEASED YOU MADE IT. COME IN, COME IN.
THE 4TH IS TOMORROW, AND THERE'S STILL SO MUCH TO DO.
THE ESCAPIST! YOUR MORTAL ENEMY IS RIGHT IN FRONT OF YOU. HOW MANY OF YOUR GOOD FRIENDS DID HE CAPTURE? HOW MANY TIMES DID HE ESCAPE PAINFUL AND DESERVED DEATH?
...THE PRESIDENT WANTED A PUPPET SHOW, AND WITH YOUR ESCAPE TRICKS, THIS'LL BE A JULY 4TH THOSE ORPHANS WON'T EVER FORGET.
ABE, YOU'VE ALWAYS HELPED THOSE LESS FORTUNATE. HOW COULD I NOT HELP WITH SUCH A GOOD CAUSE?
THE WHITE HOUSE JULY 4TH, 1955 INDEPENDENCE DAY CELEBRATION!
WATCH! THE GREATEST PUPPET SHOW EVER! KIDS! DESIGN YOUR OWN MARIONETTES! ALSO! ICE CREAM! CAKE! PLUS! THE WORLD-FAMOUS HERO THE ESCAPIST PERFORMS DEATH-DEFYING ESCAPES BEFORE YOUR VERY EYES!
"PUPPET SHOW"? HOW APPROPRIATE, AS THESE FOOLS WILL SOON LEARN. BUT FOR NOW, GO ABOUT YOUR WORK, AND FOR GOD'S SAKE -- PAY ATTENTION!
THANKS, BUT WE ALL DO WHAT WE HAVE TO. C'MON. LET ME SHOW YOU THE PLANS...

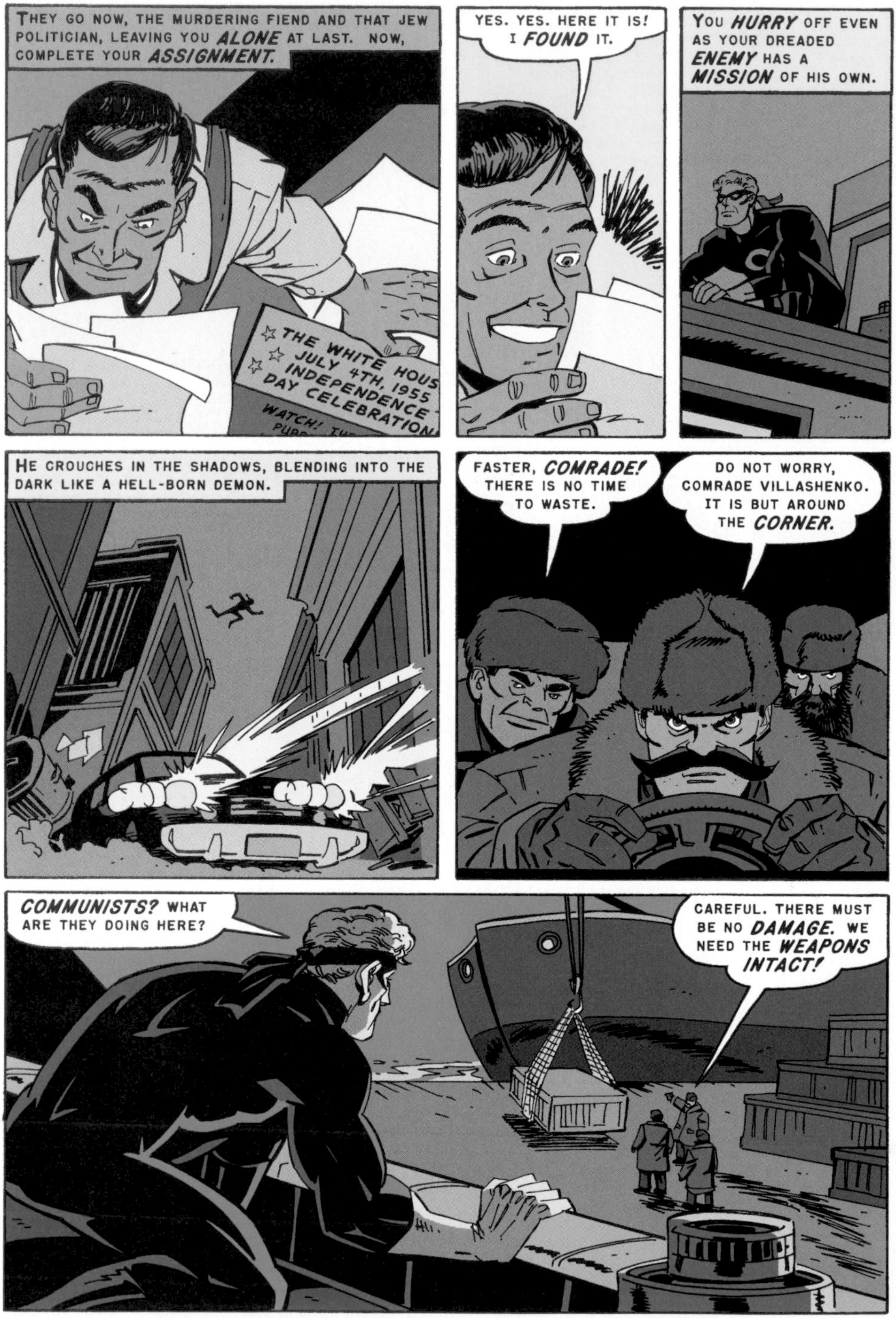
THEY GO NOW, THE MURDERING FIEND AND THAT JEW POLITICIAN, LEAVING YOU ALONE AT LAST. NOW, COMPLETE YOUR ASSIGNMENT.
THE WHITE HOUS
JULY 4TH, 1955
INDEPENDENCE
DAY CELEBRATION
WATCH!
YES. YES. HERE IT IS! I FOUND IT.
YOU HURRY OFF EVEN AS YOUR DREADED ENEMY HAS A MISSION OF HIS OWN.
HE CROUCHES IN THE SHADOWS, BLENDING INTO THE DARK LIKE A HELL-BORN DEMON.
FASTER, COMRADE! THERE IS NO TIME TO WASTE.
DO NOT WORRY, COMRADE VILLASHENKO. IT IS BUT AROUND THE CORNER.
COMMUNISTS? WHAT ARE THEY DOING HERE?
CAREFUL. THERE MUST BE NO DAMAGE. WE NEED THE WEAPONS INTACT!

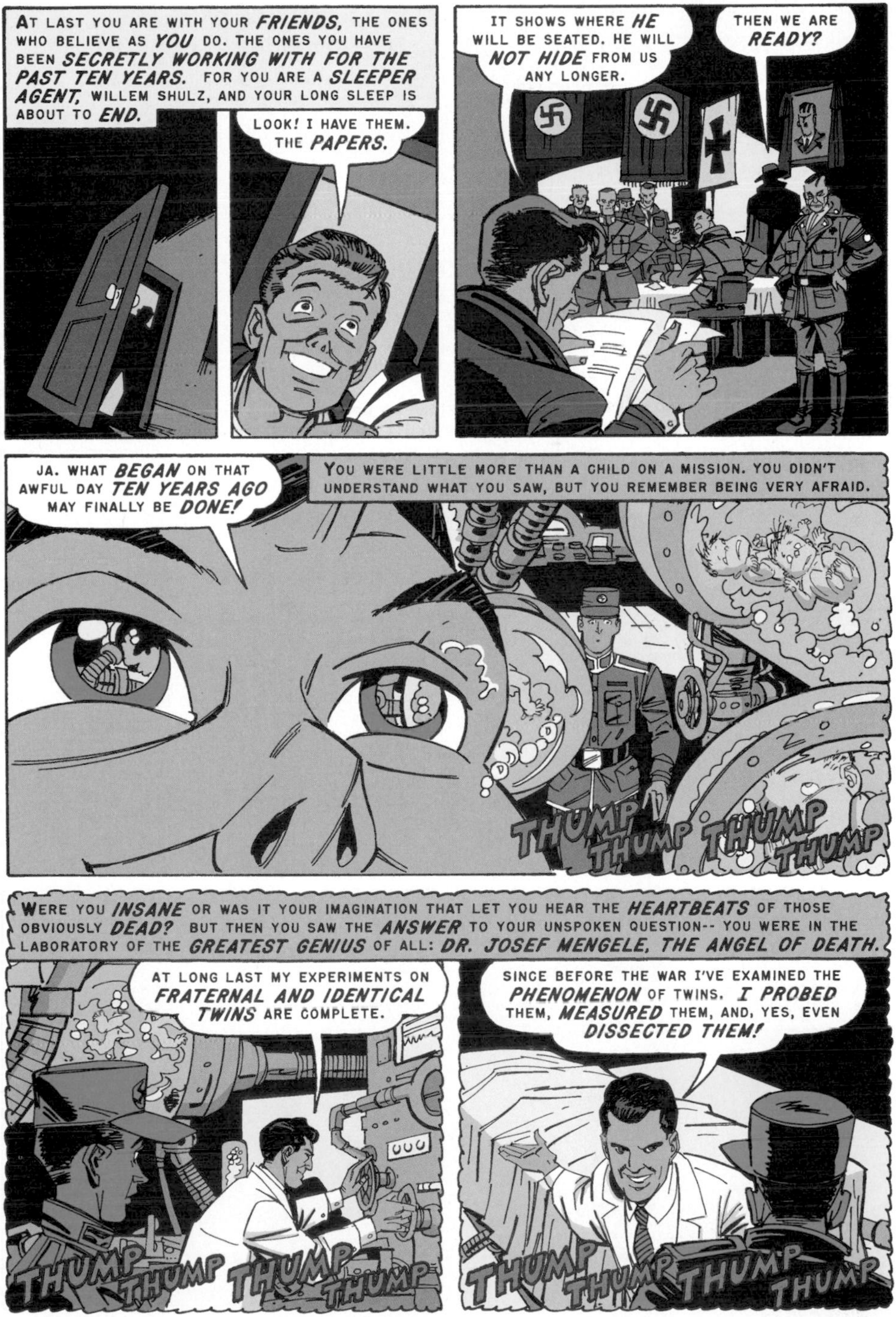
AT LAST YOU ARE WITH YOUR FRIENDS, THE ONES WHO BELIEVE AS YOU DO. THE ONES YOU HAVE BEEN SECRETLY WORKING WITH FOR THE PAST TEN YEARS. FOR YOU ARE A SLEEPER AGENT, WILLEM SHULZ, AND YOUR LONG SLEEP IS ABOUT TO END.
LOOK! I HAVE THEM. THE PAPERS.
IT SHOWS WHERE HE WILL BE SEATED. HE WILL NOT HIDE FROM US ANY LONGER.
THEN WE ARE READY?
JA. WHAT BEGAN ON THAT AWFUL DAY TEN YEARS AGO MAY FINALLY BE DONE!
YOU WERE LITTLE MORE THAN A CHILD ON A MISSION. YOU DIDN'T UNDERSTAND WHAT YOU SAW, BUT YOU REMEMBER BEING VERY AFRAID.
THUMP THUMP THUMP THUMP
WERE YOU INSANE OR WAS IT YOUR IMAGINATION THAT LET YOU HEAR THE HEARTBEATS OF THOSE OBVIOUSLY DEAD? BUT THEN YOU SAW THE ANSWER TO YOUR UNSPOKEN QUESTION-- YOU WERE IN THE LABORATORY OF THE GREATEST GENIUS OF ALL: DR. JOSEF MENGELE, THE ANGEL OF DEATH.
AT LONG LAST MY EXPERIMENTS ON FRATERNAL AND IDENTICAL TWINS ARE COMPLETE.
THUMP THUMP THUMP THUMP
SINCE BEFORE THE WAR I'VE EXAMINED THE PHENOMENON OF TWINS. I PROBED THEM, MEASURED THEM, AND, YES, EVEN DISSECTED THEM!
THUMP THUMP THUMP THUMP

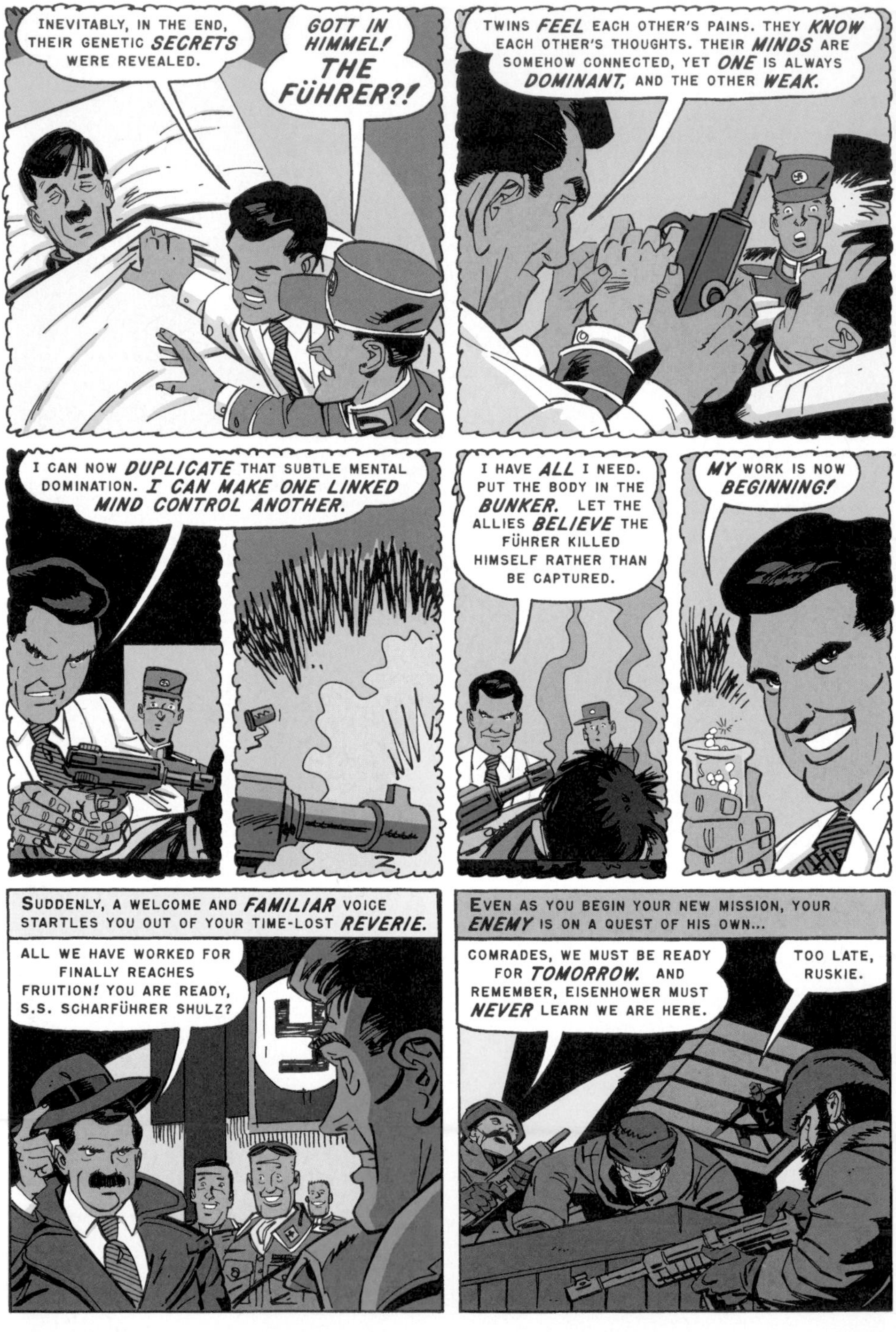
INEVITABLY, IN THE END, THEIR GENETIC SECRETS WERE REVEALED.
GOTT IN HIMMEL! THE FÜHRER?!
TWINS FEEL EACH OTHER'S PAINS. THEY KNOW EACH OTHER'S THOUGHTS. THEIR MINDS ARE SOMEHOW CONNECTED, YET ONE IS ALWAYS DOMINANT, AND THE OTHER WEAK.
I CAN NOW DUPLICATE THAT SUBTLE MENTAL DOMINATION. I CAN MAKE ONE LINKED MIND CONTROL ANOTHER.
I HAVE ALL I NEED. PUT THE BODY IN THE BUNKER. LET THE ALLIES BELIEVE THE FÜHRER KILLED HIMSELF RATHER THAN BE CAPTURED.
MY WORK IS NOW BEGINNING!
SUDDENLY, A WELCOME AND FAMILIAR VOICE STARTLES YOU OUT OF YOUR TIME-LOST REVERIE.
ALL WE HAVE WORKED FOR FINALLY REACHES FRUITION! YOU ARE READY, S.S. SCHARFÜHRER SHULZ?
EVEN AS YOU BEGIN YOUR NEW MISSION, YOUR ENEMY IS ON A QUEST OF HIS OWN...
COMRADES, WE MUST BE READY FOR TOMORROW. AND REMEMBER, EISENHOWER MUST NEVER LEARN WE ARE HERE.
TOO LATE, RUSKIE.

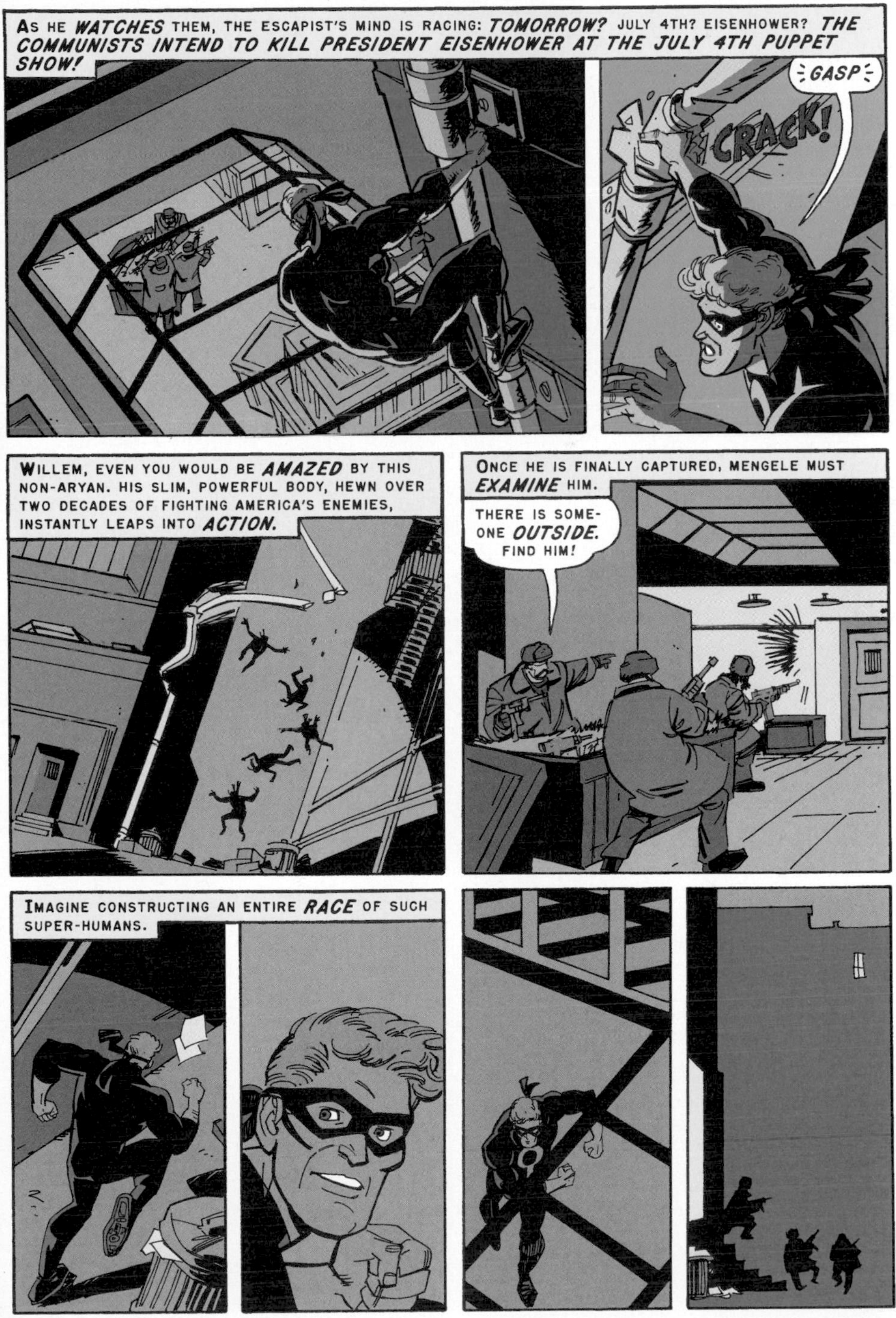
AS HE WATCHES THEM, THE ESCAPIST'S MIND IS RACING: TOMORROW? JULY 4TH? EISENHOWER? THE COMMUNISTS INTEND TO KILL PRESIDENT EISENHOWER AT THE JULY 4TH PUPPET SHOW!
GASP
CRACK!
WILLEM, EVEN YOU WOULD BE AMAZED BY THIS NON-ARYAN. HIS SLIM, POWERFUL BODY, HEWN OVER TWO DECADES OF FIGHTING AMERICA'S ENEMIES, INSTANTLY LEAPS INTO ACTION.
ONCE HE IS FINALLY CAPTURED, MENGELE MUST EXAMINE HIM.
THERE IS SOME-ONE OUTSIDE. FIND HIM!
IMAGINE CONSTRUCTING AN ENTIRE RACE OF SUCH SUPER-HUMANS.

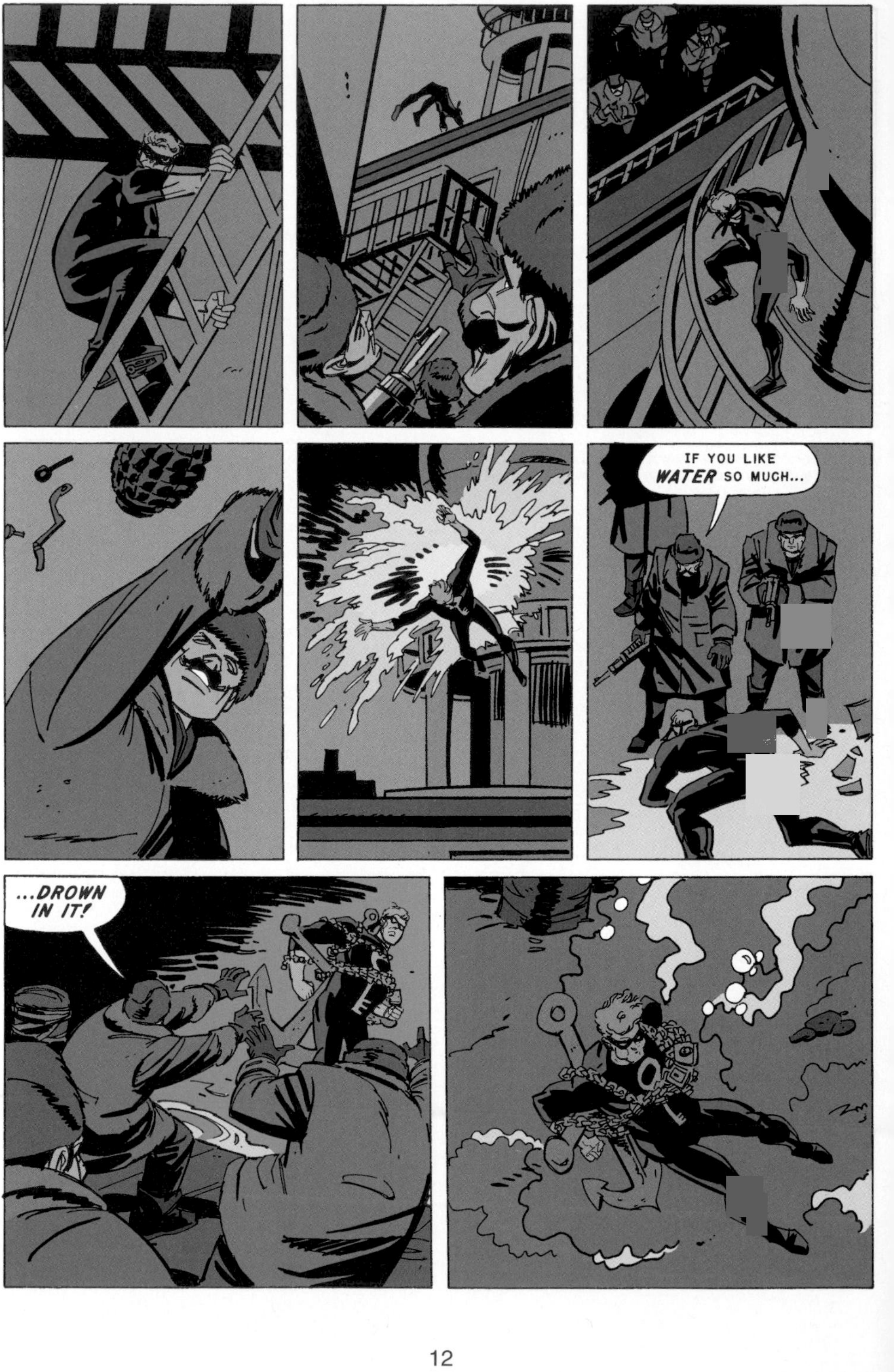
IF YOU LIKE WATER SO MUCH...
...DROWN IN IT!

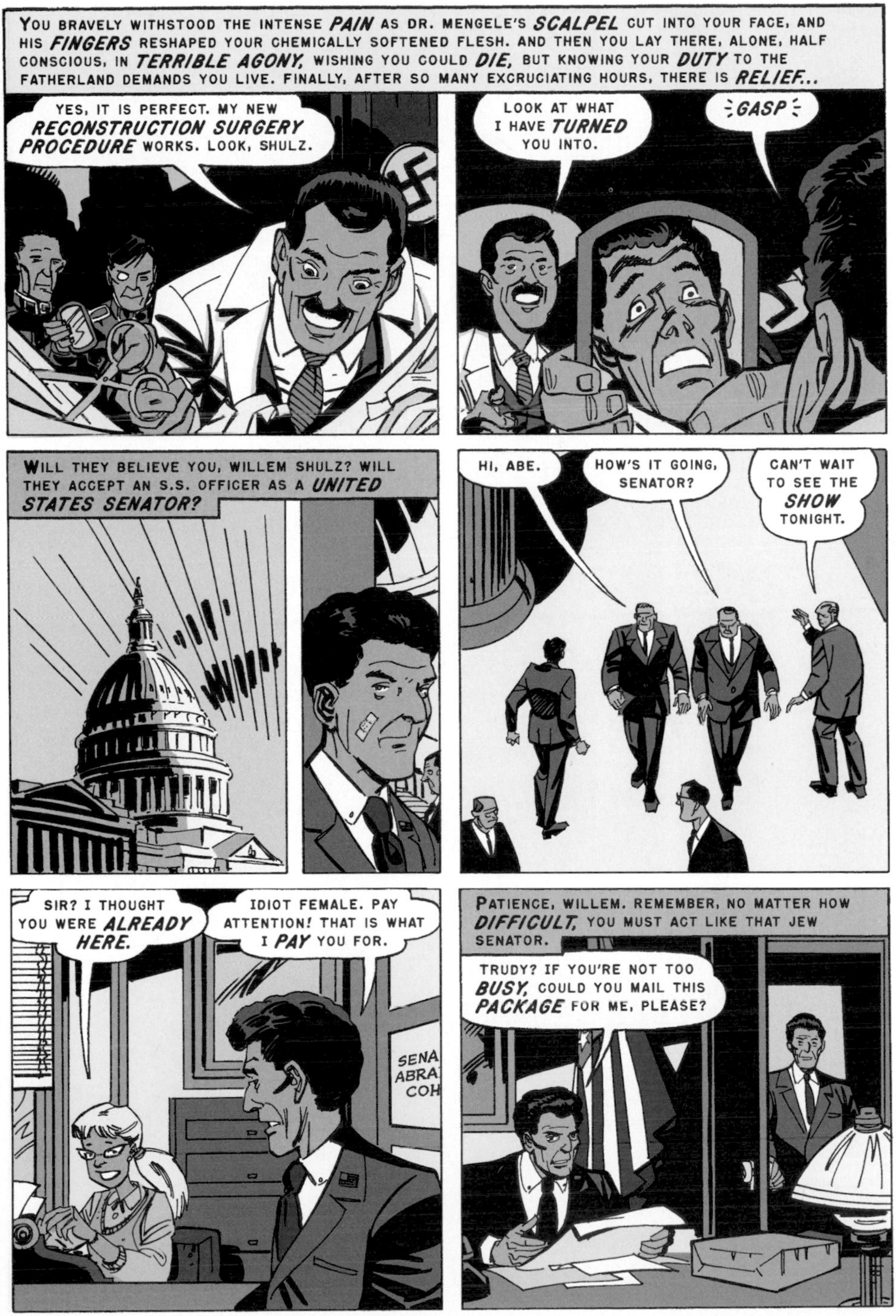
YOU BRAVELY WITHSTOOD THE INTENSE PAIN AS DR. MENGELE'S SCALPEL CUT INTO YOUR FACE, AND HIS FINGERS RESHAPED YOUR CHEMICALLY SOFTENED FLESH. AND THEN YOU LAY THERE, ALONE, HALF CONSCIOUS, IN TERRIBLE AGONY, WISHING YOU COULD DIE, BUT KNOWING YOUR DUTY TO THE FATHERLAND DEMANDS YOU LIVE. FINALLY, AFTER SO MANY EXCRUCIATING HOURS, THERE IS RELIEF...
YES, IT IS PERFECT. MY NEW RECONSTRUCTION SURGERY PROCEDURE WORKS. LOOK, SHULZ.
LOOK AT WHAT I HAVE TURNED YOU INTO.
GASP
WILL THEY BELIEVE YOU, WILLEM SHULZ? WILL THEY ACCEPT AN S.S. OFFICER AS A UNITED STATES SENATOR?
HI, ABE.
HOW'S IT GOING, SENATOR?
CAN'T WAIT TO SEE THE SHOW TONIGHT.
SIR? I THOUGHT YOU WERE ALREADY HERE.
IDIOT FEMALE. PAY ATTENTION! THAT IS WHAT I PAY YOU FOR.
SENA
ABRA
COH
PATIENCE, WILLEM. REMEMBER, NO MATTER HOW DIFFICULT, YOU MUST ACT LIKE THAT JEW SENATOR.
TRUDY? IF YOU'RE NOT TOO BUSY, COULD YOU MAIL THIS PACKAGE FOR ME, PLEASE?

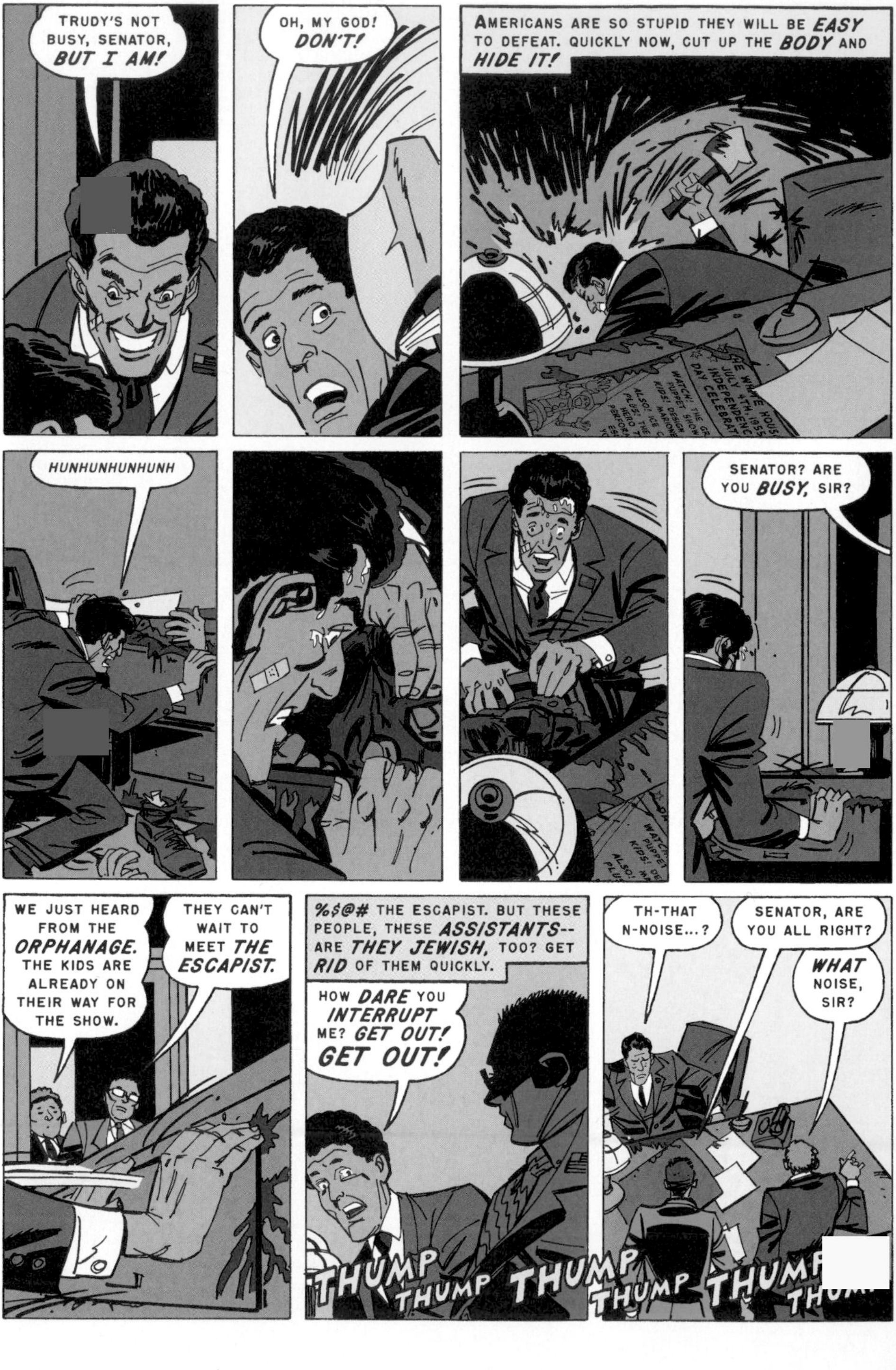

TRUDY'S NOT BUSY, SENATOR, BUT I AM!
OH, MY GOD! DON'T!
AMERICANS ARE SO STUPID THEY WILL BE EASY TO DEFEAT. QUICKLY NOW, CUT UP THE BODY AND HIDE IT!
HUNHUNHUNHUNH
SENATOR? ARE YOU BUSY, SIR?
WE JUST HEARD FROM THE ORPHANAGE. THE KIDS ARE ALREADY ON THEIR WAY FOR THE SHOW.
THEY CAN'T WAIT TO MEET THE ESCAPIST.
%$@# THE ESCAPIST. BUT THESE PEOPLE, THESE ASSISTANTS-- ARE THEY JEWISH, TOO? GET RID OF THEM QUICKLY.
HOW DARE YOU INTERRUPT ME? GET OUT! GET OUT!
TH-THAT N-NOISE...?
SENATOR, ARE YOU ALL RIGHT?
WHAT NOISE, SIR?
THUMP THUMP THUMP THUMP THUM

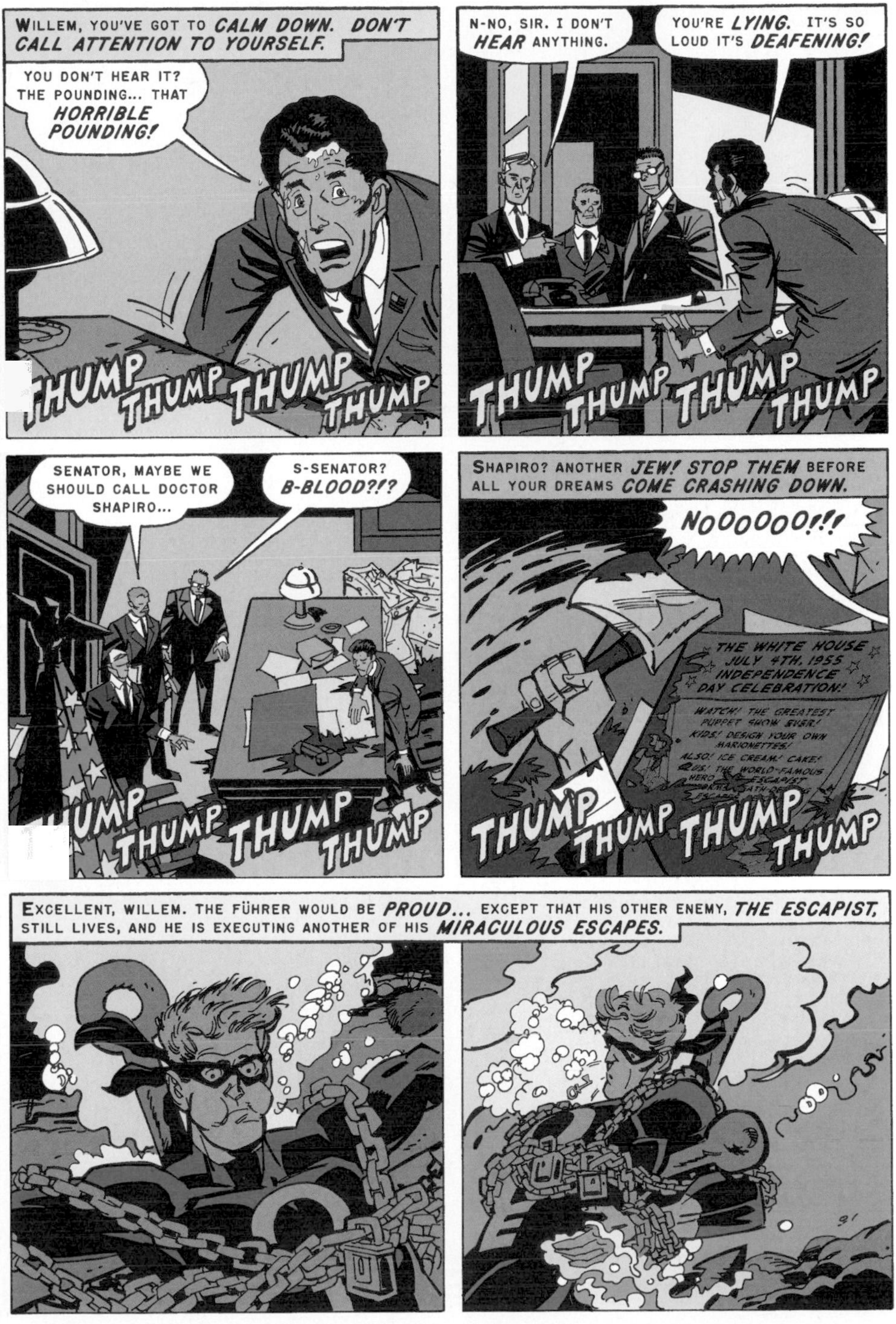
WILLEM, YOU'VE GOT TO CALM DOWN. DON'T CALL ATTENTION TO YOURSELF.
YOU DON'T HEAR IT? THE POUNDING... THAT HORRIBLE POUNDING!
THUMP THUMP THUMP THUMP
N-NO, SIR. I DON'T HEAR ANYTHING.
YOU'RE LYING. IT'S SO LOUD IT'S DEAFENING!
THUMP THUMP THUMP THUMP
SENATOR, MAYBE WE SHOULD CALL DOCTOR SHAPIRO...
S-SENATOR? B-BLOOD?!?
UMP THUMP THUMP THUMP
SHAPIRO? ANOTHER JEW! STOP THEM BEFORE ALL YOUR DREAMS COME CRASHING DOWN.
NOOOOOO!!!
THE WHITE HOUSE JULY 4TH, 1955 INDEPENDENCE DAY CELEBRATION!
WATCH! THE GREATEST PUPPET SHOW EVER!
KIDS! DESIGN YOUR OWN MARIONETTES!
ALSO! ICE CREAM! CAKE!
THUMP THUMP THUMP THUMP
EXCELLENT, WILLEM. THE FÜHRER WOULD BE PROUD... EXCEPT THAT HIS OTHER ENEMY, THE ESCAPIST, STILL LIVES, AND HE IS EXECUTING ANOTHER OF HIS MIRACULOUS ESCAPES.

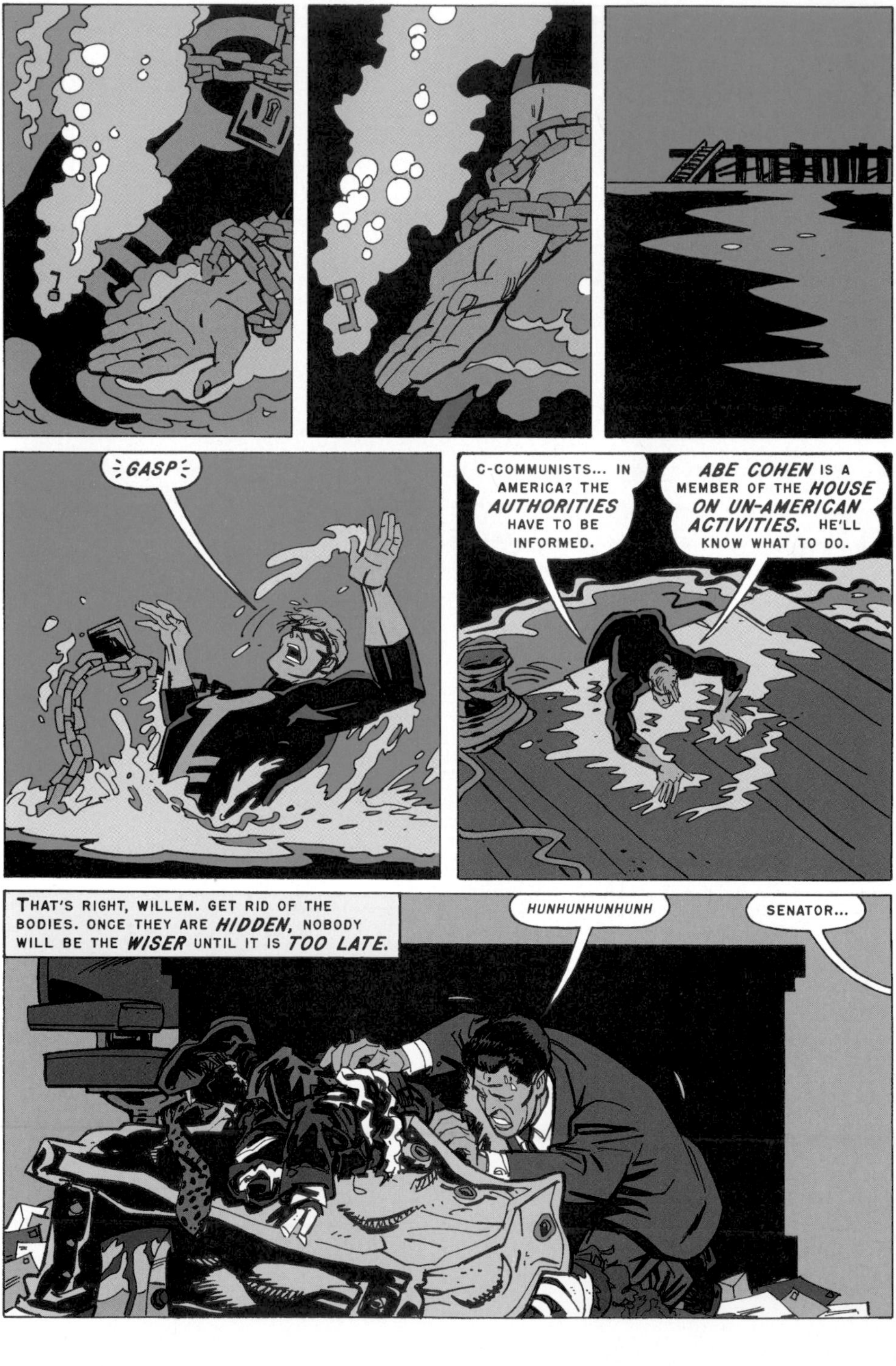
GASP
C-COMMUNISTS... IN AMERICA? THE AUTHORITIES HAVE TO BE INFORMED.
ABE COHEN IS A MEMBER OF THE HOUSE ON UN-AMERICAN ACTIVITIES. HE'LL KNOW WHAT TO DO.
THAT'S RIGHT, WILLEM. GET RID OF THE BODIES. ONCE THEY ARE HIDDEN, NOBODY WILL BE THE WISER UNTIL IT IS TOO LATE.
HUNHUNHUNHUNH
SENATOR...

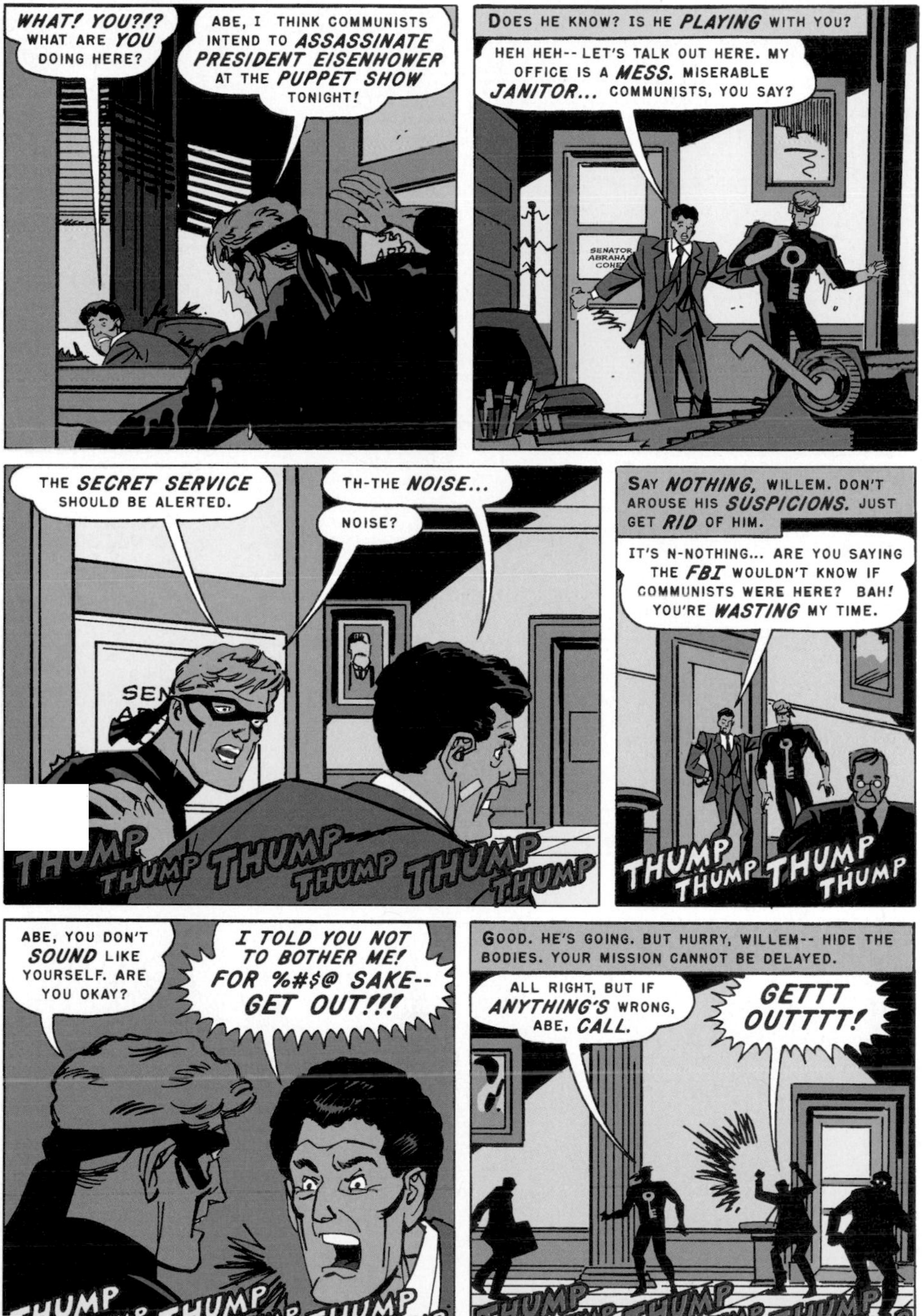
WHAT! YOU?!? WHAT ARE YOU DOING HERE?
ABE, I THINK COMMUNISTS INTEND TO ASSASSINATE PRESIDENT EISENHOWER AT THE PUPPET SHOW TONIGHT!
DOES HE KNOW? IS HE PLAYING WITH YOU?
HEH HEH-- LET'S TALK OUT HERE. MY OFFICE IS A MESS. MISERABLE JANITOR... COMMUNISTS, YOU SAY?
SENATOR ABRAHA COHE
THE SECRET SERVICE SHOULD BE ALERTED.
TH-THE NOISE...
NOISE?
THUMP THUMP THUMP THUMP THUMP THUMP
SAY NOTHING, WILLEM. DON'T AROUSE HIS SUSPICIONS. JUST GET RID OF HIM.
IT'S N-NOTHING... ARE YOU SAYING THE FBI WOULDN'T KNOW IF COMMUNISTS WERE HERE? BAH! YOU'RE WASTING MY TIME.
THUMP THUMP THUMP THUMP
ABE, YOU DON'T SOUND LIKE YOURSELF. ARE YOU OKAY?
I TOLD YOU NOT TO BOTHER ME! FOR %#$@ SAKE-- GET OUT!!!
THUMP THUMP THUMP THUMP THUMP THUMP
GOOD. HE'S GOING. BUT HURRY, WILLEM-- HIDE THE BODIES. YOUR MISSION CANNOT BE DELAYED.
ALL RIGHT, BUT IF ANYTHING'S WRONG, ABE, CALL.
GETTT OUTTTTT!
THUMP THUMP THUMP THUMP THUMP THUMP

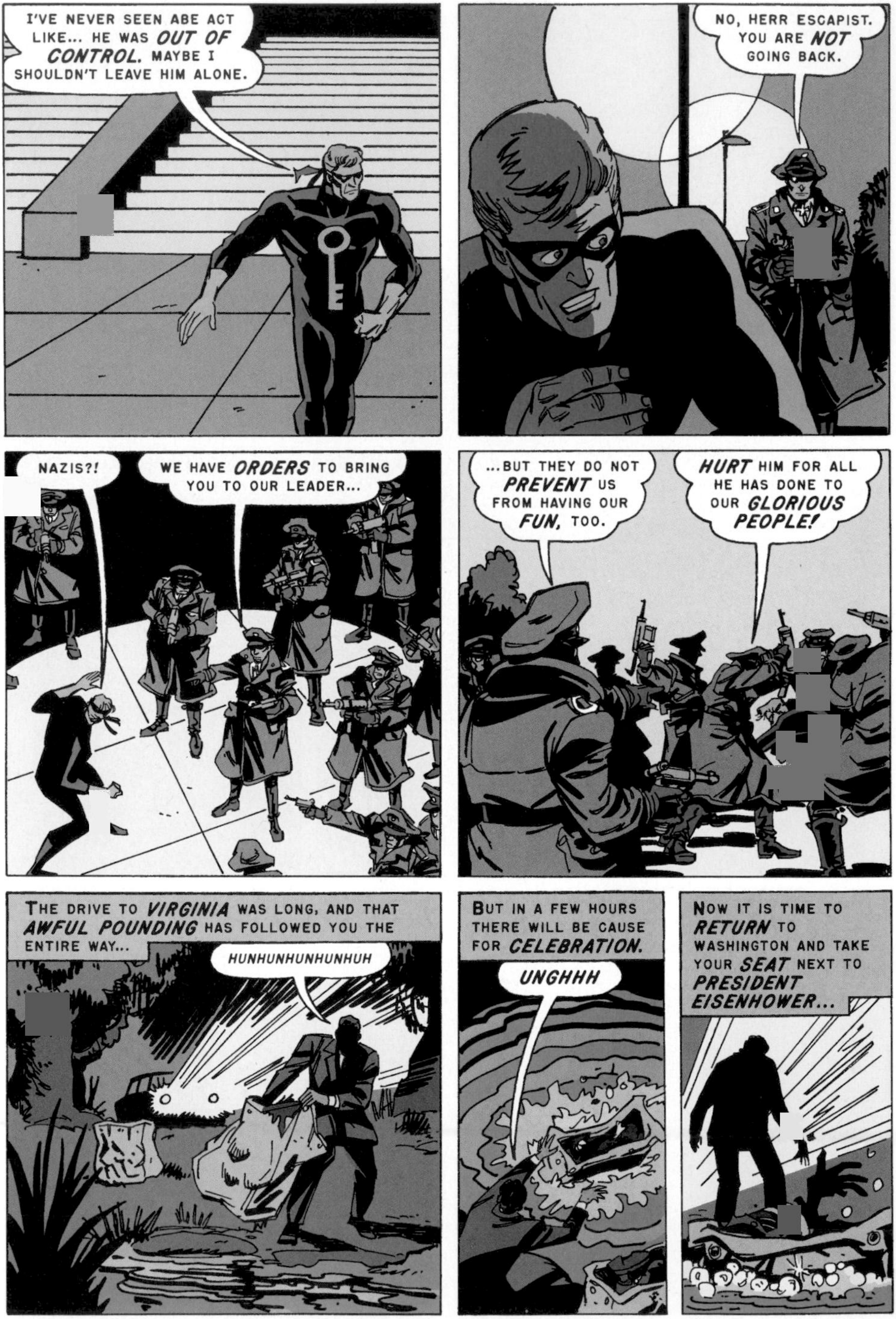
I'VE NEVER SEEN ABE ACT LIKE... HE WAS OUT OF CONTROL. MAYBE I SHOULDN'T LEAVE HIM ALONE.
NO, HERR ESCAPIST. YOU ARE NOT GOING BACK.
NAZIS?!
WE HAVE ORDERS TO BRING YOU TO OUR LEADER...
...BUT THEY DO NOT PREVENT US FROM HAVING OUR FUN, TOO.
HURT HIM FOR ALL HE HAS DONE TO OUR GLORIOUS PEOPLE!
THE DRIVE TO VIRGINIA WAS LONG, AND THAT AWFUL POUNDING HAS FOLLOWED YOU THE ENTIRE WAY...
HUNHUNHUNHUNHUH
BUT IN A FEW HOURS THERE WILL BE CAUSE FOR CELEBRATION.
UNGHHH
NOW IT IS TIME TO RETURN TO WASHINGTON AND TAKE YOUR SEAT NEXT TO PRESIDENT EISENHOWER...

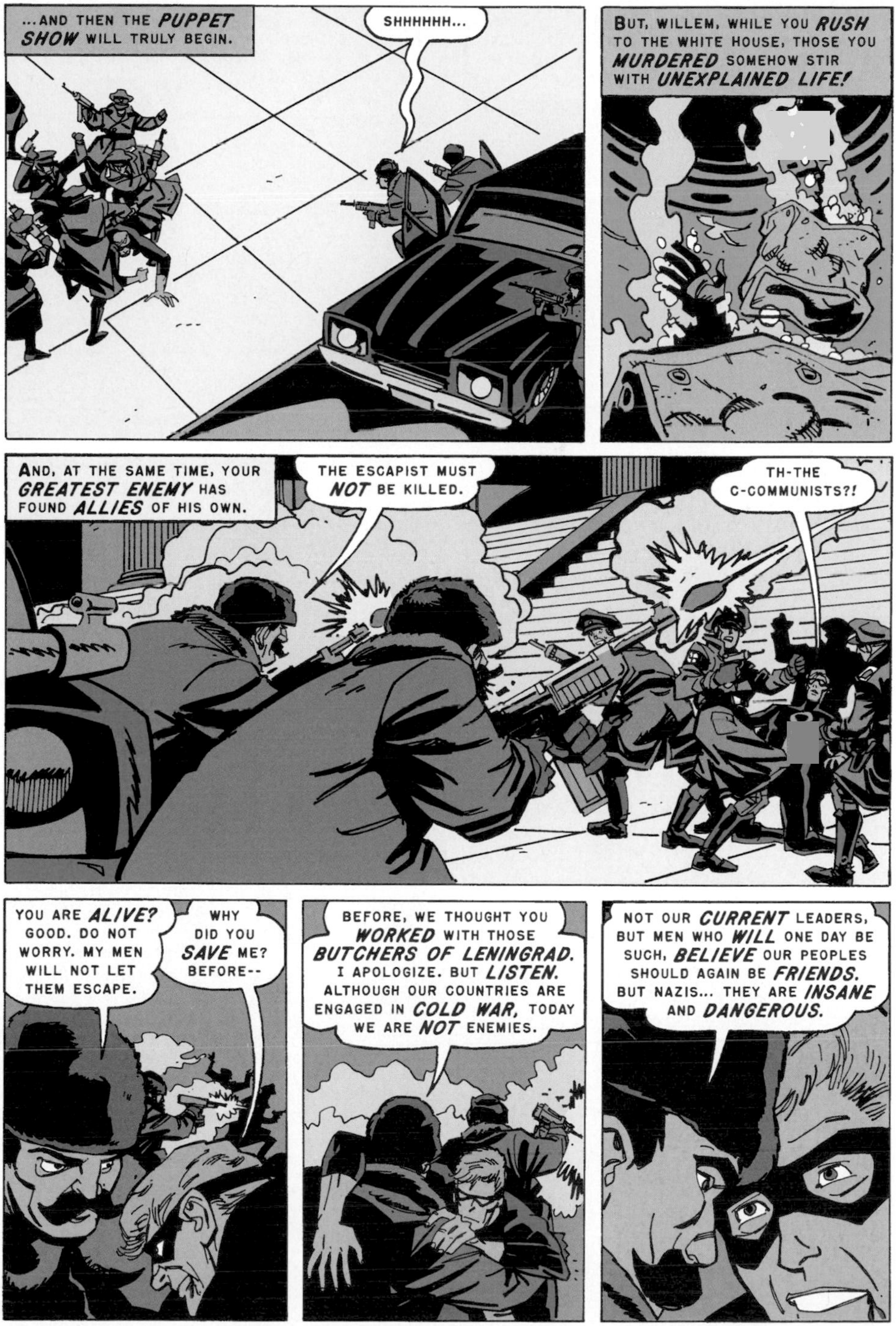
...AND THEN THE PUPPET SHOW WILL TRULY BEGIN.
SHHHHHH...
BUT, WILLEM, WHILE YOU RUSH TO THE WHITE HOUSE, THOSE YOU MURDERED SOMEHOW STIR WITH UNEXPLAINED LIFE!
AND, AT THE SAME TIME, YOUR GREATEST ENEMY HAS FOUND ALLIES OF HIS OWN.
THE ESCAPIST MUST NOT BE KILLED.
TH-THE C-COMMUNISTS?!
YOU ARE ALIVE? GOOD. DO NOT WORRY. MY MEN WILL NOT LET THEM ESCAPE.
WHY DID YOU SAVE ME? BEFORE--
BEFORE, WE THOUGHT YOU WORKED WITH THOSE BUTCHERS OF LENINGRAD. I APOLOGIZE. BUT LISTEN. ALTHOUGH OUR COUNTRIES ARE ENGAGED IN COLD WAR, TODAY WE ARE NOT ENEMIES.
NOT OUR CURRENT LEADERS, BUT MEN WHO WILL ONE DAY BE SUCH, BELIEVE OUR PEOPLES SHOULD AGAIN BE FRIENDS. BUT NAZIS... THEY ARE INSANE AND DANGEROUS.

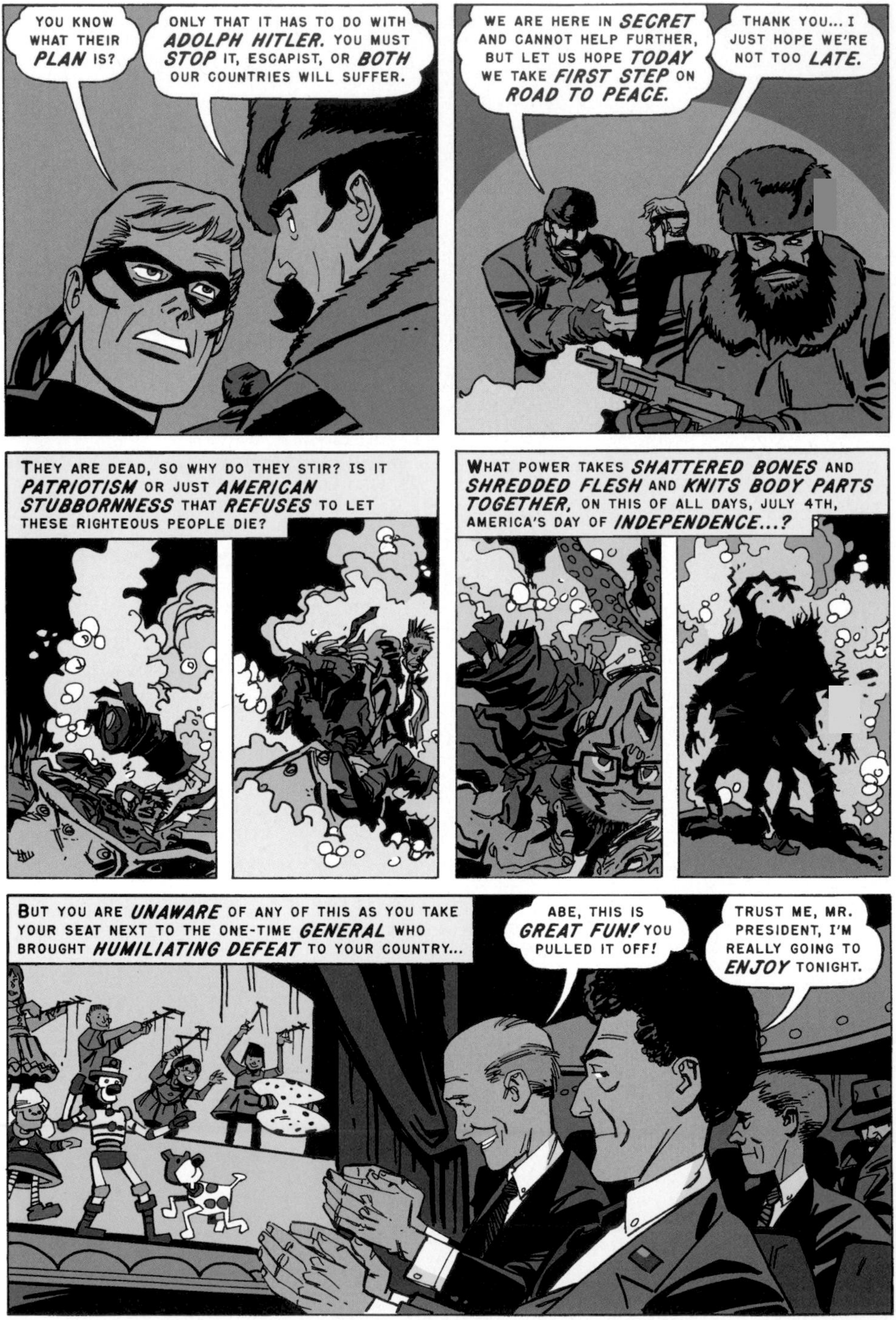

YOU KNOW WHAT THEIR PLAN IS?
ONLY THAT IT HAS TO DO WITH ADOLPH HITLER. YOU MUST STOP IT, ESCAPIST, OR BOTH OUR COUNTRIES WILL SUFFER.
WE ARE HERE IN SECRET AND CANNOT HELP FURTHER, BUT LET US HOPE TODAY WE TAKE FIRST STEP ON ROAD TO PEACE.
THANK YOU... I JUST HOPE WE'RE NOT TOO LATE.
THEY ARE DEAD, SO WHY DO THEY STIR? IS IT PATRIOTISM OR JUST AMERICAN STUBBORNNESS THAT REFUSES TO LET THESE RIGHTEOUS PEOPLE DIE?
WHAT POWER TAKES SHATTERED BONES AND SHREDDED FLESH AND KNITS BODY PARTS TOGETHER, ON THIS OF ALL DAYS, JULY 4TH, AMERICA'S DAY OF INDEPENDENCE...?
BUT YOU ARE UNAWARE OF ANY OF THIS AS YOU TAKE YOUR SEAT NEXT TO THE ONE-TIME GENERAL WHO BROUGHT HUMILIATING DEFEAT TO YOUR COUNTRY...
ABE, THIS IS GREAT FUN! YOU PULLED IT OFF!
TRUST ME, MR. PRESIDENT, I'M REALLY GOING TO ENJOY TONIGHT.

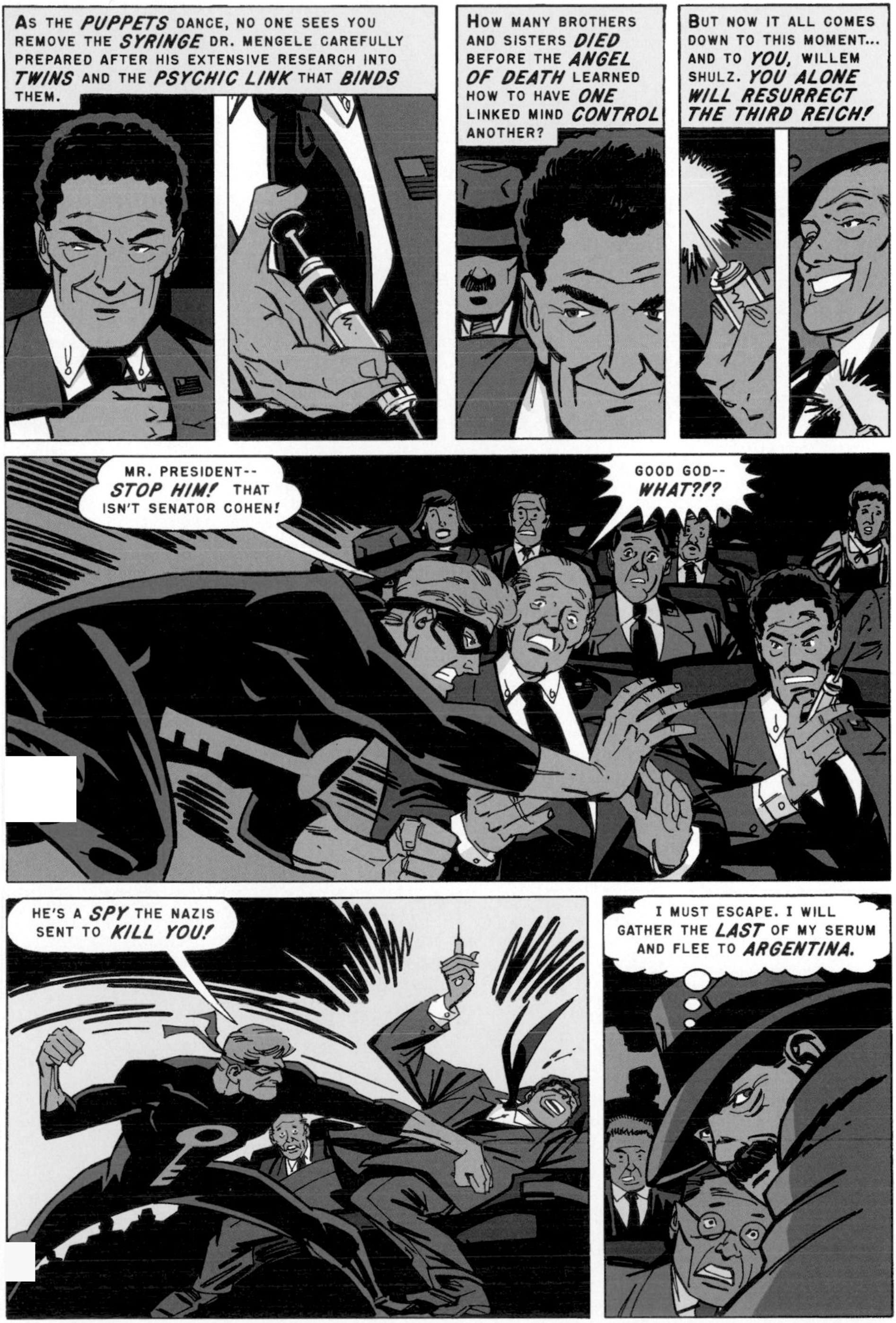
AS THE PUPPETS DANCE, NO ONE SEES YOU REMOVE THE SYRINGE DR. MENGELE CAREFULLY PREPARED AFTER HIS EXTENSIVE RESEARCH INTO TWINS AND THE PSYCHIC LINK THAT BINDS THEM.
HOW MANY BROTHERS AND SISTERS DIED BEFORE THE ANGEL OF DEATH LEARNED HOW TO HAVE ONE LINKED MIND CONTROL ANOTHER?
BUT NOW IT ALL COMES DOWN TO THIS MOMENT... AND TO YOU, WILLEM SHULZ. YOU ALONE WILL RESURRECT THE THIRD REICH!
MR. PRESIDENT-- STOP HIM! THAT ISN'T SENATOR COHEN!
GOOD GOD-- WHAT?!?
HE'S A SPY THE NAZIS SENT TO KILL YOU!
I MUST ESCAPE. I WILL GATHER THE LAST OF MY SERUM AND FLEE TO ARGENTINA.

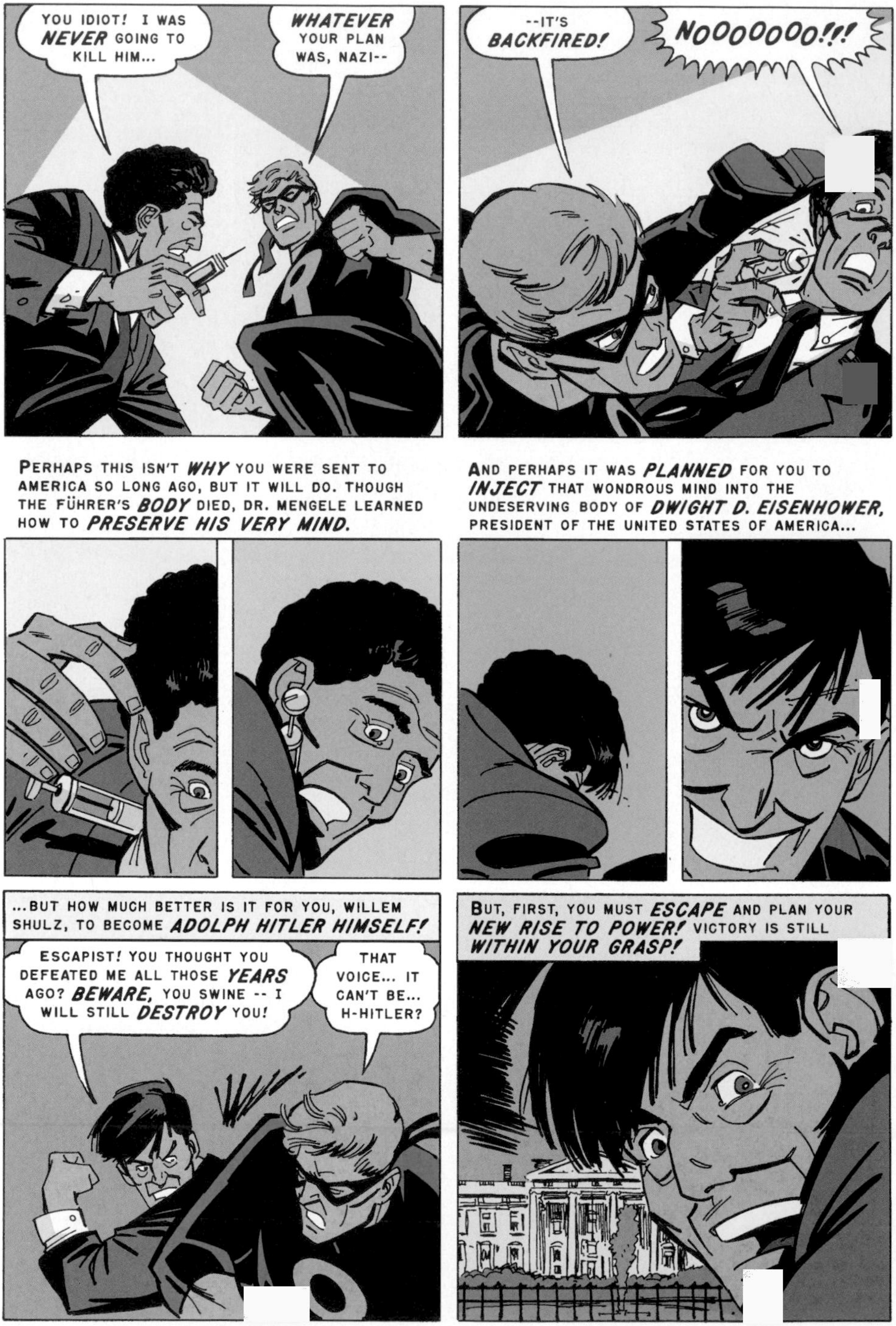
YOU IDIOT! I WAS NEVER GOING TO KILL HIM...
WHATEVER YOUR PLAN WAS, NAZI--
--IT'S BACKFIRED!
NOOOOOOOO!!!
PERHAPS THIS ISN'T WHY YOU WERE SENT TO AMERICA SO LONG AGO, BUT IT WILL DO. THOUGH THE FÜHRER'S BODY DIED, DR. MENGELE LEARNED HOW TO PRESERVE HIS VERY MIND.
AND PERHAPS IT WAS PLANNED FOR YOU TO INJECT THAT WONDROUS MIND INTO THE UNDESERVING BODY OF DWIGHT D. EISENHOWER, PRESIDENT OF THE UNITED STATES OF AMERICA...
...BUT HOW MUCH BETTER IS IT FOR YOU, WILLEM SHULZ, TO BECOME ADOLPH HITLER HIMSELF!
ESCAPIST! YOU THOUGHT YOU DEFEATED ME ALL THOSE YEARS AGO? BEWARE, YOU SWINE -- I WILL STILL DESTROY YOU!
THAT VOICE... IT CAN'T BE... H-HITLER?
BUT, FIRST, YOU MUST ESCAPE AND PLAN YOUR NEW RISE TO POWER! VICTORY IS STILL WITHIN YOUR GRASP!

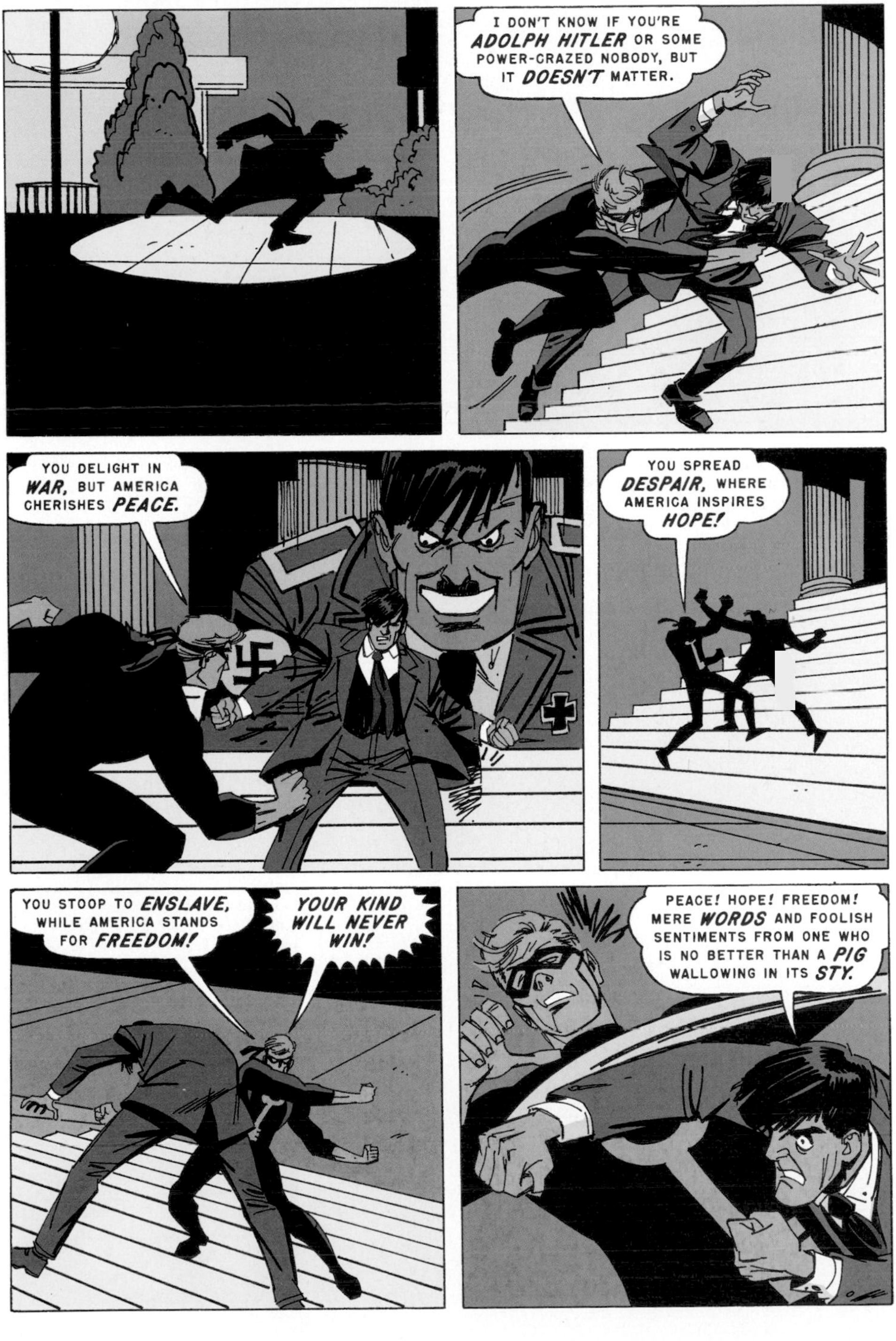
I DON'T KNOW IF YOU'RE ADOLPH HITLER OR SOME POWER-CRAZED NOBODY, BUT IT DOESN'T MATTER.
YOU DELIGHT IN WAR, BUT AMERICA CHERISHES PEACE.
YOU SPREAD DESPAIR, WHERE AMERICA INSPIRES HOPE!
YOU STOOP TO ENSLAVE, WHILE AMERICA STANDS FOR FREEDOM!
YOUR KIND WILL NEVER WIN!
PEACE! HOPE! FREEDOM! MERE WORDS AND FOOLISH SENTIMENTS FROM ONE WHO IS NO BETTER THAN A PIG WALLOWING IN ITS STY.

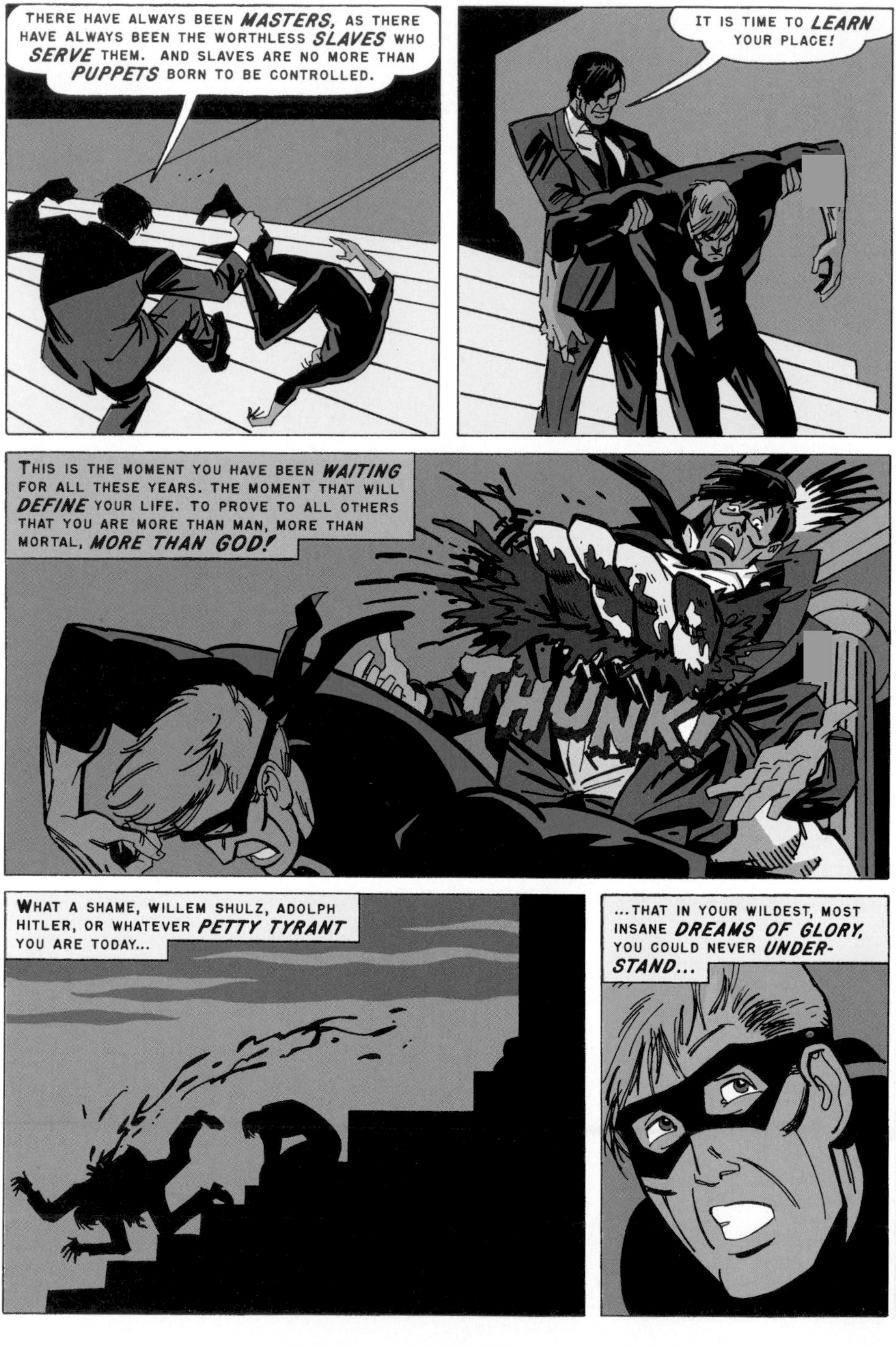
THERE HAVE ALWAYS BEEN MASTERS, AS THERE HAVE ALWAYS BEEN THE WORTHLESS SLAVES WHO SERVE THEM. AND SLAVES ARE NO MORE THAN PUPPETS BORN TO BE CONTROLLED.
IT IS TIME TO LEARN YOUR PLACE!
THIS IS THE MOMENT YOU HAVE BEEN WAITING FOR ALL THESE YEARS. THE MOMENT THAT WILL DEFINE YOUR LIFE. TO PROVE TO ALL OTHERS THAT YOU ARE MORE THAN MAN, MORE THAN MORTAL, MORE THAN GOD!
THUNK!
WHAT A SHAME, WILLEM SHULZ, ADOLPH HITLER, OR WHATEVER PETTY TYRANT YOU ARE TODAY...
...THAT IN YOUR WILDEST, MOST INSANE DREAMS OF GLORY, YOU COULD NEVER UNDER-STAND...

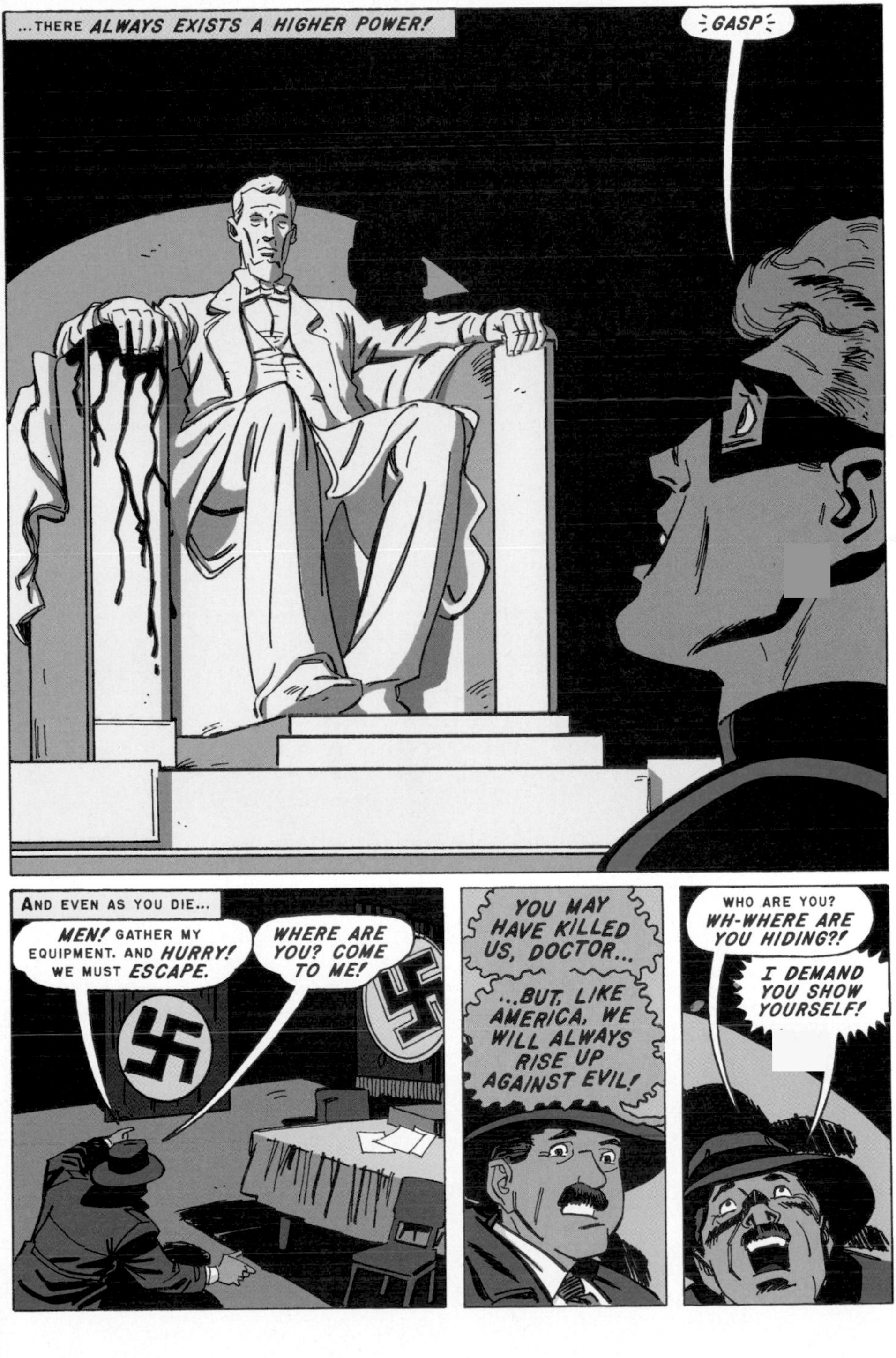
...THERE ALWAYS EXISTS A HIGHER POWER!
GASP
AND EVEN AS YOU DIE...
MEN! GATHER MY EQUIPMENT. AND HURRY! WE MUST ESCAPE.
WHERE ARE YOU? COME TO ME!
YOU MAY HAVE KILLED US, DOCTOR...
...BUT, LIKE AMERICA, WE WILL ALWAYS RISE UP AGAINST EVIL!
WHO ARE YOU? WH-WHERE ARE YOU HIDING?!
I DEMAND YOU SHOW YOURSELF!

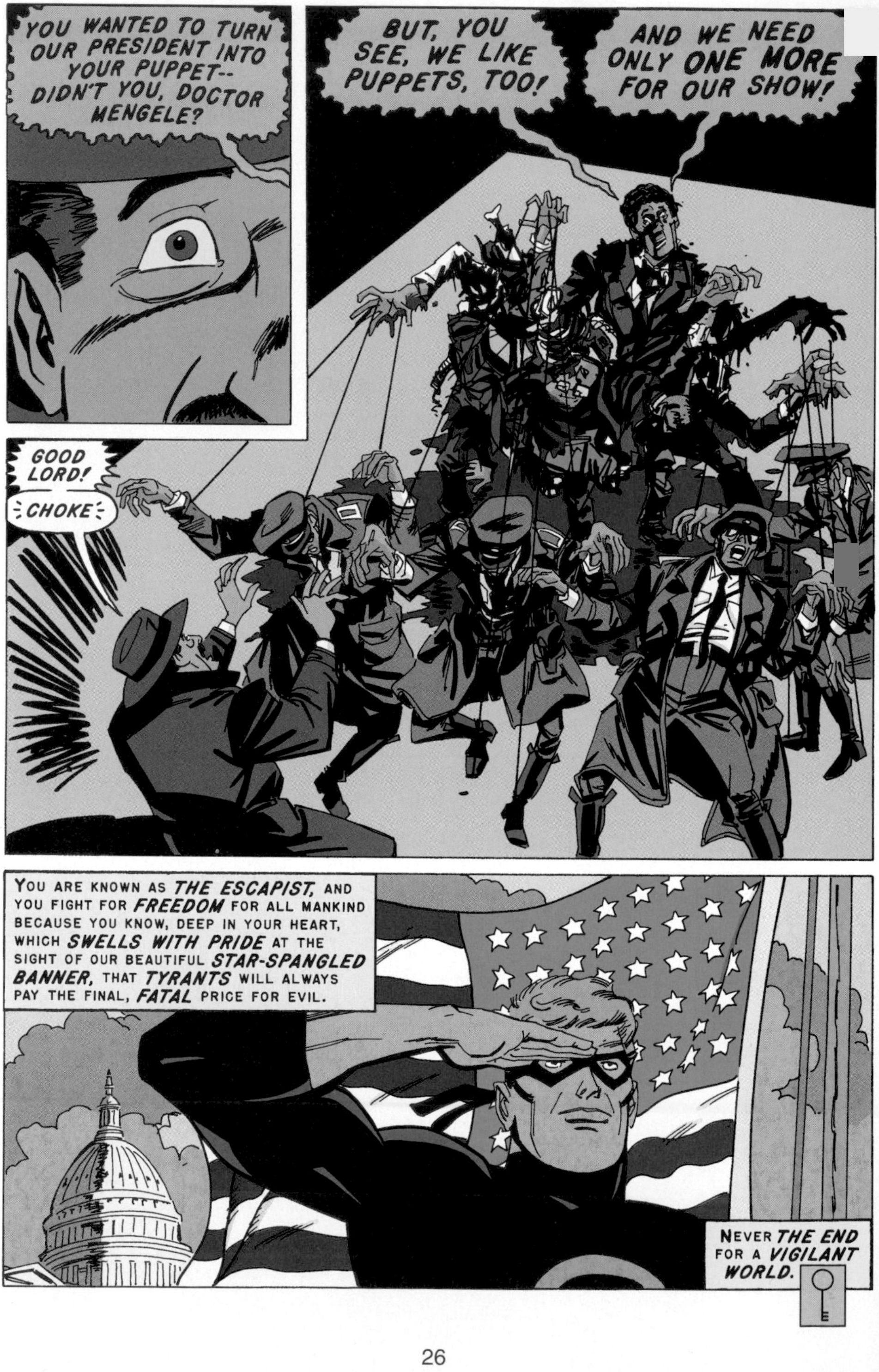
YOU WANTED TO TURN OUR PRESIDENT INTO YOUR PUPPET-- DIDN'T YOU, DOCTOR MENGELE?
BUT, YOU SEE, WE LIKE PUPPETS, TOO!
AND WE NEED ONLY ONE MORE FOR OUR SHOW!
GOOD LORD!
CHOKE
YOU ARE KNOWN AS THE ESCAPIST, AND YOU FIGHT FOR FREEDOM FOR ALL MANKIND BECAUSE YOU KNOW, DEEP IN YOUR HEART, WHICH SWELLS WITH PRIDE AT THE SIGHT OF OUR BEAUTIFUL STAR-SPANGLED BANNER, THAT TYRANTS WILL ALWAYS PAY THE FINAL, FATAL PRICE FOR EVIL.
NEVER THE END FOR A VIGILANT WORLD.

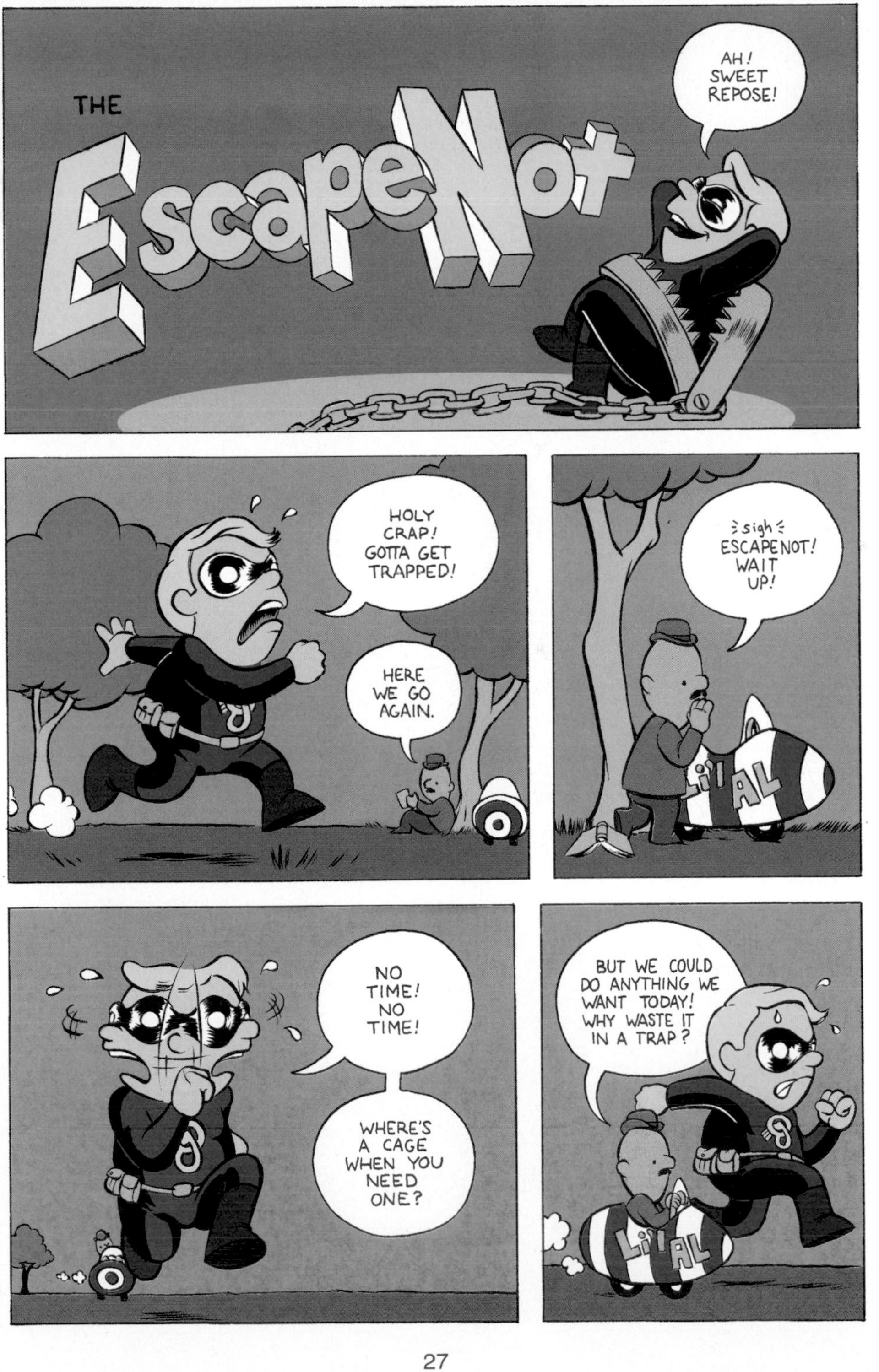
THE
EscapeNot
AH! SWEET REPOSE!
HOLY CRAP! GOTTA GET TRAPPED!
HERE WE GO AGAIN.
sigh
ESCAPENOT! WAIT UP!
LI'L AL
NO TIME! NO TIME!
WHERE'S A CAGE WHEN YOU NEED ONE?
BUT WE COULD DO ANYTHING WE WANT TODAY! WHY WASTE IT IN A TRAP?
LI'L AL

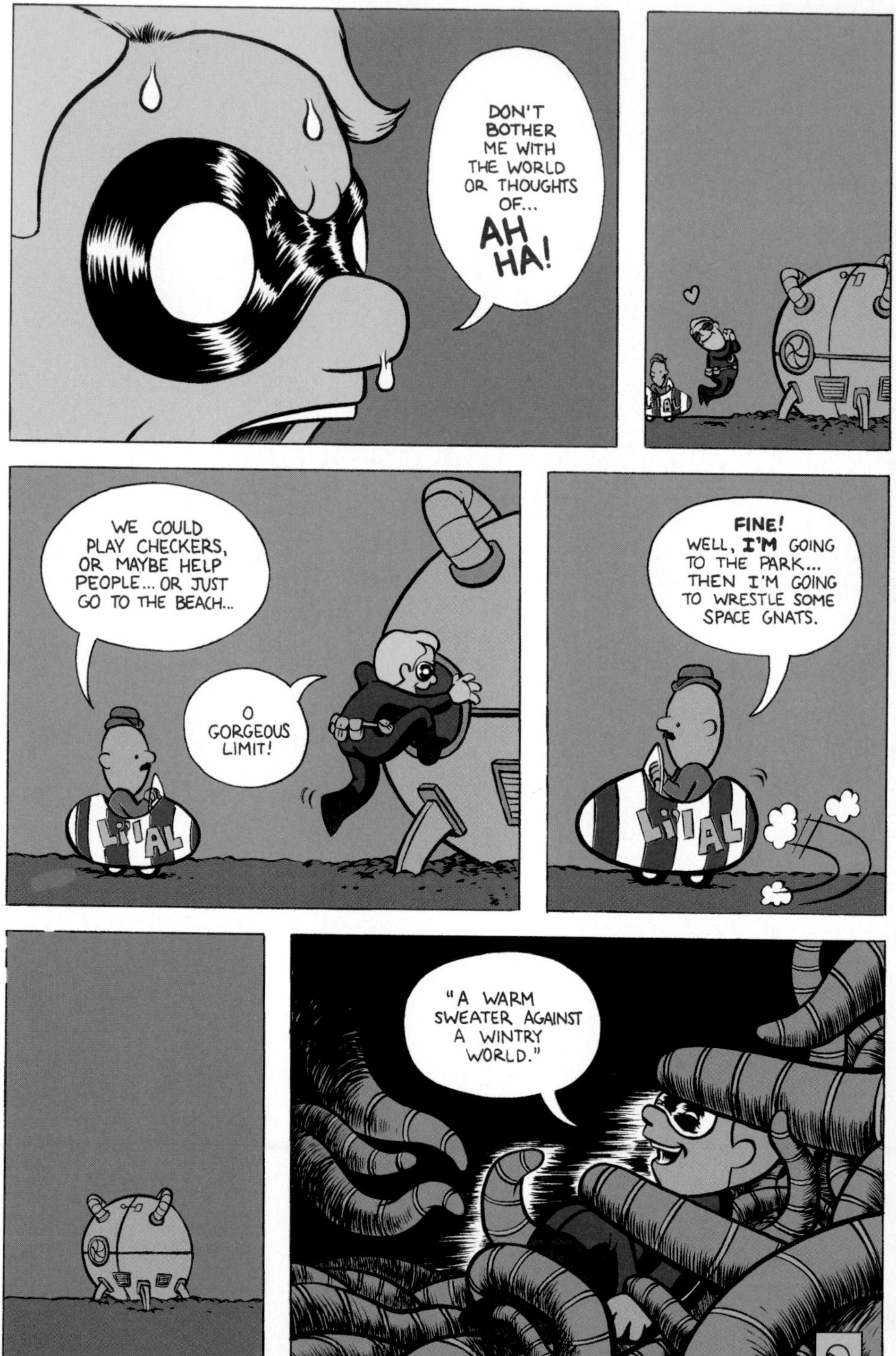
DON'T BOTHER ME WITH THE WORLD OR THOUGHTS OF... AH HA!
WE COULD PLAY CHECKERS, OR MAYBE HELP PEOPLE... OR JUST GO TO THE BEACH...
O GORGEOUS LIMIT!
LIL' AL
FINE! WELL, I'M GOING TO THE PARK... THEN I'M GOING TO WRESTLE SOME SPACE GNATS.
LIL' AL
"A WARM SWEATER AGAINST A WINTRY WORLD."

THOUGH THE ESCAPIST IS THE ***GREATEST HERO*** THE ***FORCES OF LIBERATION*** HAVE EVER KNOWN, EVEN ***HE*** CANNOT ELUDE ***DEATH*** FOREVER! SOMEDAY, IN THE FUTURE, ***OTHERS*** WILL CARRY ON THE MANTLE OF THE ***ESCAPIST...*** AS SEEN IN THIS CLASSIC STORY BY AWARD-WINNING SCI-FI SCRIBE ***CYRIL M. CUTTER***. CUTTER PENNED DOZENS OF TELEPLAYS, EDITED A VARIETY OF GENERAL INTEREST MAGAZINES, AND WROTE HUNDREDS OF LEGENDARY SHORT STORIES. SADLY, HE IS NO LONGER WITH US...BUT IN THIS VERY SPECIAL ***EDITOR'S CHOICE REPRINT***, YOU, READER, CAN ONCE AGAIN ***THRILL*** TO THE ***ROCKET-BLASTING ADVENTURES OF...***

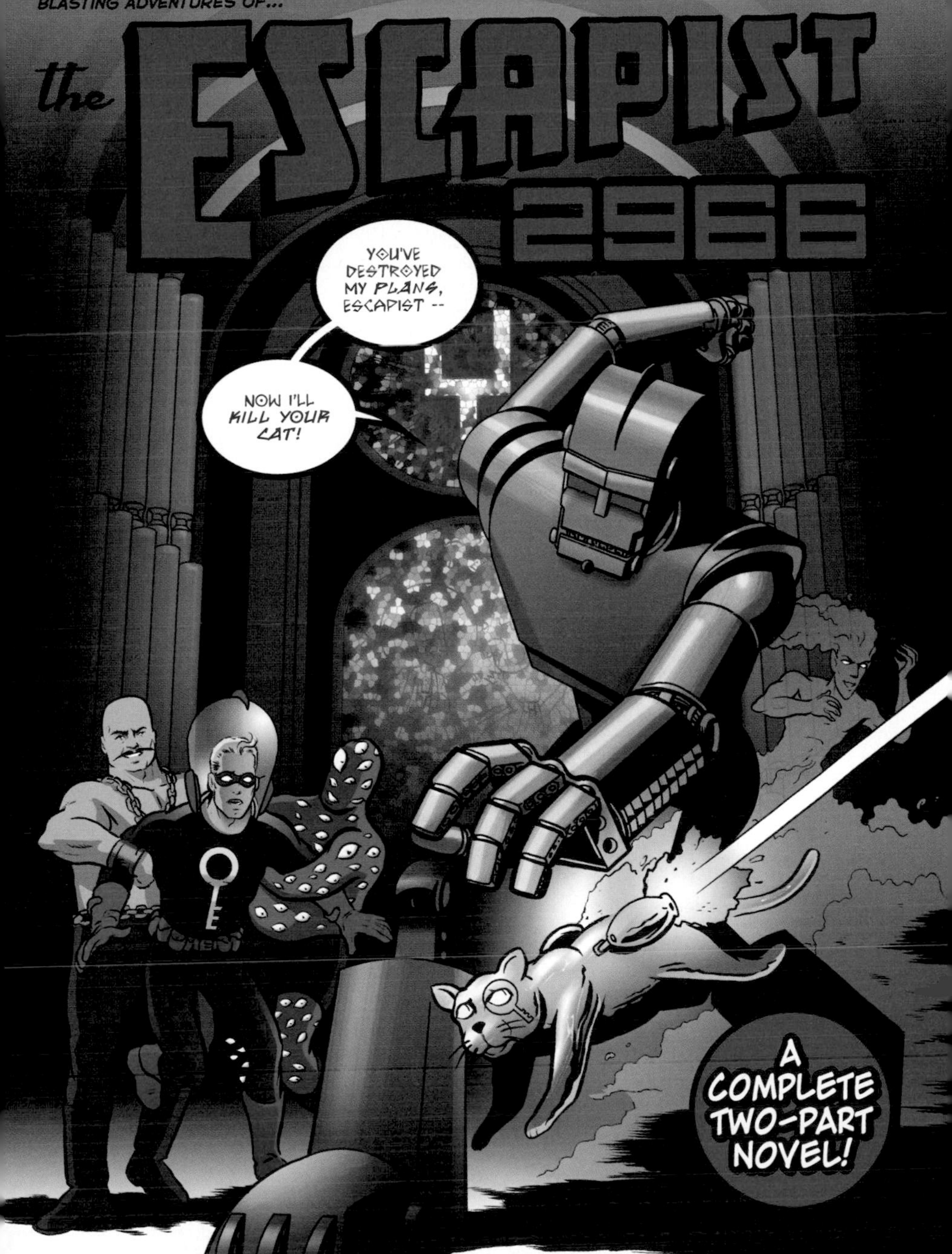

the ESCAPIST
2966
YOU'VE DESTROYED MY PLANS, ESCAPIST --
NOW I'LL KILL YOUR CAT!
A COMPLETE TWO-PART NOVEL!

...AND WHAT OF THE ESCAPIST?

THIS IS A **TOUGH** ONE!

MY ARCH-ENEMIES, THE **IRON CHAIN**, HAVE TRAPPED ME IN THIS **GIANT CLAM** — AT THE BOTTOM OF THE **MARIANAS TRENCH***...

*EDITOR'S NOTE: AT 32,842 FEET BELOW SEA LEVEL, THE MARIANAS TRENCH IS THE DEEPEST POINT ON THE OCEAN FLOOR!

...AND IF I **DO** BREAK LOOSE, THE EXPLOSION FROM THIS **TORPEX DEPTH CHARGE*** WILL **KILL** ME!

BUT I'VE **GOT** TO GET **FREE!** THOSE MONSTERS ARE GOING TO **KILL** PRESIDENT **JOHNSON!**

*EDITOR'S NOTE: TORPEX, WHICH IS 50% MORE POWERFUL THAN TNT, WAS USED IN DEPTH CHARGES BEGINNING LATE IN WORLD WAR II!

LET'S SEE — THAT DEPTH CHARGE IS DETONATED BY **IMPACT**, NOT **HEAT** —

SO IF I CAN JUST **WARM UP** THE SURROUNDING **WATER** WITH THIS **OXY-ACETYLENE TORCH** —

VOILÀ!

JUST LIKE **COOKING CLAMS** FOR **DINNER** — THEY OPEN BY **THEMSELVES!**

GOOD THING I'VE GOT ON MY **SCUBA*** GEAR!

*EDITOR'S NOTE: SCUBA: SELF-CONTAINED UNDERWATER BREATHING APPARATUS!

TIME TO LIVE UP TO MY REPUTATION AS THE **CHAMPION OF DEMOCRACY*** —

*EDITOR'S NOTE: DEMOCRACY -- THE ONLY FORM OF GOVERNMENT IN THE DAMN WORLD WORTH FIGHTING FOR -- DATES BACK...

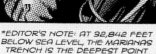

DAYDREAMING AGAIN?

30

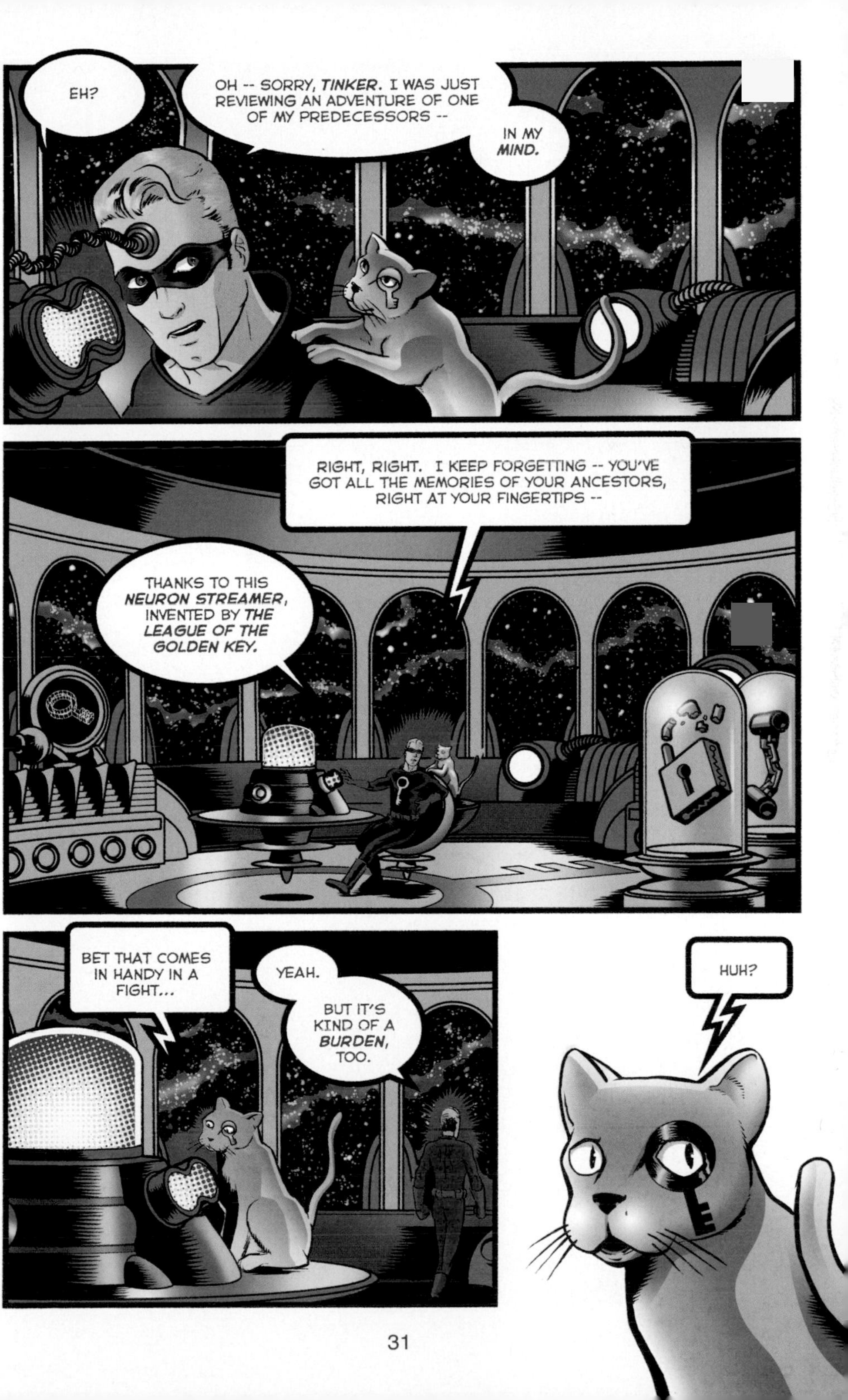

EH?
OH -- SORRY, TINKER. I WAS JUST REVIEWING AN ADVENTURE OF ONE OF MY PREDECESSORS --
IN MY MIND.
RIGHT, RIGHT. I KEEP FORGETTING -- YOU'VE GOT ALL THE MEMORIES OF YOUR ANCESTORS, RIGHT AT YOUR FINGERTIPS --
THANKS TO THIS NEURON STREAMER, INVENTED BY THE LEAGUE OF THE GOLDEN KEY.
BET THAT COMES IN HANDY IN A FIGHT...
YEAH.
BUT IT'S KIND OF A BURDEN, TOO.
HUH?

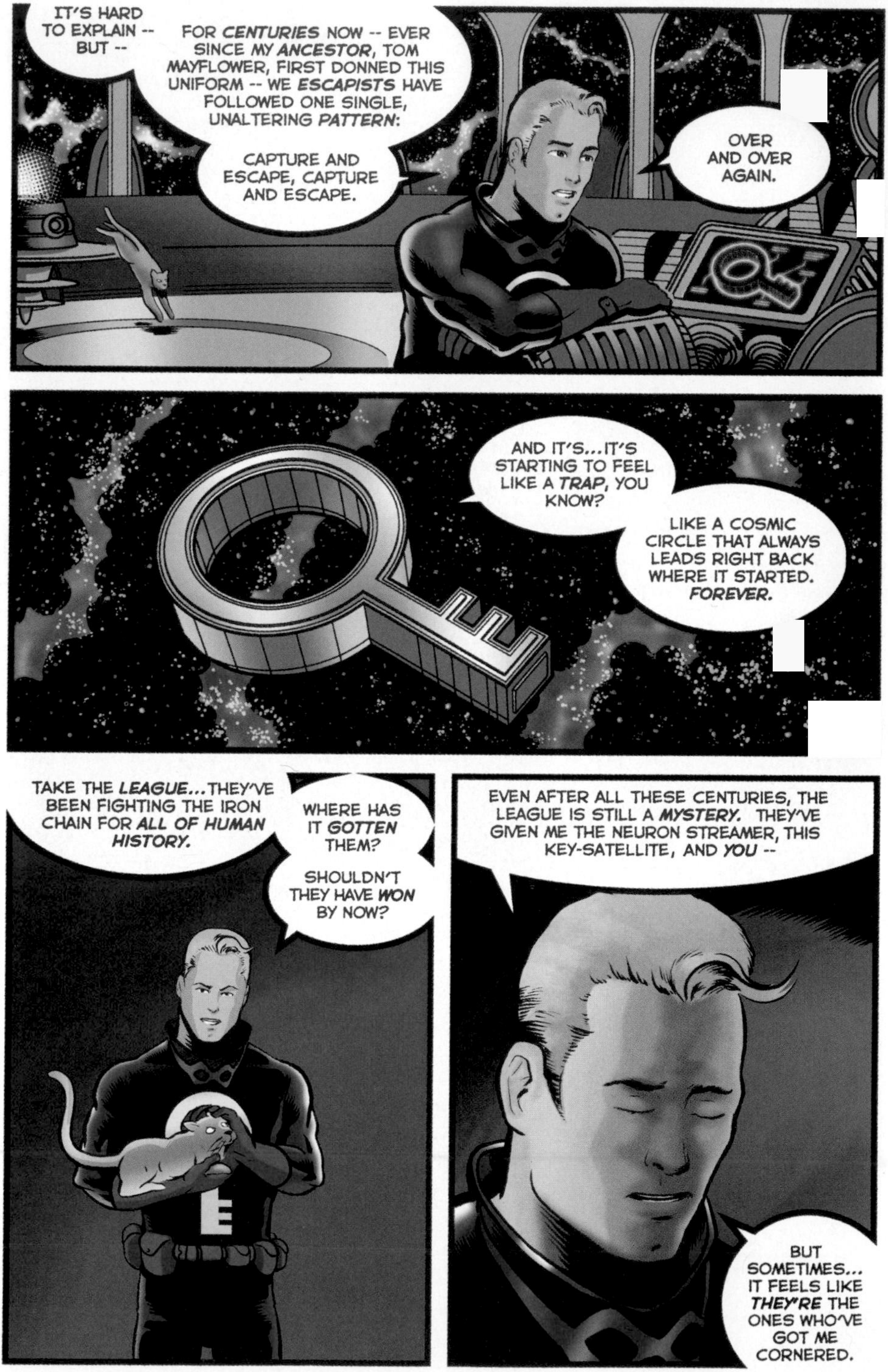
IT'S HARD TO EXPLAIN -- BUT --
FOR CENTURIES NOW -- EVER SINCE MY ANCESTOR, TOM MAYFLOWER, FIRST DONNED THIS UNIFORM -- WE ESCAPISTS HAVE FOLLOWED ONE SINGLE, UNALTERING PATTERN:
CAPTURE AND ESCAPE, CAPTURE AND ESCAPE.
OVER AND OVER AGAIN.
AND IT'S...IT'S STARTING TO FEEL LIKE A TRAP, YOU KNOW?
LIKE A COSMIC CIRCLE THAT ALWAYS LEADS RIGHT BACK WHERE IT STARTED. FOREVER.
TAKE THE LEAGUE...THEY'VE BEEN FIGHTING THE IRON CHAIN FOR ALL OF HUMAN HISTORY.
WHERE HAS IT GOTTEN THEM?
SHOULDN'T THEY HAVE WON BY NOW?
EVEN AFTER ALL THESE CENTURIES, THE LEAGUE IS STILL A MYSTERY. THEY'VE GIVEN ME THE NEURON STREAMER, THIS KEY-SATELLITE, AND YOU --
BUT SOMETIMES... IT FEELS LIKE THEY'RE THE ONES WHO'VE GOT ME CORNERED.

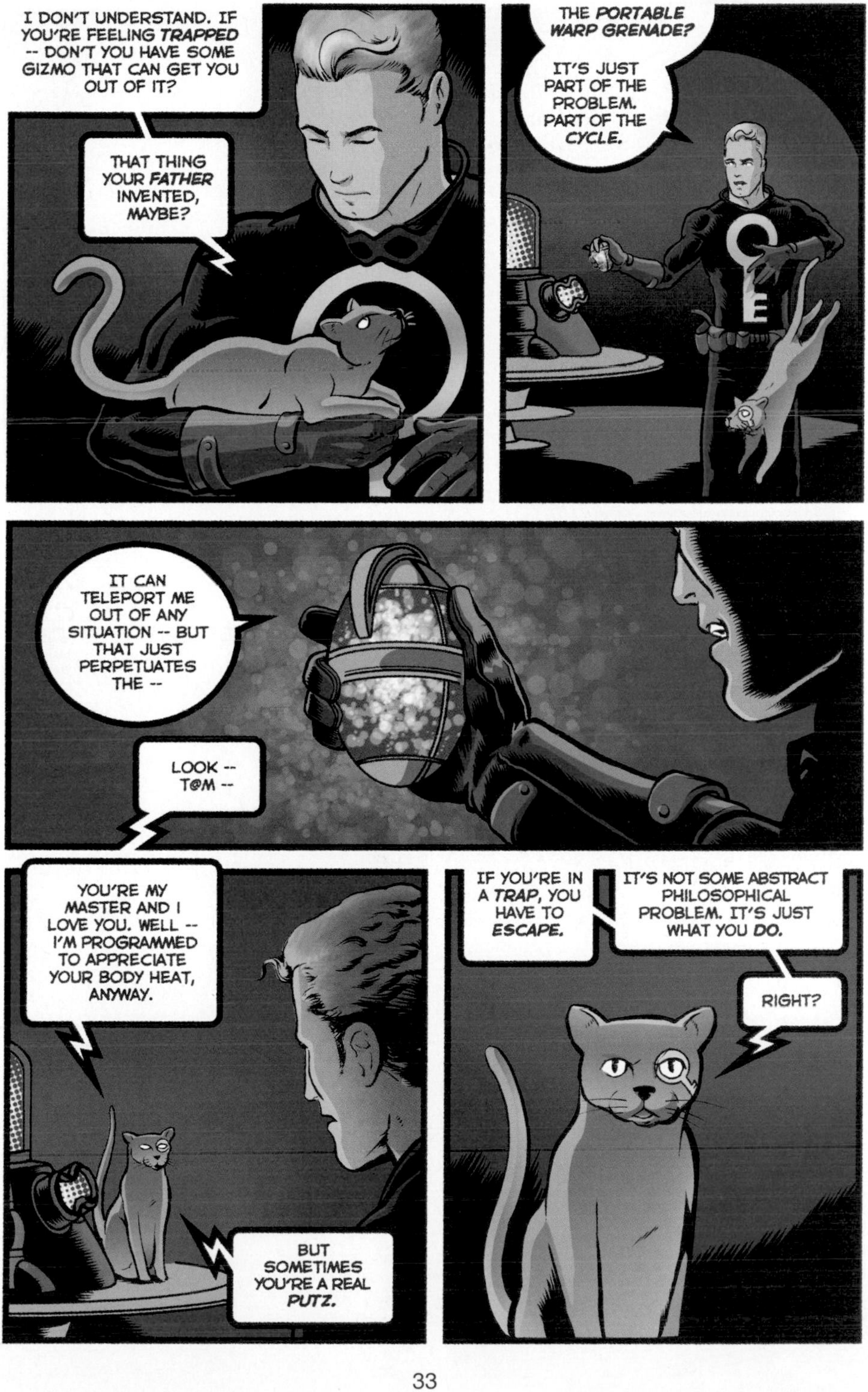
I DON'T UNDERSTAND. IF YOU'RE FEELING *TRAPPED* -- DON'T YOU HAVE SOME GIZMO THAT CAN GET YOU OUT OF IT?
THAT THING YOUR *FATHER* INVENTED, MAYBE?
THE *PORTABLE WARP GRENADE?*
IT'S JUST PART OF THE PROBLEM. PART OF THE *CYCLE.*
IT CAN TELEPORT ME OUT OF ANY SITUATION -- BUT THAT JUST PERPETUATES THE --
LOOK -- T@M --
YOU'RE *MY* MASTER AND I LOVE YOU. WELL -- I'M PROGRAMMED TO APPRECIATE YOUR BODY HEAT, ANYWAY.
BUT SOMETIMES YOU'RE A REAL *PUTZ.*
IF YOU'RE IN A *TRAP,* YOU HAVE TO *ESCAPE.*
IT'S NOT SOME ABSTRACT PHILOSOPHICAL PROBLEM. IT'S JUST WHAT YOU *DO.*
RIGHT?

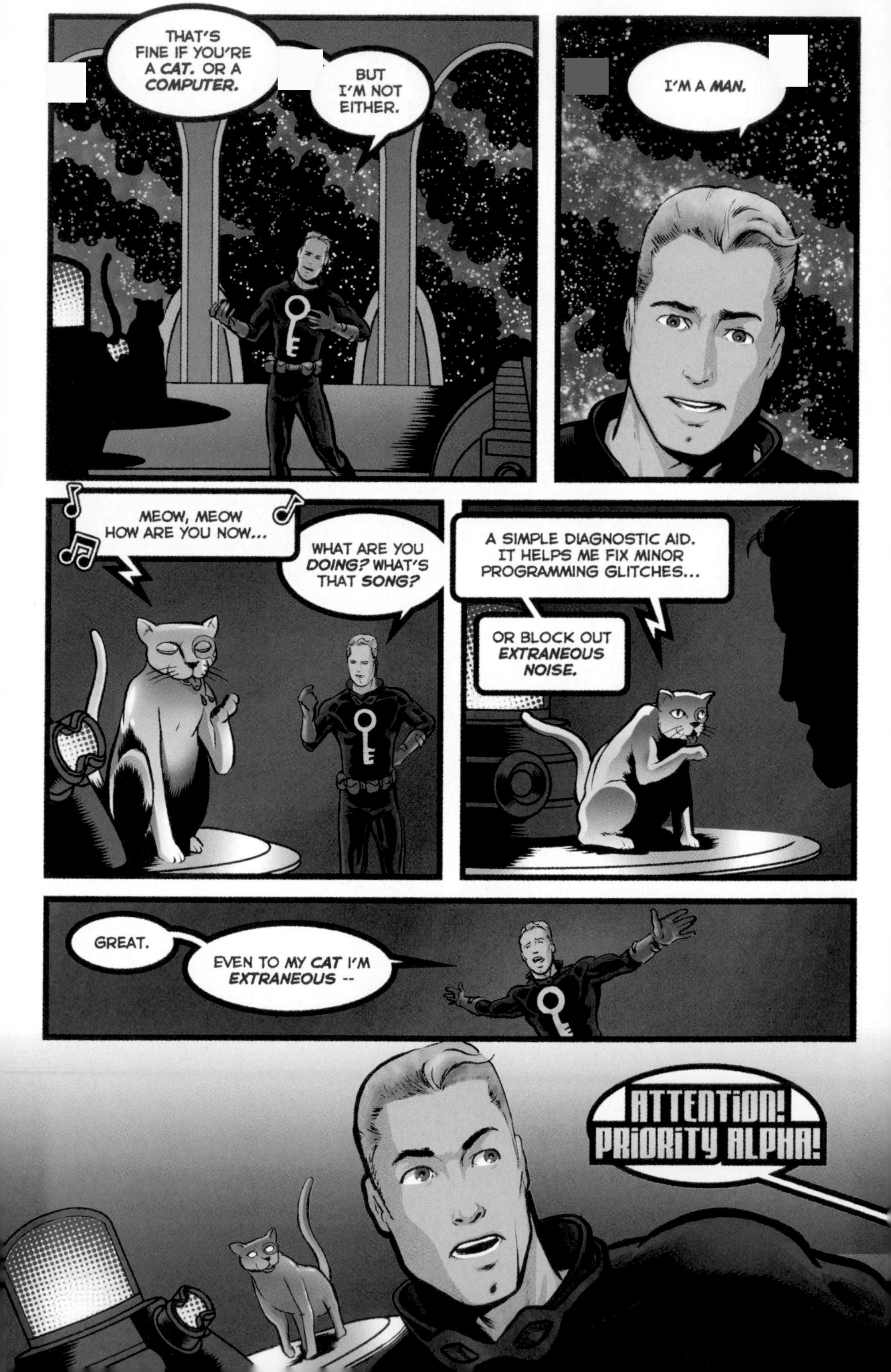
THAT'S FINE IF YOU'RE A CAT. OR A COMPUTER.
BUT I'M NOT EITHER.
I'M A MAN.
MEOW, MEOW HOW ARE YOU NOW...
WHAT ARE YOU DOING? WHAT'S THAT SONG?
A SIMPLE DIAGNOSTIC AID. IT HELPS ME FIX MINOR PROGRAMMING GLITCHES...
OR BLOCK OUT EXTRANEOUS NOISE.
GREAT.
EVEN TO MY CAT I'M EXTRANEOUS --
ATTENTION! PRIORITY ALPHA!

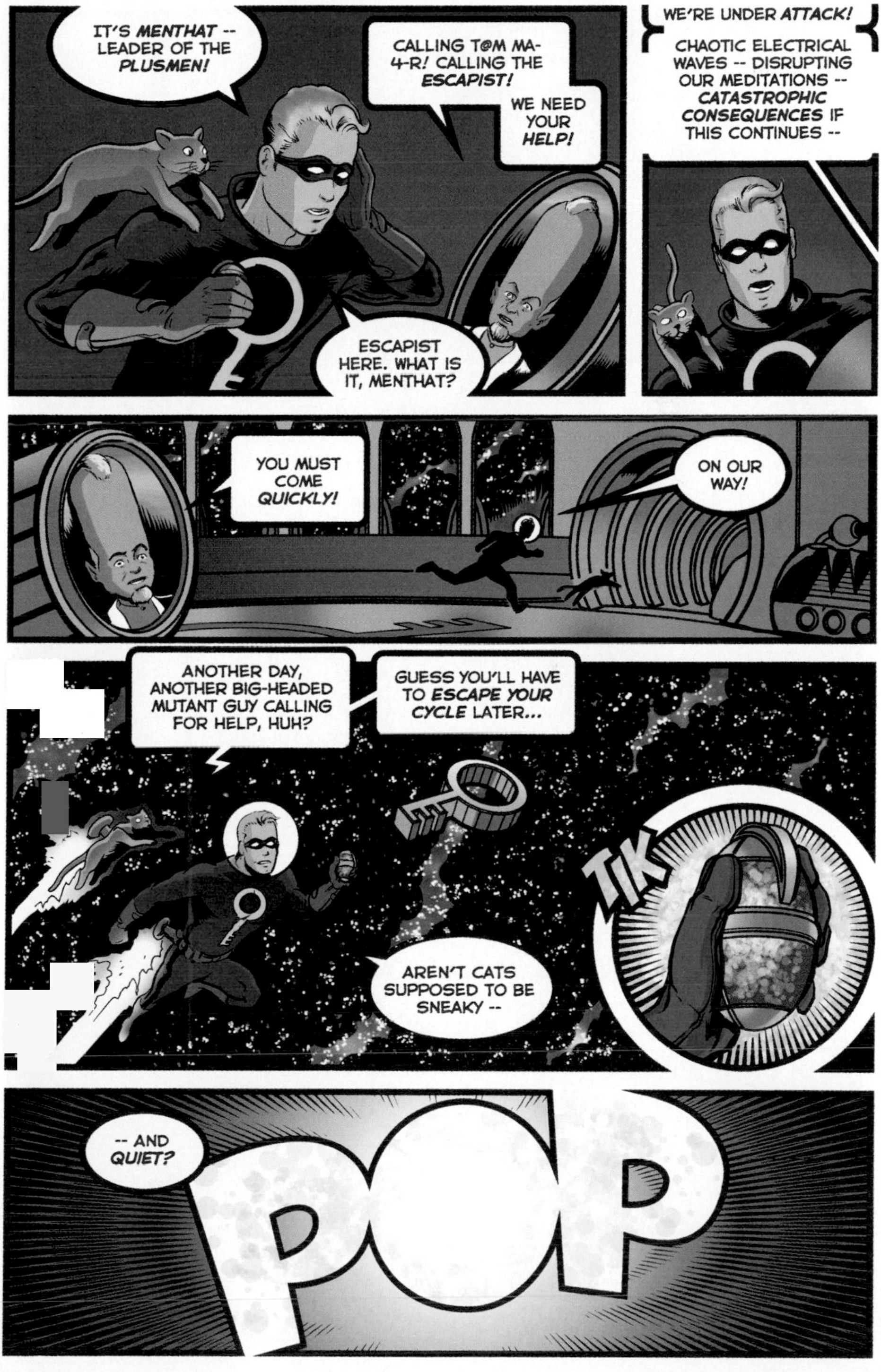
IT'S MENTHAT -- LEADER OF THE PLUSMEN!
CALLING T@M MA-4-R! CALLING THE ESCAPIST!
WE NEED YOUR HELP!
ESCAPIST HERE. WHAT IS IT, MENTHAT?
WE'RE UNDER ATTACK!
CHAOTIC ELECTRICAL WAVES -- DISRUPTING OUR MEDITATIONS -- CATASTROPHIC CONSEQUENCES IF THIS CONTINUES --
YOU MUST COME QUICKLY!
ON OUR WAY!
ANOTHER DAY, ANOTHER BIG-HEADED MUTANT GUY CALLING FOR HELP, HUH?
GUESS YOU'LL HAVE TO ESCAPE YOUR CYCLE LATER...
TK
AREN'T CATS SUPPOSED TO BE SNEAKY --
-- AND QUIET?
POP

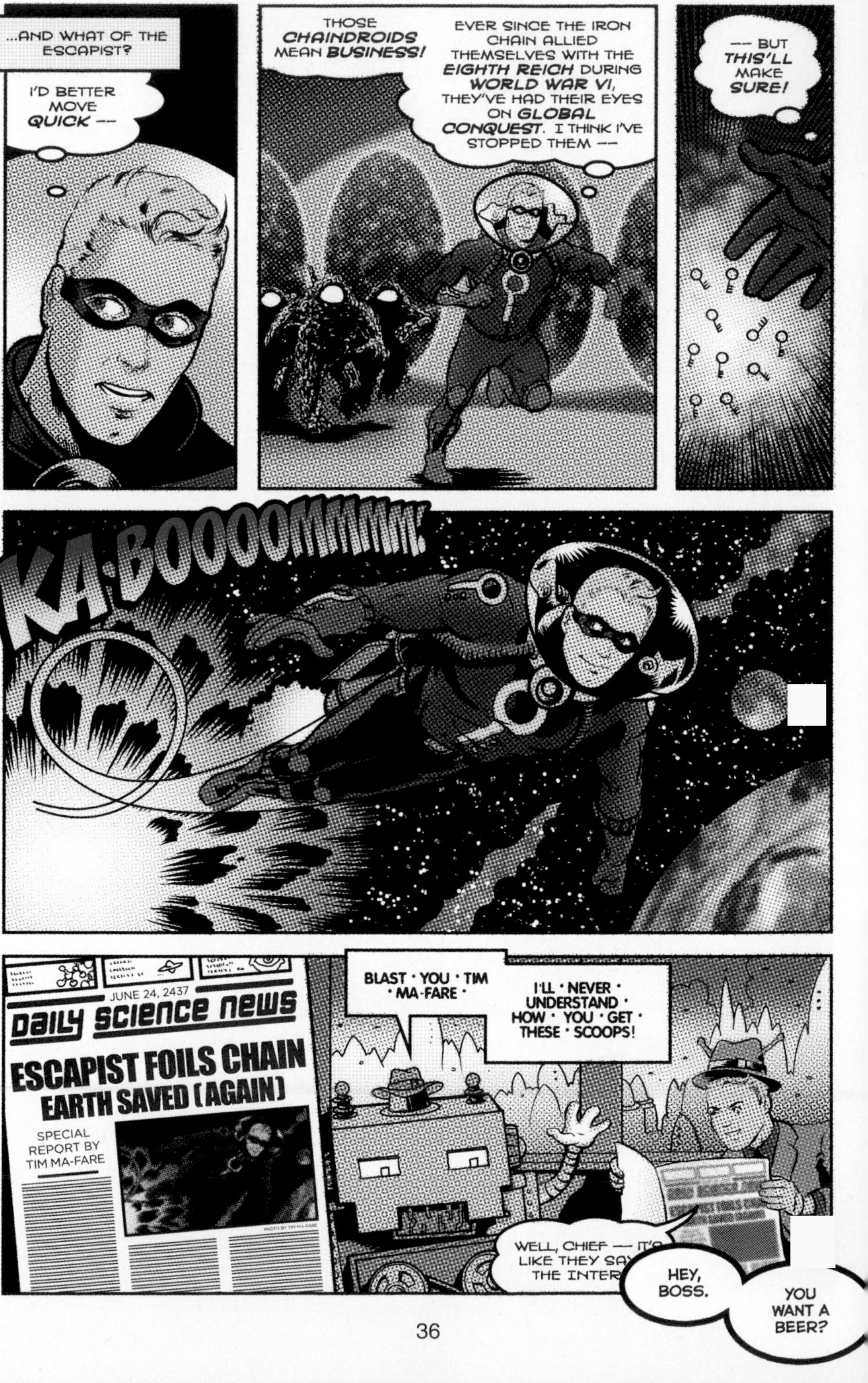
...AND WHAT OF THE ESCAPIST?
I'D BETTER MOVE QUICK --
THOSE CHAINDROIDS MEAN BUSINESS!
EVER SINCE THE IRON CHAIN ALLIED THEMSELVES WITH THE EIGHTH REICH DURING WORLD WAR VI, THEY'VE HAD THEIR EYES ON GLOBAL CONQUEST. I THINK I'VE STOPPED THEM --
-- BUT THIS'LL MAKE SURE!
KA-BOOOOMMMM!
JUNE 24, 2437
daily science news
ESCAPIST FOILS CHAIN
EARTH SAVED (AGAIN)
SPECIAL REPORT BY TIM MA-FARE
PHOTO BY TIM MA-FARE
BLAST · YOU · TIM · MA-FARE ·
I'LL · NEVER · UNDERSTAND · HOW · YOU · GET · THESE · SCOOPS!
WELL, CHIEF -- IT'S LIKE THEY SA THE INTER
HEY, BOSS.
YOU WANT A BEER?

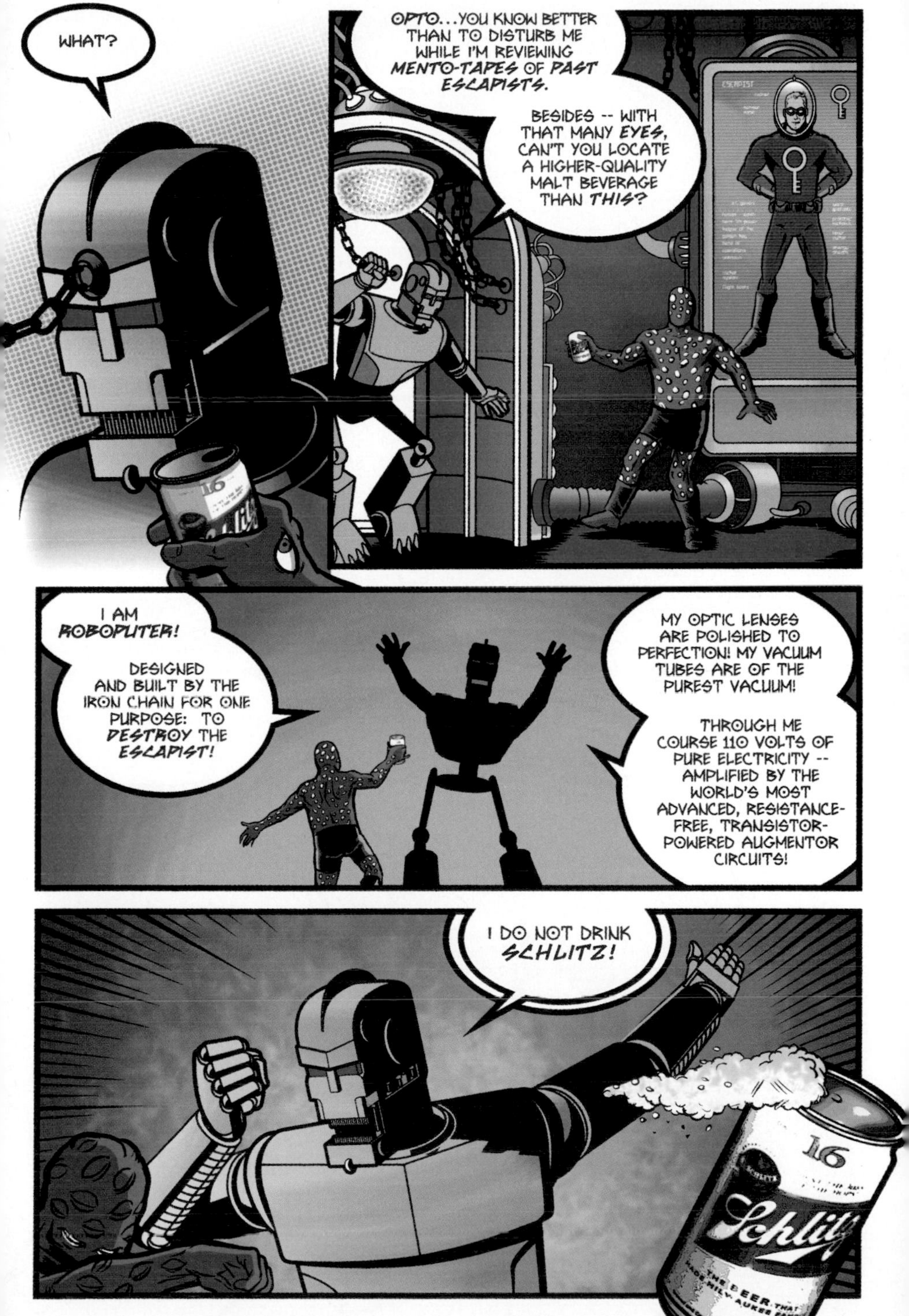
WHAT?
OPTO...YOU KNOW BETTER THAN TO DISTURB ME WHILE I'M REVIEWING MENTO-TAPES OF PAST ESCAPISTS.
BESIDES -- WITH THAT MANY EYES, CAN'T YOU LOCATE A HIGHER-QUALITY MALT BEVERAGE THAN THIS?
I AM ROBOPUTER!
DESIGNED AND BUILT BY THE IRON CHAIN FOR ONE PURPOSE: TO DESTROY THE ESCAPIST!
MY OPTIC LENSES ARE POLISHED TO PERFECTION! MY VACUUM TUBES ARE OF THE PUREST VACUUM!
THROUGH ME COURSE 110 VOLTS OF PURE ELECTRICITY -- AMPLIFIED BY THE WORLD'S MOST ADVANCED, RESISTANCE-FREE, TRANSISTOR-POWERED AUGMENTOR CIRCUITS!
I DO NOT DRINK SCHLITZ!
Schlitz

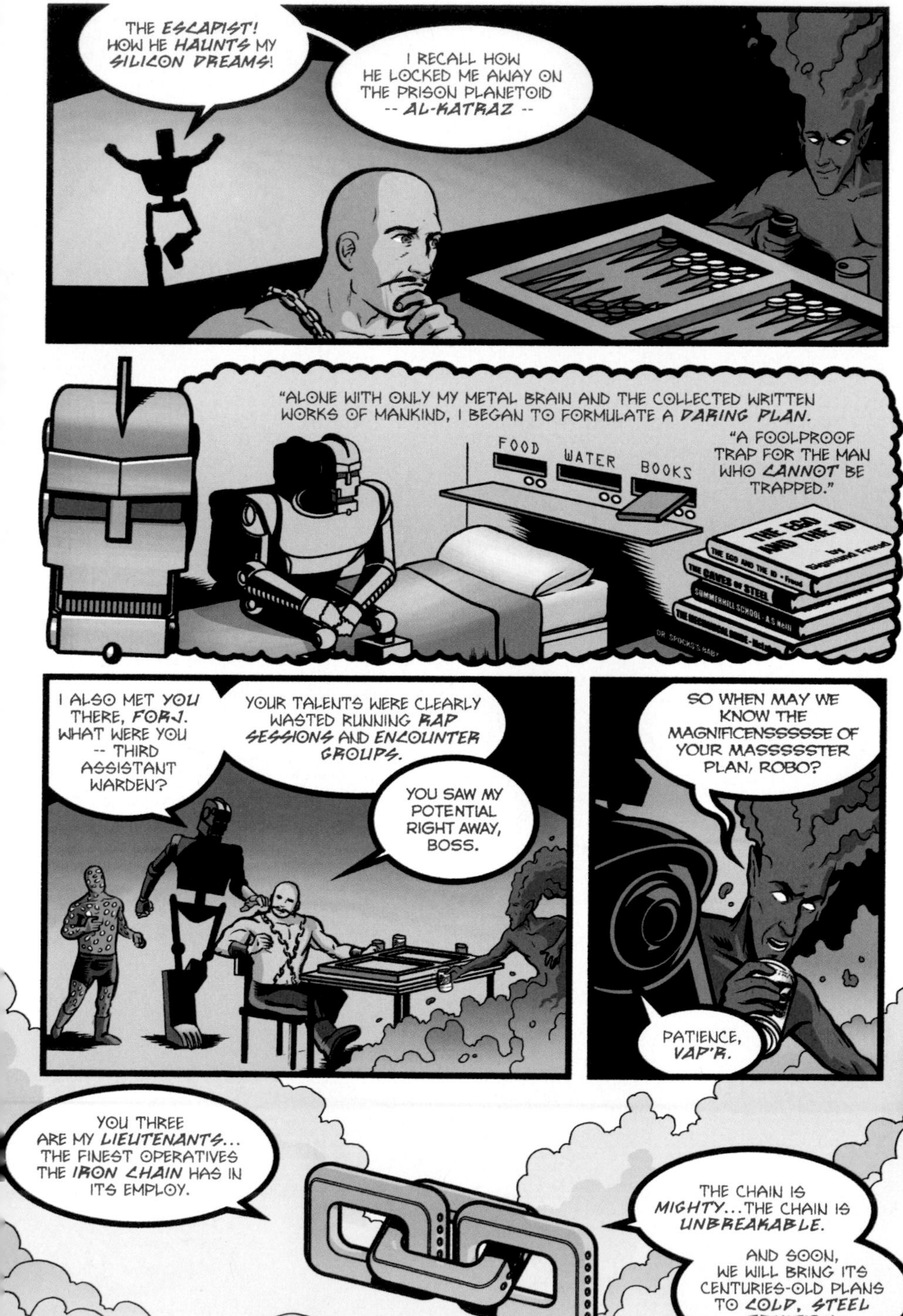
THE ESCAPIST! HOW HE HAUNTS MY SILICON DREAMS!
I RECALL HOW HE LOCKED ME AWAY ON THE PRISON PLANETOID -- AL-KATRAZ --
"ALONE WITH ONLY MY METAL BRAIN AND THE COLLECTED WRITTEN WORKS OF MANKIND, I BEGAN TO FORMULATE A DARING PLAN.
FOOD
WATER
BOOKS
"A FOOLPROOF TRAP FOR THE MAN WHO CANNOT BE TRAPPED."
THE EGO AND THE ID by Sigmund Freud
THE EGO AND THE ID • Freud
THE CAVES OF STEEL
SUMMERHILL SCHOOL · A.S. Neill
DR. SPOCK'S BABY
I ALSO MET YOU THERE, FORJ. WHAT WERE YOU -- THIRD ASSISTANT WARDEN?
YOUR TALENTS WERE CLEARLY WASTED RUNNING RAP SESSIONS AND ENCOUNTER GROUPS.
YOU SAW MY POTENTIAL RIGHT AWAY, BOSS.
SO WHEN MAY WE KNOW THE MAGNIFICENSSSSSE OF YOUR MASSSSSTER PLAN, ROBO?
PATIENCE, VAP'R.
YOU THREE ARE MY LIEUTENANTS... THE FINEST OPERATIVES THE IRON CHAIN HAS IN ITS EMPLOY.
THE CHAIN IS MIGHTY...THE CHAIN IS UNBREAKABLE.
AND SOON, WE WILL BRING ITS CENTURIES-OLD PLANS TO COLD, STEEL FRUITION.

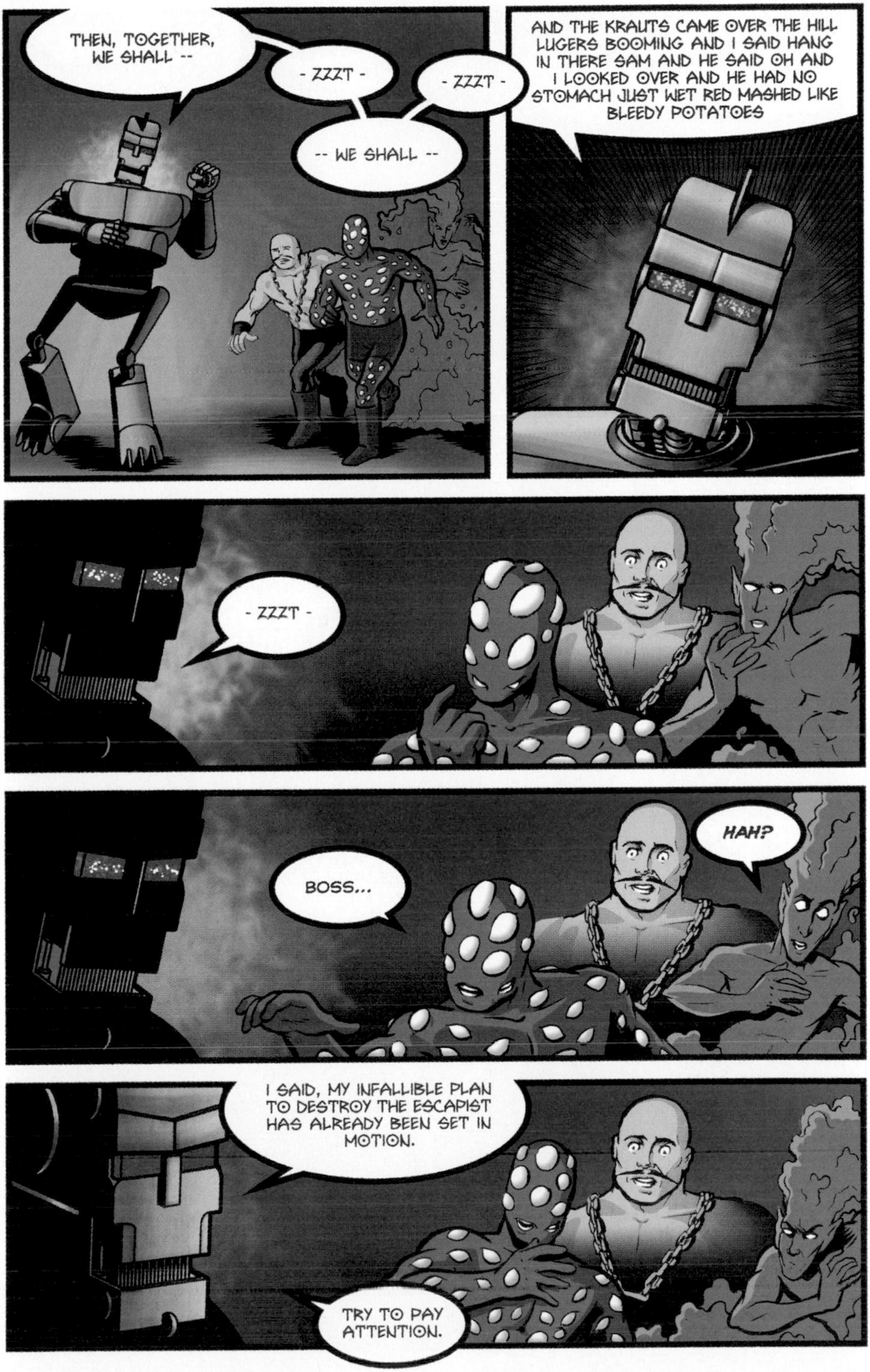
THEN, TOGETHER, WE SHALL --
- ZZZT -
- ZZZT -
-- WE SHALL --
AND THE KRAUTS CAME OVER THE HILL LUGERS BOOMING AND I SAID HANG IN THERE SAM AND HE SAID OH AND I LOOKED OVER AND HE HAD NO STOMACH JUST WET RED MASHED LIKE BLEEDY POTATOES
- ZZZT -
BOSS...
HAH?
I SAID, MY INFALLIBLE PLAN TO DESTROY THE ESCAPIST HAS ALREADY BEEN SET IN MOTION.
TRY TO PAY ATTENTION.

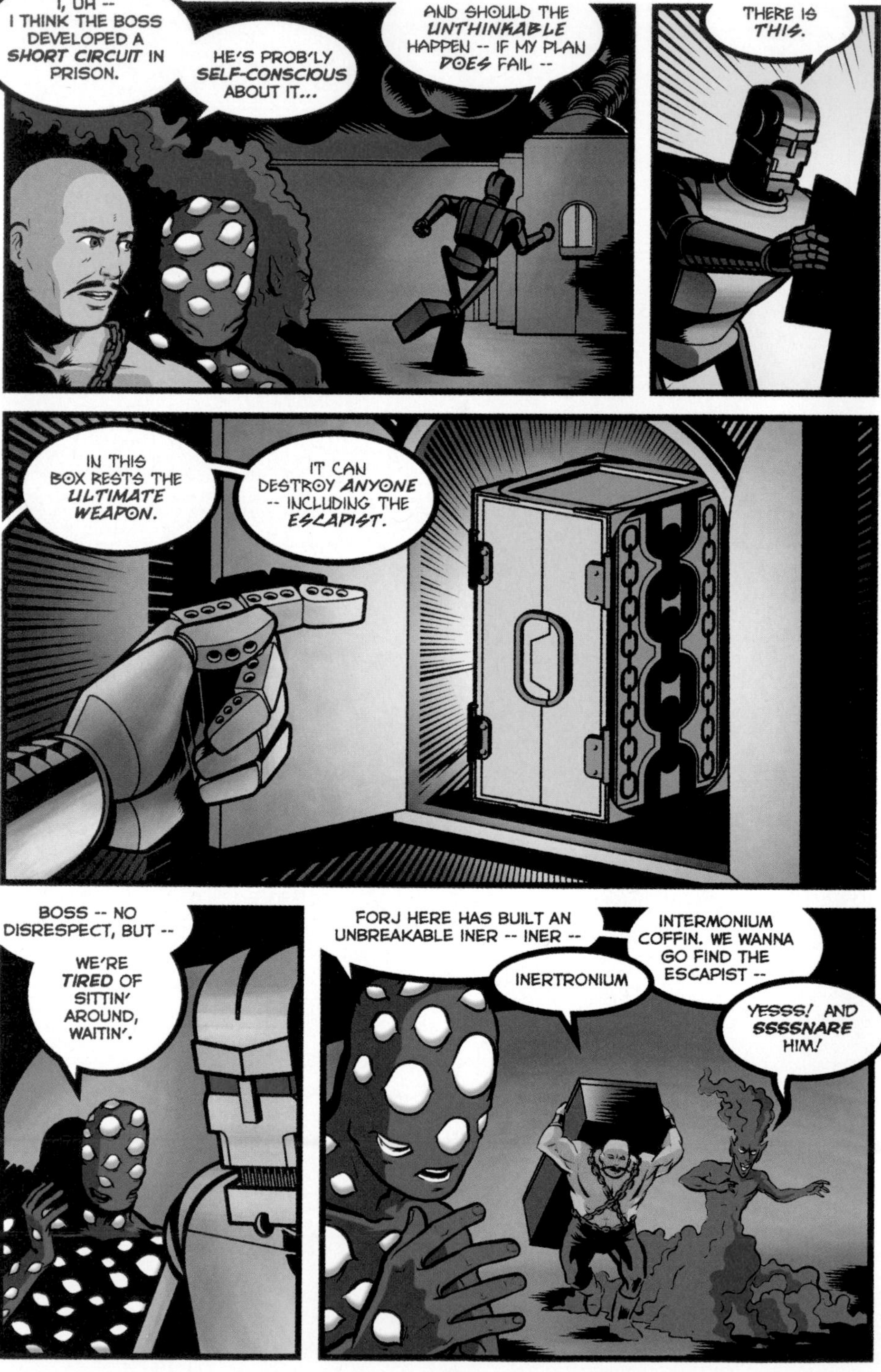

I, UH -- I THINK THE BOSS DEVELOPED A SHORT CIRCUIT IN PRISON.
HE'S PROB'LY SELF-CONSCIOUS ABOUT IT...
AND SHOULD THE UNTHINKABLE HAPPEN -- IF MY PLAN DOES FAIL --
THERE IS THIS.
IN THIS BOX RESTS THE ULTIMATE WEAPON.
IT CAN DESTROY ANYONE -- INCLUDING THE ESCAPIST.
BOSS -- NO DISRESPECT, BUT --
WE'RE TIRED OF SITTIN' AROUND, WAITIN'.
FORJ HERE HAS BUILT AN UNBREAKABLE INER -- INER --
INERTRONIUM
INTERMONIUM COFFIN. WE WANNA GO FIND THE ESCAPIST --
YESSS! AND SSSSNARE HIM!

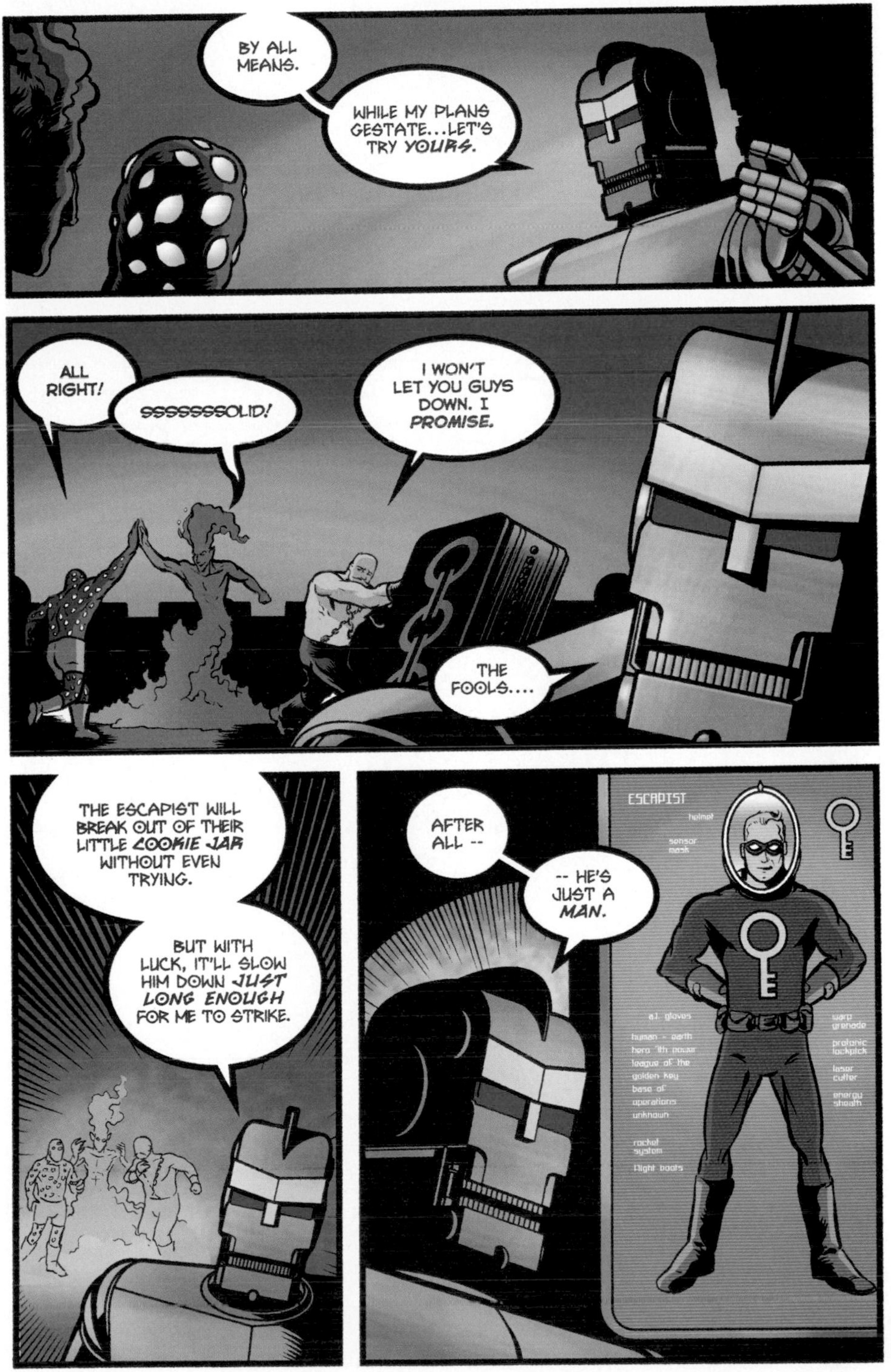
BY ALL MEANS.
WHILE MY PLANS GESTATE...LET'S TRY YOURS.
ALL RIGHT!
SSSSSSSOLID!
I WON'T LET YOU GUYS DOWN. I PROMISE.
THE FOOLS....
THE ESCAPIST WILL BREAK OUT OF THEIR LITTLE COOKIE JAR WITHOUT EVEN TRYING.
BUT WITH LUCK, IT'LL SLOW HIM DOWN JUST LONG ENOUGH FOR ME TO STRIKE.
AFTER ALL --
-- HE'S JUST A MAN.
ESCAPIST
helmet
sensor mask
a.l. gloves
human - earth
league of the golden key
base of operations unknown
rocket system
flight boots
warp grenade
protonic lockpick
laser cutter
energy sheath

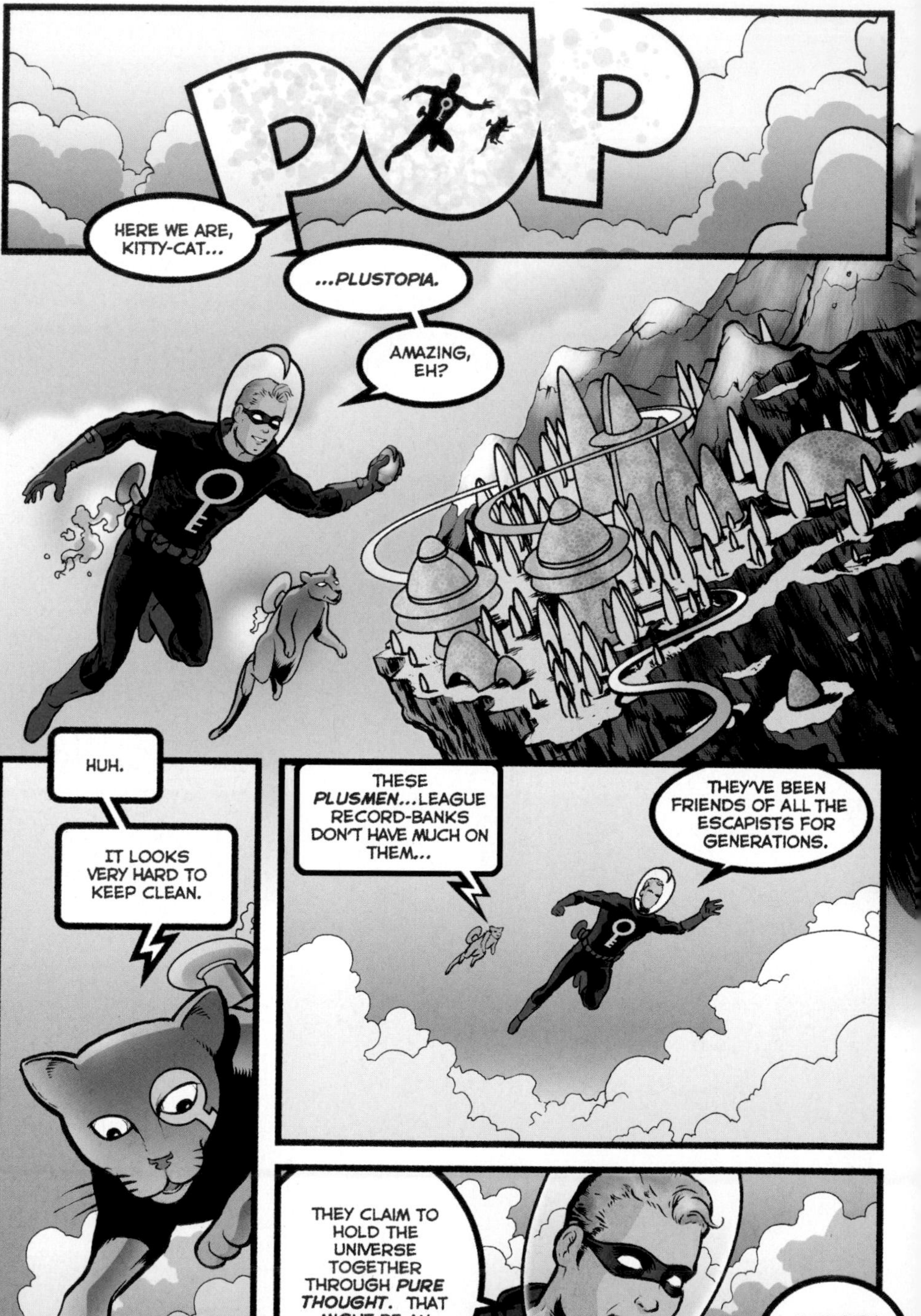
POP
HERE WE ARE, KITTY-CAT...
...PLUSTOPIA.
AMAZING, EH?
HUH.
IT LOOKS VERY HARD TO KEEP CLEAN.
THESE PLUSMEN...LEAGUE RECORD-BANKS DON'T HAVE MUCH ON THEM...
THEY'VE BEEN FRIENDS OF ALL THE ESCAPISTS FOR GENERATIONS.
THEY CLAIM TO HOLD THE UNIVERSE TOGETHER THROUGH PURE THOUGHT. THAT MIGHT BE AN EXAGGERATION --
BUT THEY ARE REALLY, REALLY SMART.

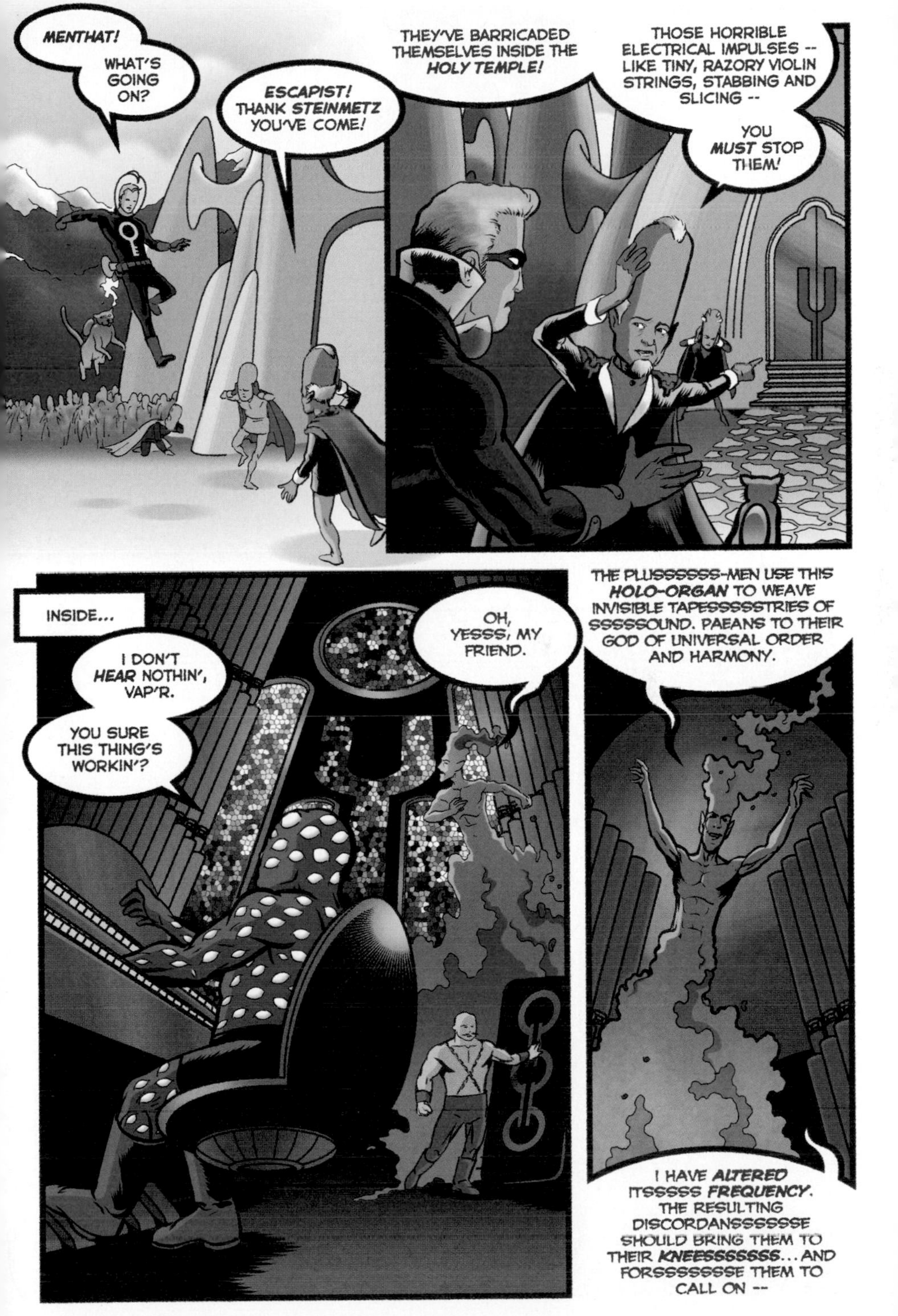
MENTHAT!
WHAT'S GOING ON?
ESCAPIST! THANK STEINMETZ YOU'VE COME!
THEY'VE BARRICADED THEMSELVES INSIDE THE HOLY TEMPLE!
THOSE HORRIBLE ELECTRICAL IMPULSES -- LIKE TINY, RAZORY VIOLIN STRINGS, STABBING AND SLICING --
YOU MUST STOP THEM!
INSIDE...
I DON'T HEAR NOTHIN', VAP'R.
YOU SURE THIS THING'S WORKIN'?
OH, YESSS, MY FRIEND.
THE PLUSSSSSSS-MEN USE THIS HOLO-ORGAN TO WEAVE INVISIBLE TAPESSSSSTRIES OF SSSSSOUND. PAEANS TO THEIR GOD OF UNIVERSAL ORDER AND HARMONY.
I HAVE ALTERED ITSSSSS FREQUENCY. THE RESULTING DISCORDANSSSSSSE SHOULD BRING THEM TO THEIR KNEESSSSSSS... AND FORSSSSSSSE THEM TO CALL ON --

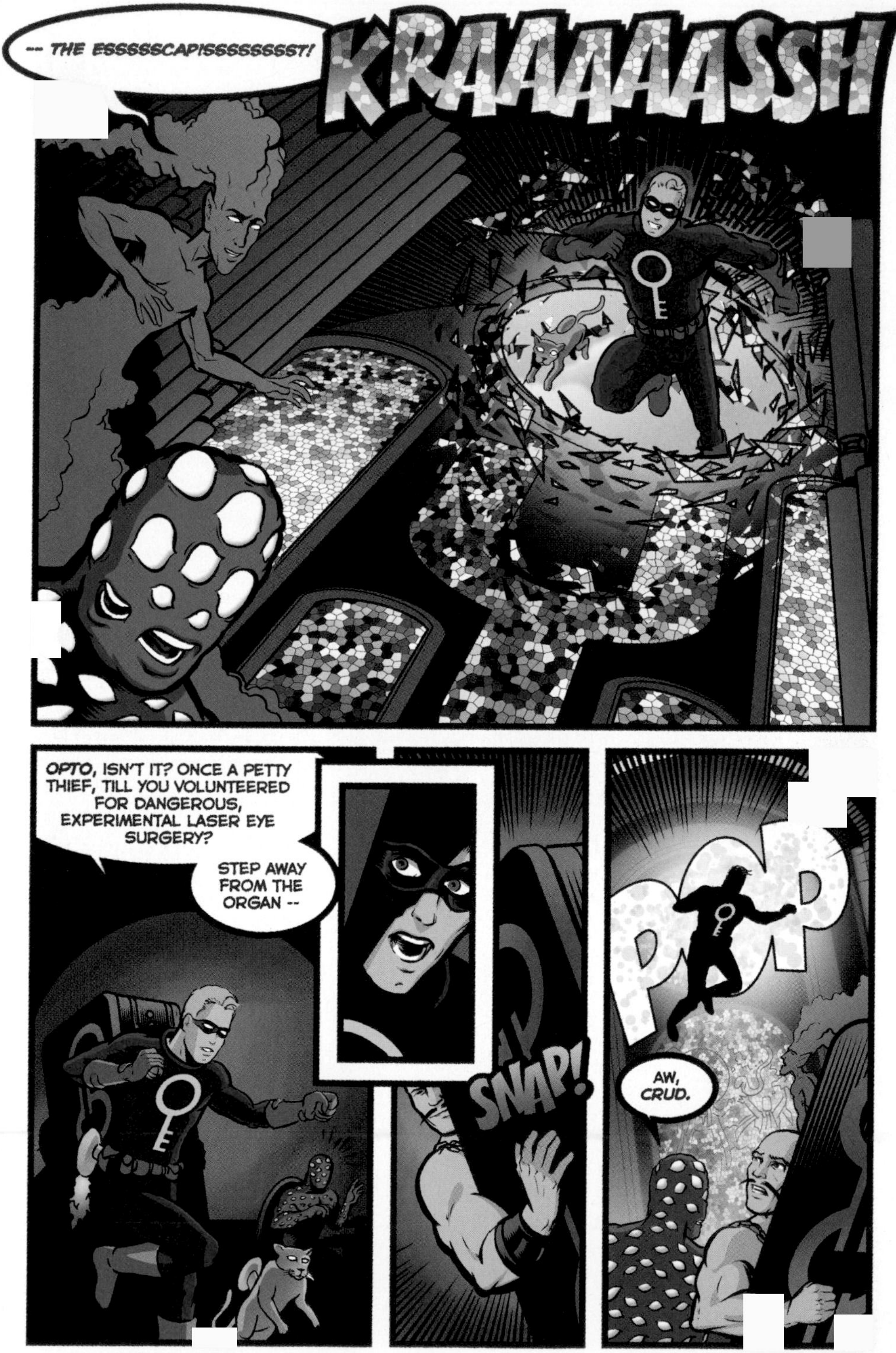
-- THE ESSSSSCAPISSSSSSSST!
KRAAAAAASSH
OPTO, ISN'T IT? ONCE A PETTY THIEF, TILL YOU VOLUNTEERED FOR DANGEROUS, EXPERIMENTAL LASER EYE SURGERY?
STEP AWAY FROM THE ORGAN --
SNAP!
POP
AW, CRUD.

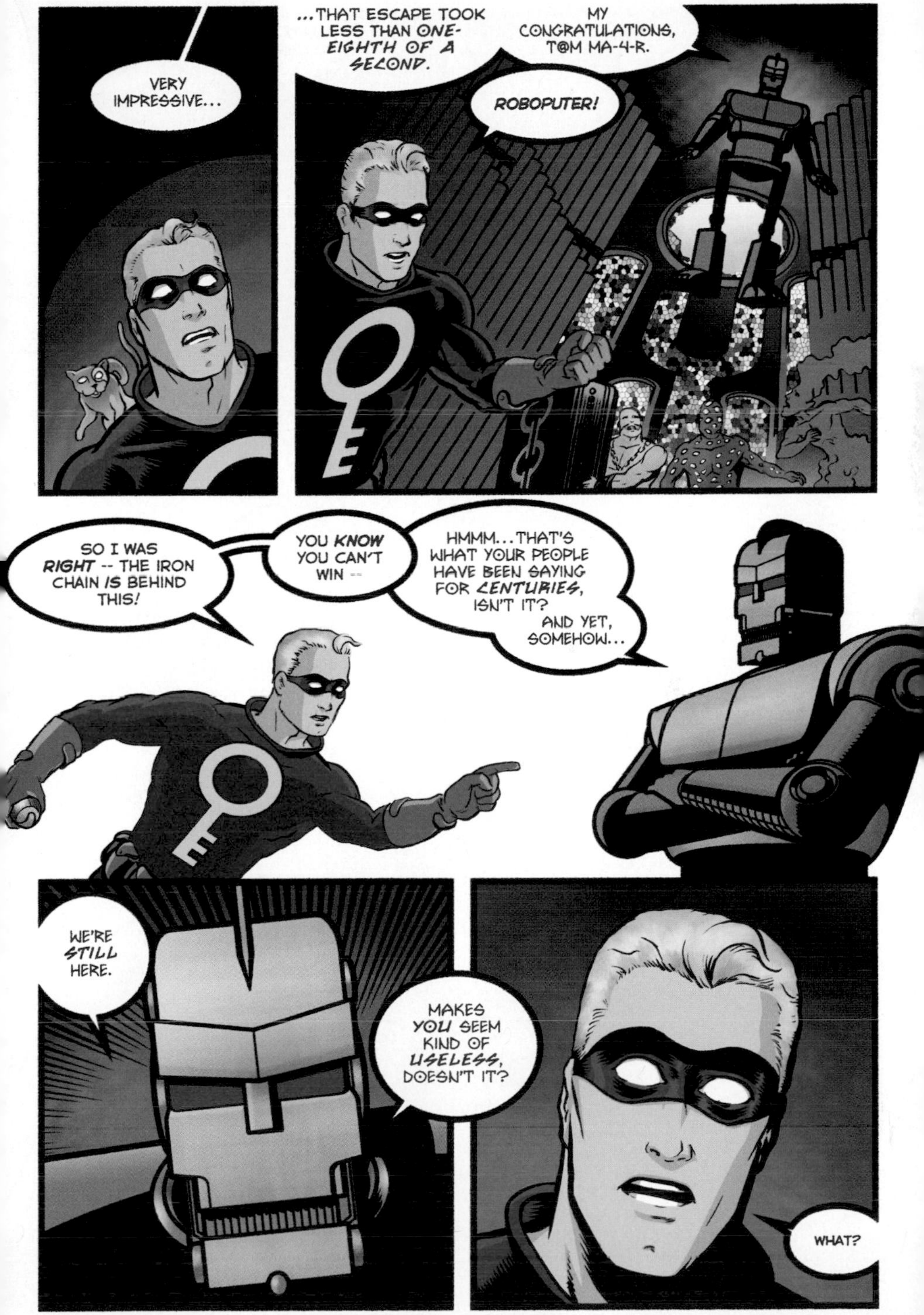
VERY IMPRESSIVE...
...THAT ESCAPE TOOK LESS THAN ONE-EIGHTH OF A SECOND.
MY CONGRATULATIONS, T@M MA-4-R.
ROBOPUTER!
SO I WAS RIGHT -- THE IRON CHAIN IS BEHIND THIS!
YOU KNOW YOU CAN'T WIN --
HMMM...THAT'S WHAT YOUR PEOPLE HAVE BEEN SAYING FOR CENTURIES, ISN'T IT?
AND YET, SOMEHOW...
WE'RE STILL HERE.
MAKES YOU SEEM KIND OF USELESS, DOESN'T IT?
WHAT?

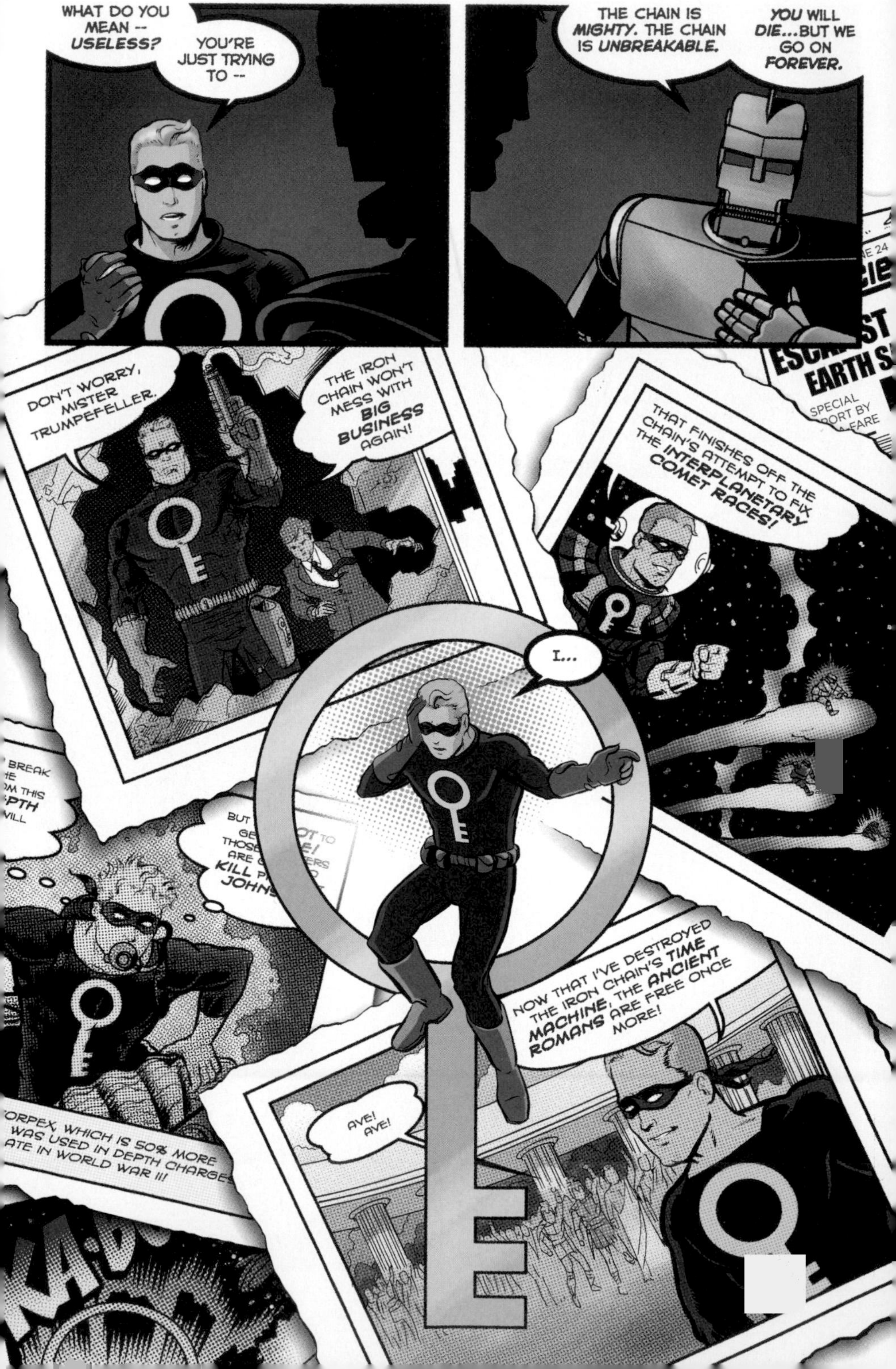

WHAT DO YOU MEAN -- USELESS?
YOU'RE JUST TRYING TO --
THE CHAIN IS MIGHTY. THE CHAIN IS UNBREAKABLE.
YOU WILL DIE...BUT WE GO ON FOREVER.
DON'T WORRY, MISTER TRUMPEFELLER.
THE IRON CHAIN WON'T MESS WITH BIG BUSINESS AGAIN!
THAT FINISHES OFF THE CHAIN'S ATTEMPT TO FIX THE INTERPLANETARY COMET RACES!
I...
NOW THAT I'VE DESTROYED THE IRON CHAIN'S TIME MACHINE, THE ANCIENT ROMANS ARE FREE ONCE MORE!
AVE! AVE!

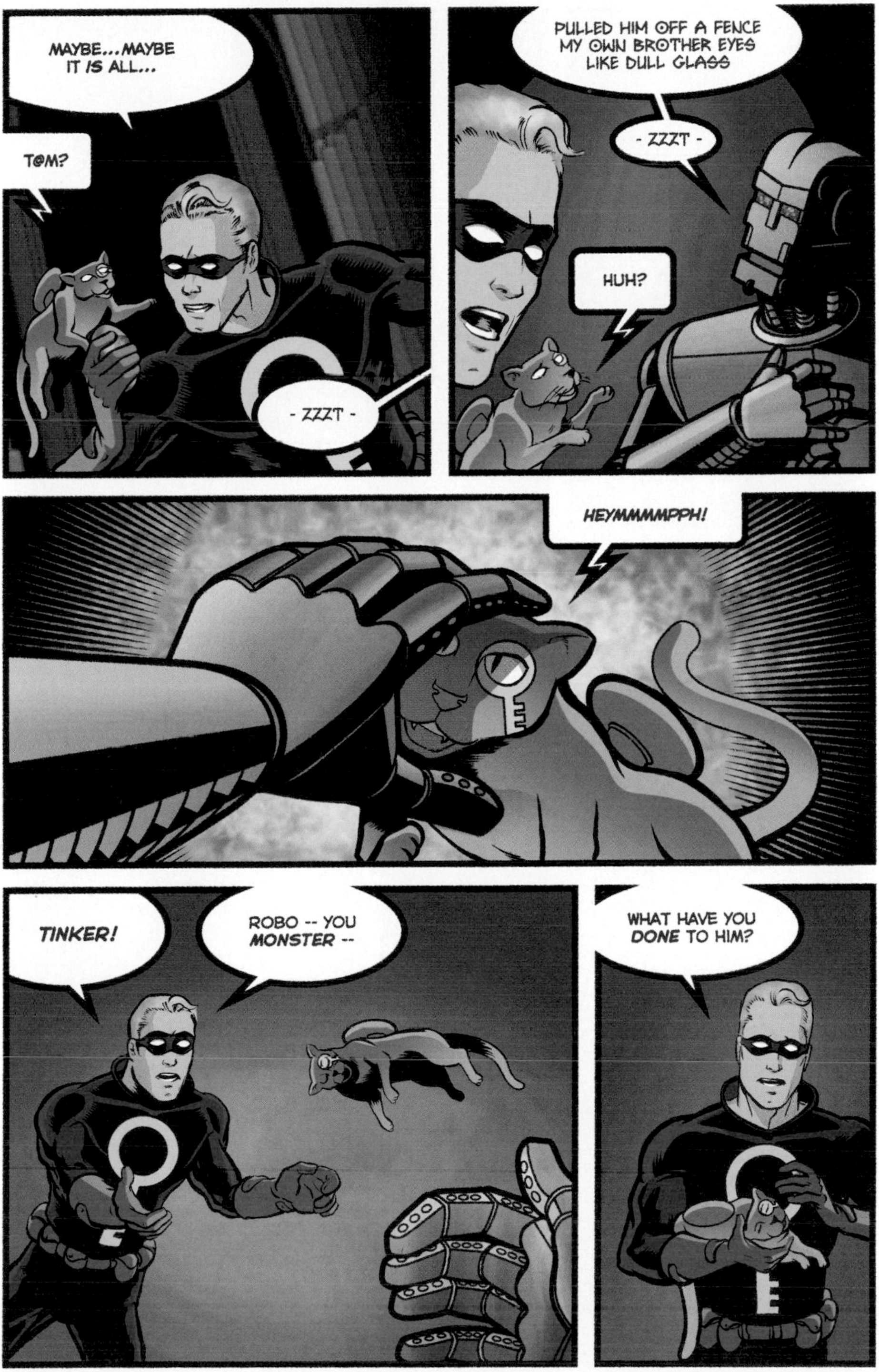
MAYBE...MAYBE IT *IS* ALL...
T@M?
- ZZZT -
PULLED HIM OFF A FENCE MY OWN BROTHER EYES LIKE DULL GLASS
- ZZZT -
HUH?
HEYMMMMPPH!
TINKER!
ROBO -- YOU *MONSTER* --
WHAT HAVE YOU *DONE* TO HIM?

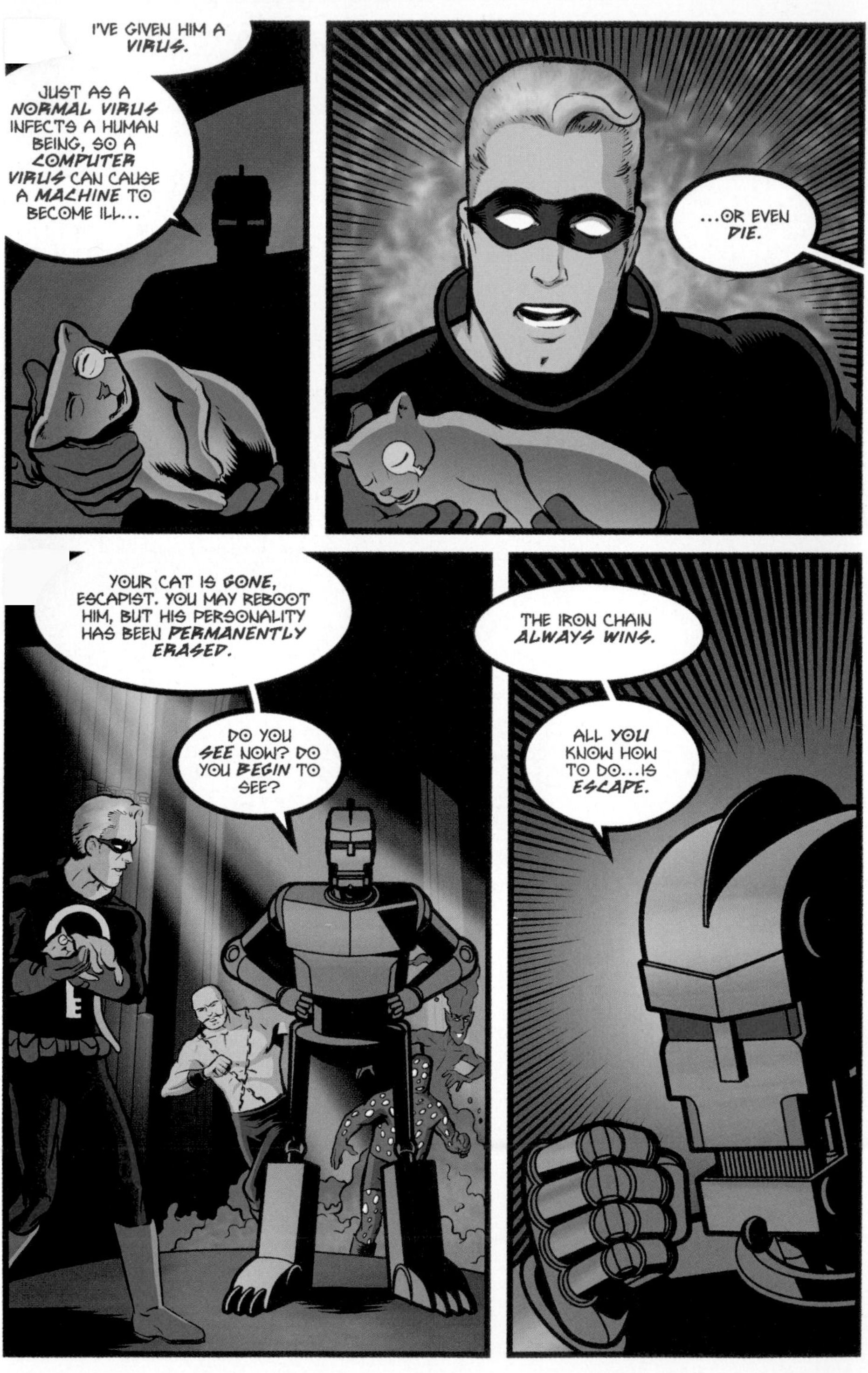
I'VE GIVEN HIM A VIRUS.
JUST AS A NORMAL VIRUS INFECTS A HUMAN BEING, SO A COMPUTER VIRUS CAN CAUSE A MACHINE TO BECOME ILL...
...OR EVEN DIE.
YOUR CAT IS GONE, ESCAPIST. YOU MAY REBOOT HIM, BUT HIS PERSONALITY HAS BEEN PERMANENTLY ERASED.
DO YOU SEE NOW? DO YOU BEGIN TO SEE?
THE IRON CHAIN ALWAYS WINS.
ALL YOU KNOW HOW TO DO...IS ESCAPE.

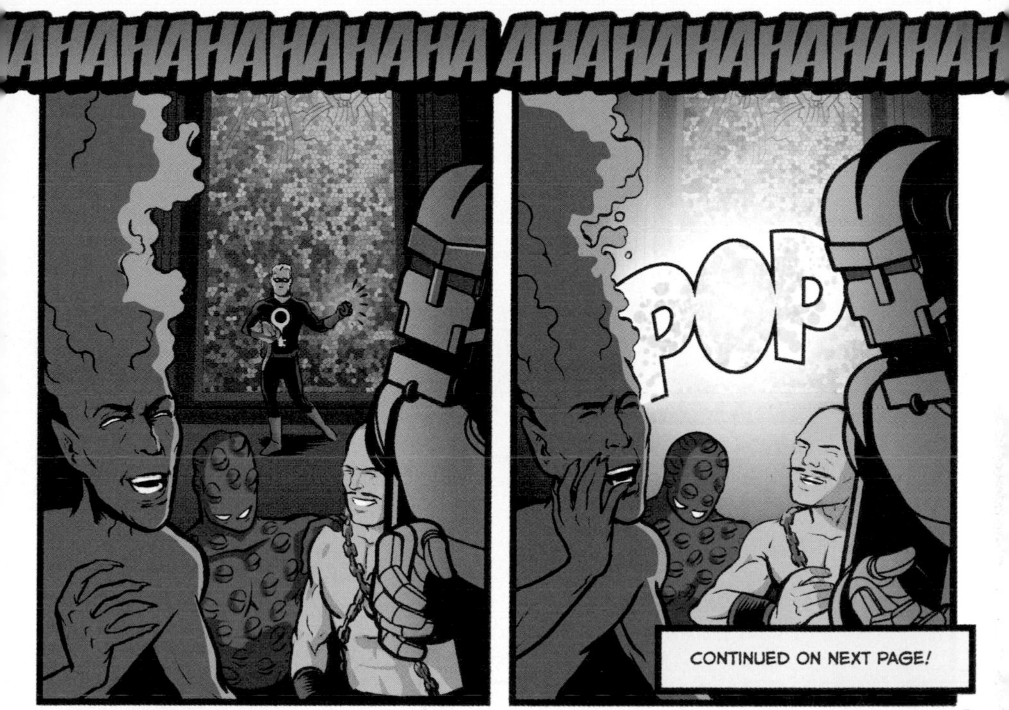

AHAHAHAHAHAHAHAHA AHAHAHAHAHAHAHAHAH
POP
CONTINUED ON NEXT PAGE!

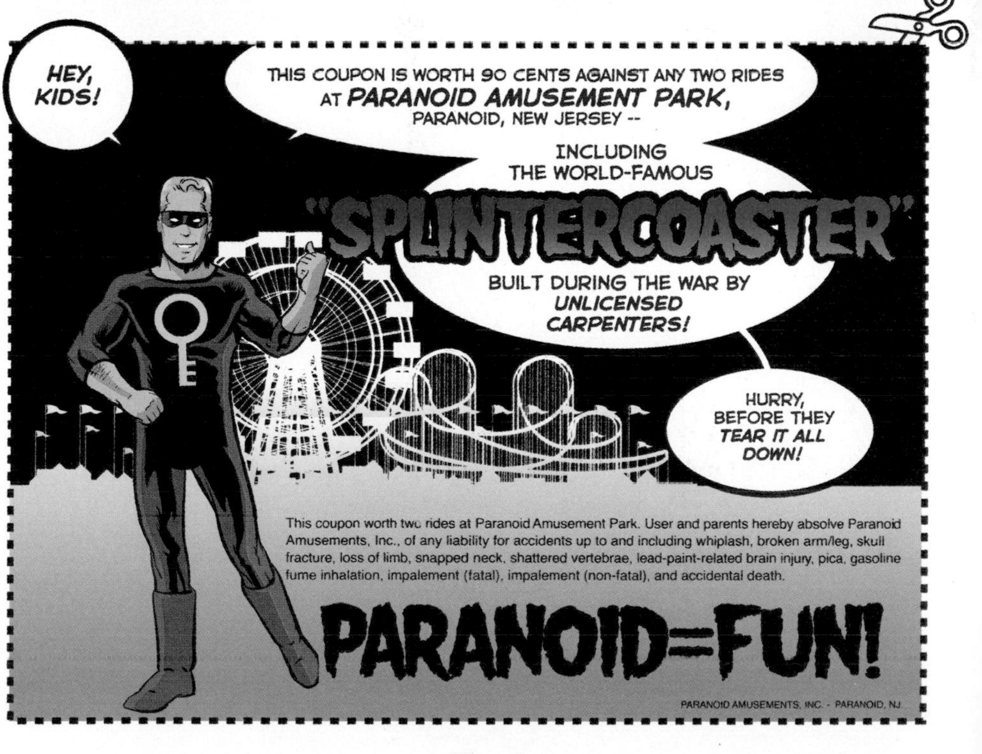

HEY, KIDS!
THIS COUPON IS WORTH 90 CENTS AGAINST ANY TWO RIDES AT PARANOID AMUSEMENT PARK, PARANOID, NEW JERSEY --
INCLUDING THE WORLD-FAMOUS
"SPLINTERCOASTER"
BUILT DURING THE WAR BY UNLICENSED CARPENTERS!
HURRY, BEFORE THEY TEAR IT ALL DOWN!
This coupon worth two rides at Paranoid Amusement Park. User and parents hereby absolve Paranoid Amusements, Inc., of any liability for accidents up to and including whiplash, broken arm/leg, skull fracture, loss of limb, snapped neck, shattered vertebrae, lead-paint-related brain injury, pica, gasoline fume inhalation, impalement (fatal), impalement (non-fatal), and accidental death.
PARANOID=FUN!
PARANOID AMUSEMENTS, INC. - PARANOID, NJ.

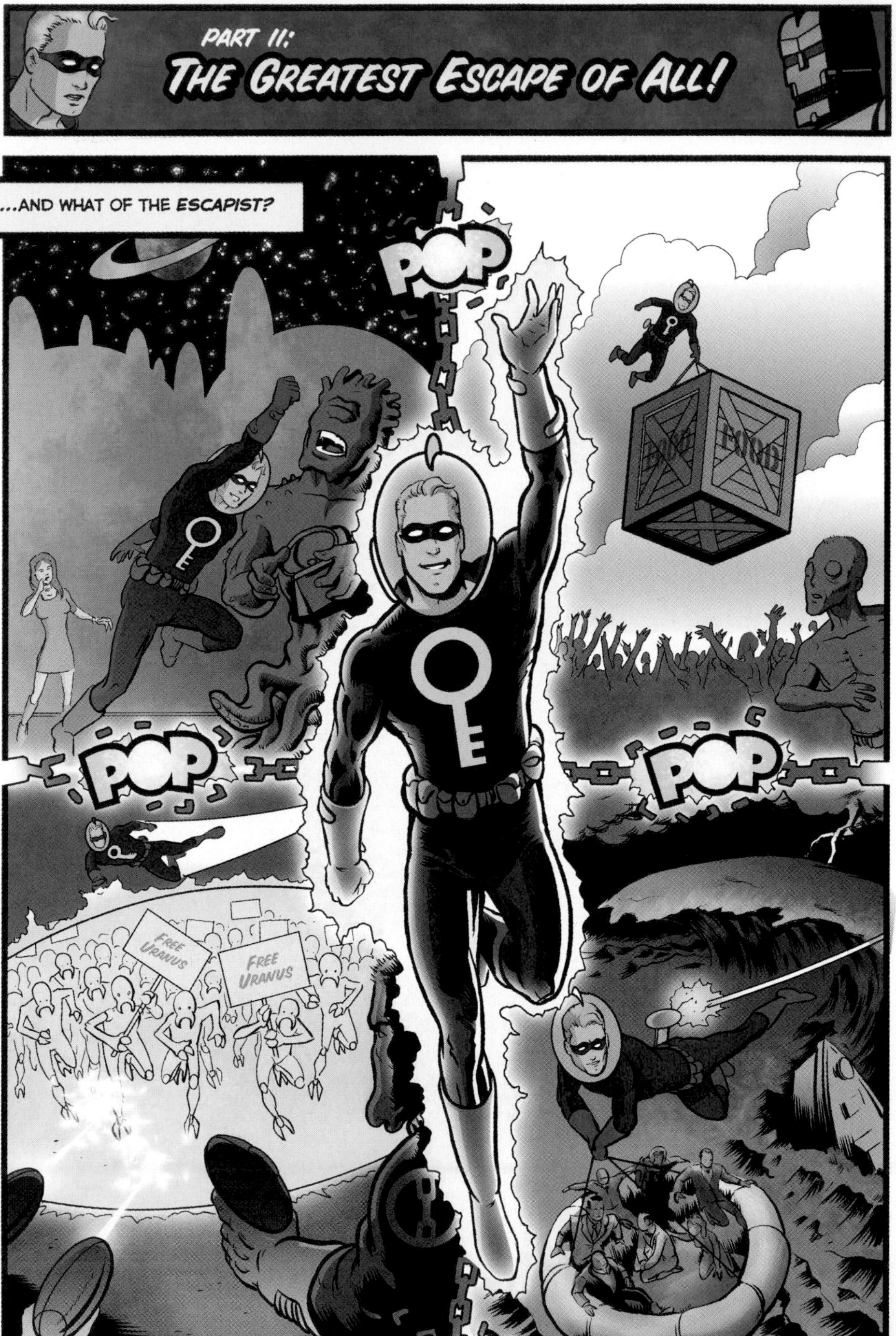
PART II:
THE GREATEST ESCAPE OF ALL!
...AND WHAT OF THE ESCAPIST?
POP
FOOD
FOOD
POP
POP
FREE URANUS
FREE URANUS
POP

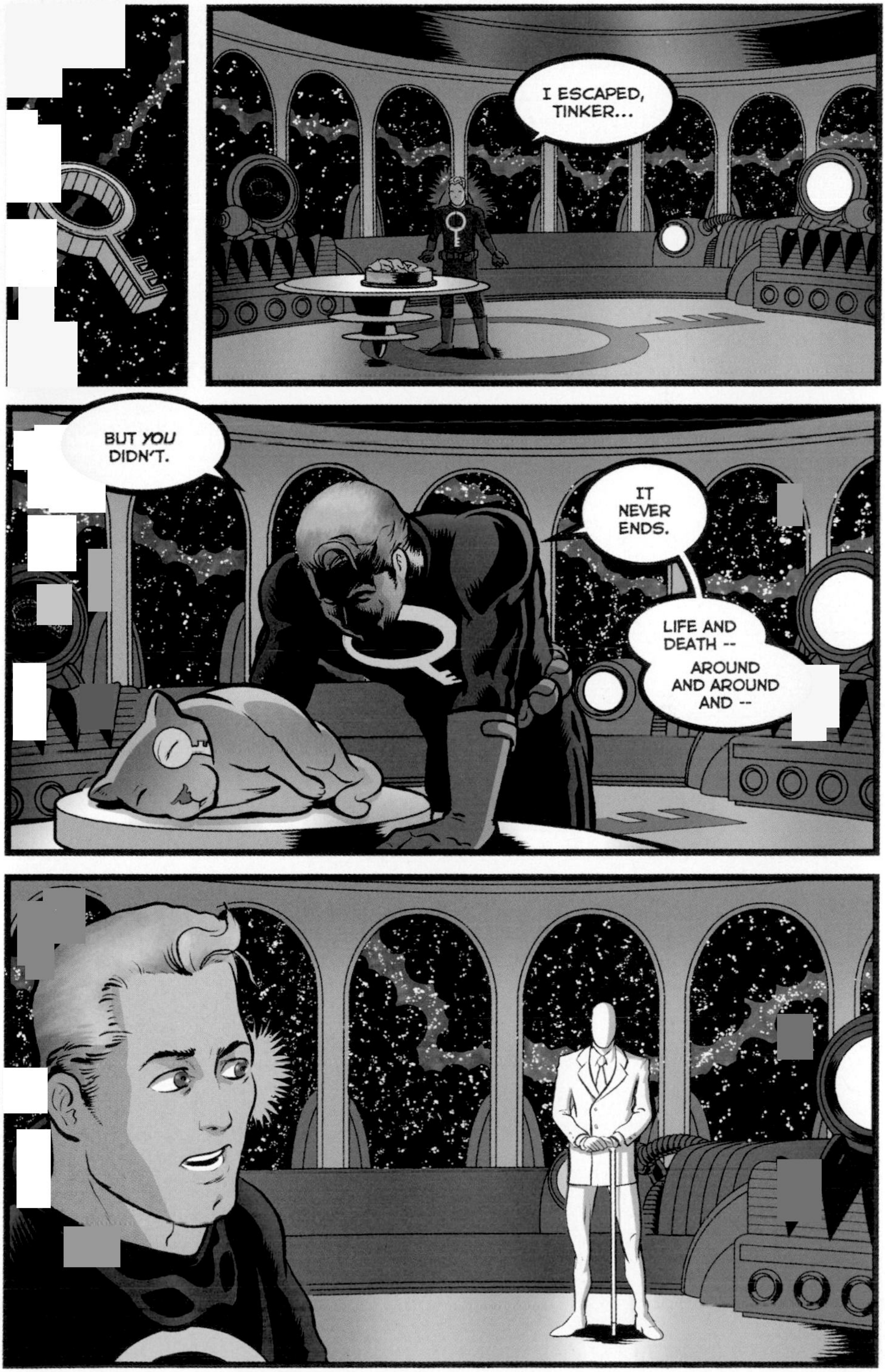
I ESCAPED, TINKER...
BUT *YOU* DIDN'T.
IT NEVER ENDS.
LIFE AND DEATH --
AROUND AND AROUND AND --

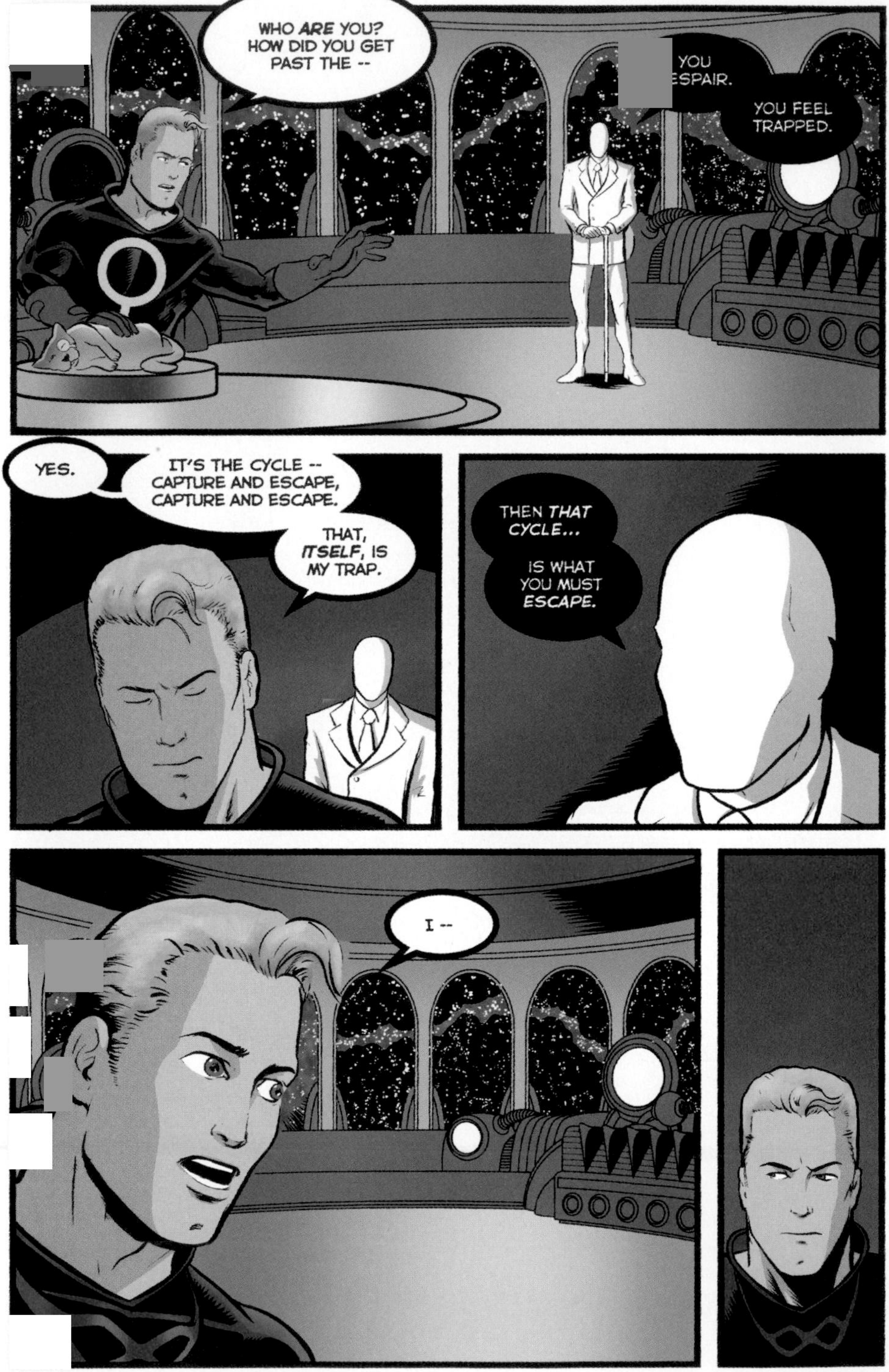
WHO ARE YOU? HOW DID YOU GET PAST THE --
YOU
ESPAIR.
YOU FEEL TRAPPED.
YES.
IT'S THE CYCLE -- CAPTURE AND ESCAPE, CAPTURE AND ESCAPE.
THAT, ITSELF, IS MY TRAP.
THEN THAT CYCLE...
IS WHAT YOU MUST ESCAPE.
I --

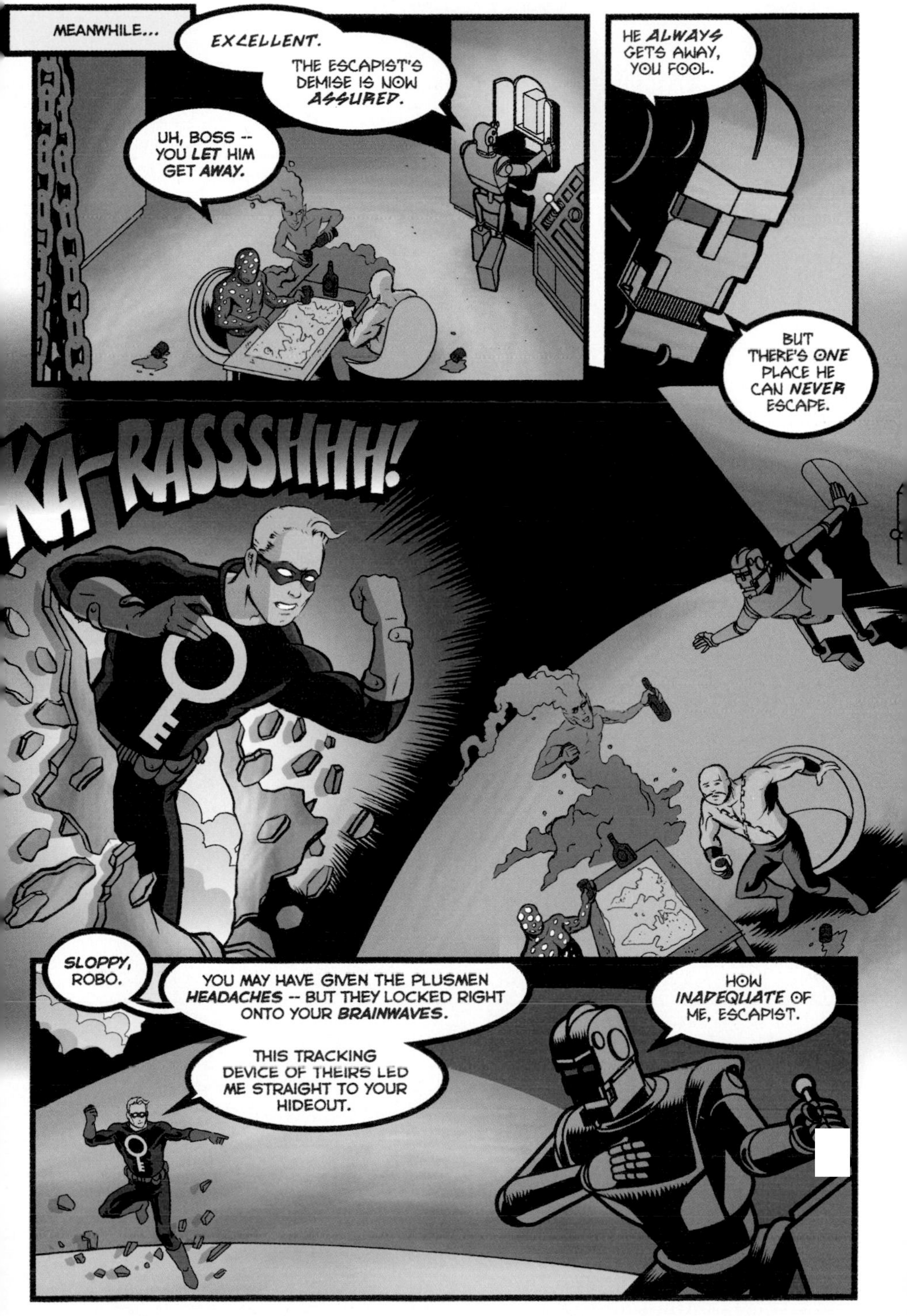
MEANWHILE...
EXCELLENT.
THE ESCAPIST'S DEMISE IS NOW ASSURED.
UH, BOSS -- YOU LET HIM GET AWAY.
HE ALWAYS GETS AWAY, YOU FOOL.
BUT THERE'S ONE PLACE HE CAN NEVER ESCAPE.
KA-RASSSHHH!
SLOPPY, ROBO.
YOU MAY HAVE GIVEN THE PLUSMEN HEADACHES -- BUT THEY LOCKED RIGHT ONTO YOUR BRAINWAVES.
THIS TRACKING DEVICE OF THEIRS LED ME STRAIGHT TO YOUR HIDEOUT.
HOW INADEQUATE OF ME, ESCAPIST.

UNLESS, OF COURSE --

I *WANTED* YOU HERE.

UUHH!

HAH!

CAN'T -- MOVE --

THAT, AS YOU HUMANS SAY, IS THE *POINT.*

I NEED YOU *STILL,* ESCAPIST -- SO I CAN USE THIS *BIPOLAR ENCEPHALIZER* --

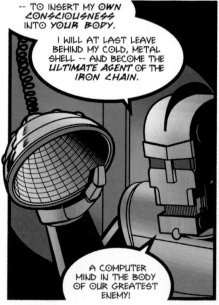

-- TO INSERT MY *OWN CONSCIOUSNESS* INTO *YOUR* BODY.

I WILL AT LAST LEAVE BEHIND MY COLD, METAL SHELL -- AND BECOME THE *ULTIMATE AGENT* OF THE *IRON CHAIN.*

A COMPUTER MIND IN THE BODY OF OUR GREATEST ENEMY!

OF COURSE --

YOUR CONSCIOUSNESS WILL THEN HAVE NOWHERE TO GO.

I'M AFRAID IT'LL JUST... *DISSIPATE.*

YESS! YESSSSSSS! DISSSSSSSSSIPATE!

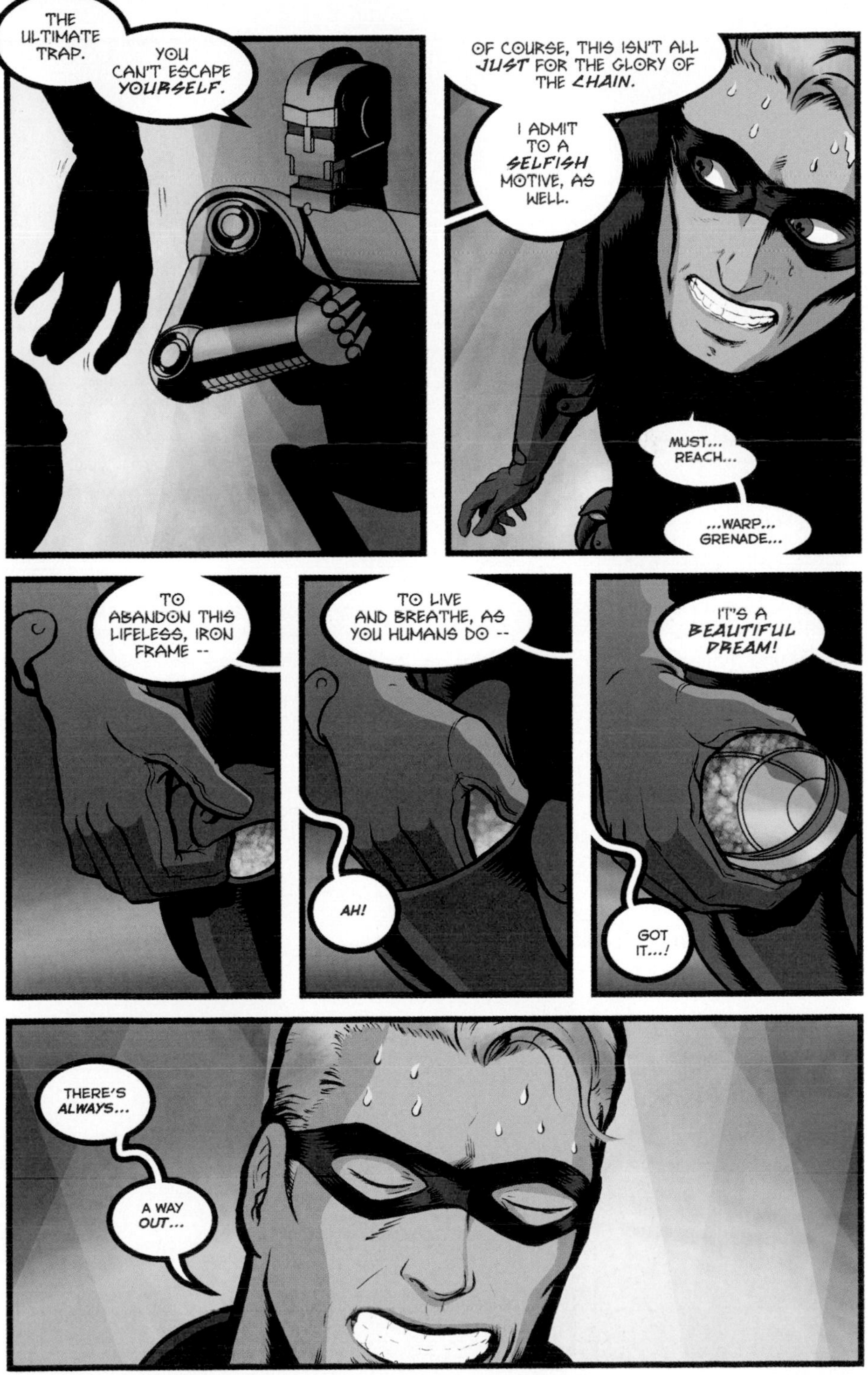
THE ULTIMATE TRAP.
YOU CAN'T ESCAPE YOURSELF.
OF COURSE, THIS ISN'T ALL JUST FOR THE GLORY OF THE CHAIN.
I ADMIT TO A SELFISH MOTIVE, AS WELL.
MUST... REACH...
...WARP... GRENADE...
TO ABANDON THIS LIFELESS, IRON FRAME --
TO LIVE AND BREATHE, AS YOU HUMANS DO --
AH!
IT'S A BEAUTIFUL DREAM!
GOT IT...!
THERE'S ALWAYS...
A WAY OUT...

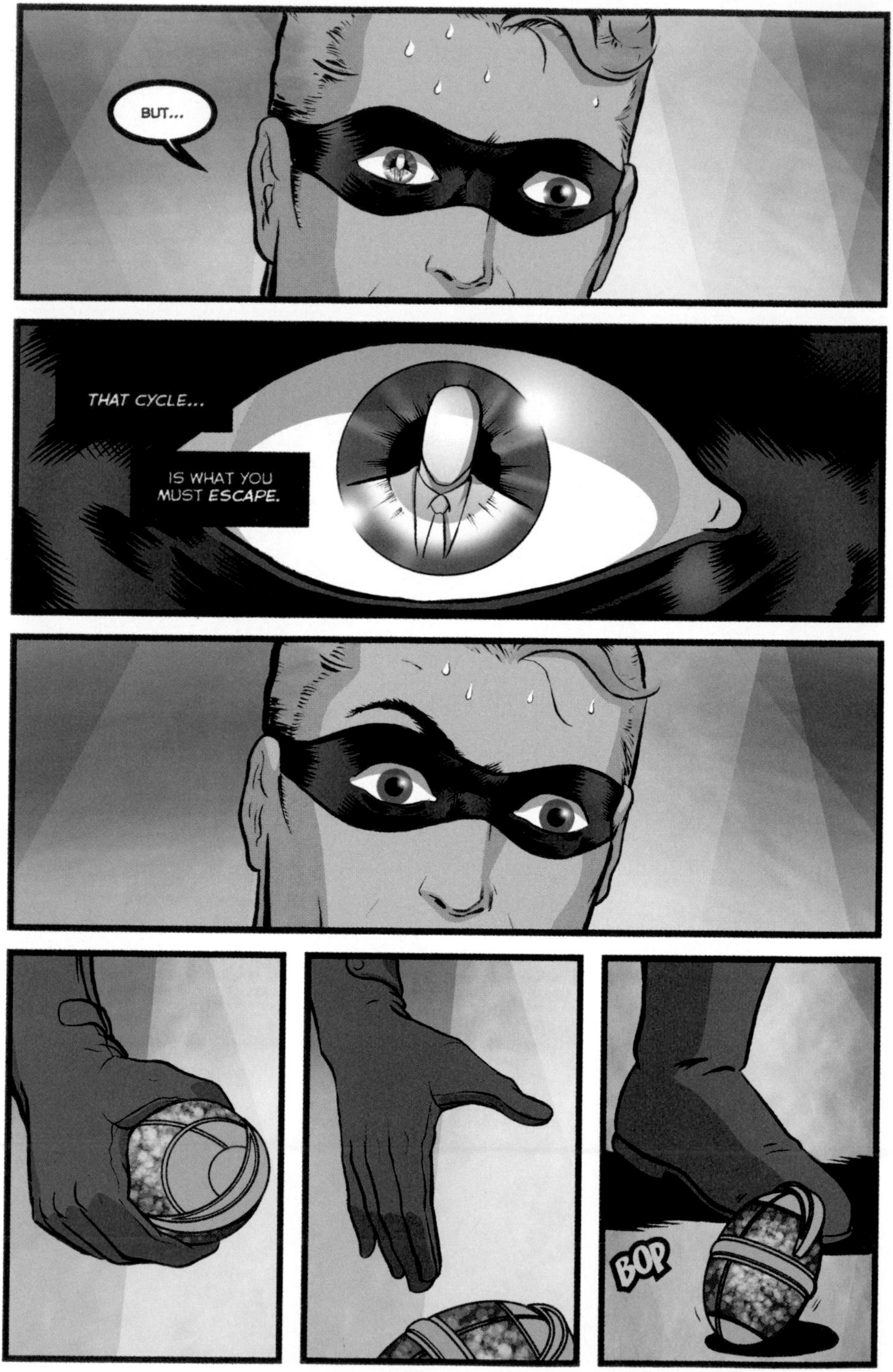
BUT...
THAT CYCLE...
IS WHAT YOU MUST ESCAPE.
BOP

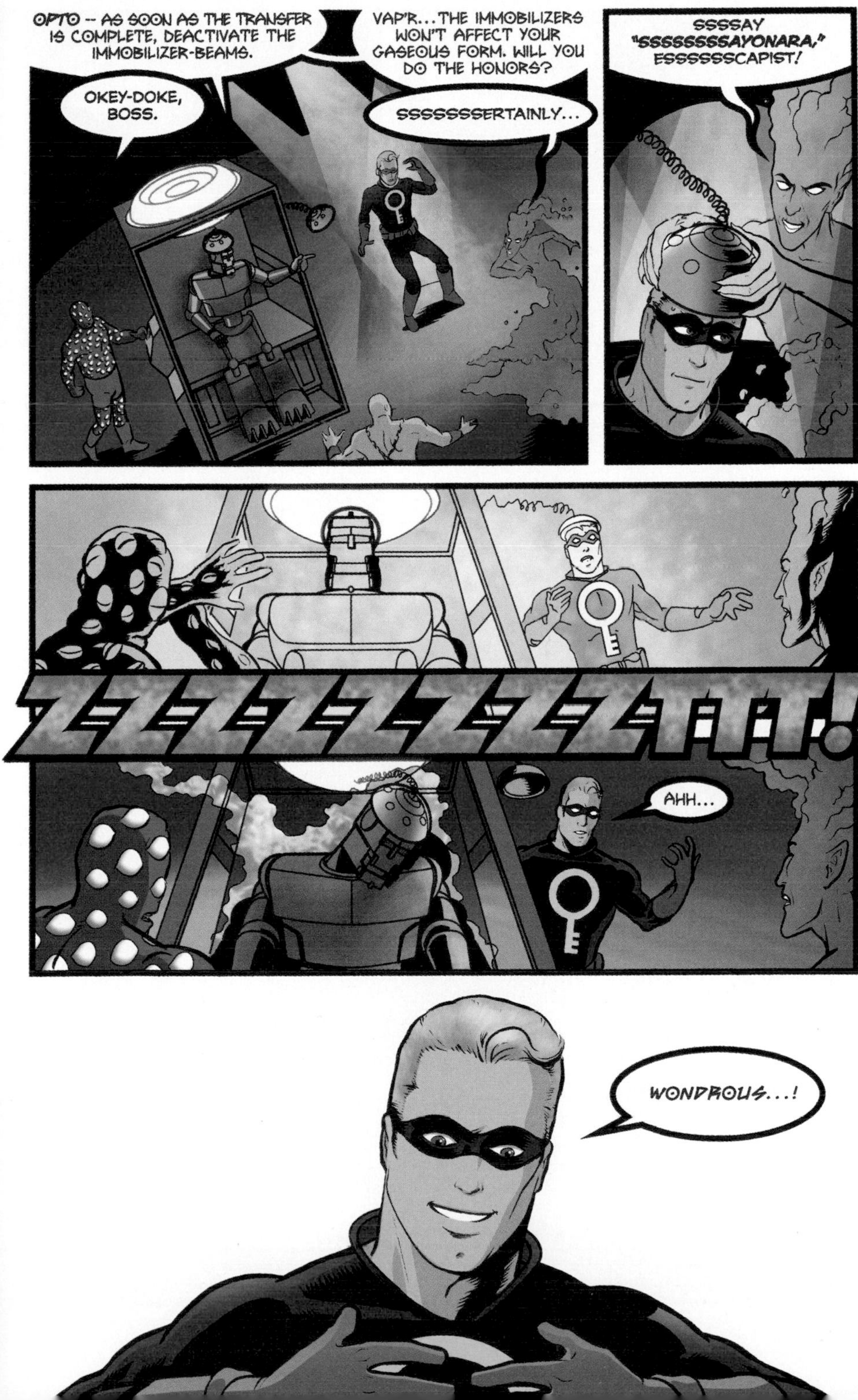
OPTO -- AS SOON AS THE TRANSFER IS COMPLETE, DEACTIVATE THE IMMOBILIZER-BEAMS.
OKEY-DOKE, BOSS.
VAP'R... THE IMMOBILIZERS WON'T AFFECT YOUR GASEOUS FORM. WILL YOU DO THE HONORS?
SSSSSSSERTAINLY...
SSSSAY "SSSSSSSSAYONARA," ESSSSSSCAPIST!
ZZZZZZZZZZAT!
AHH...
WONDROUS...!

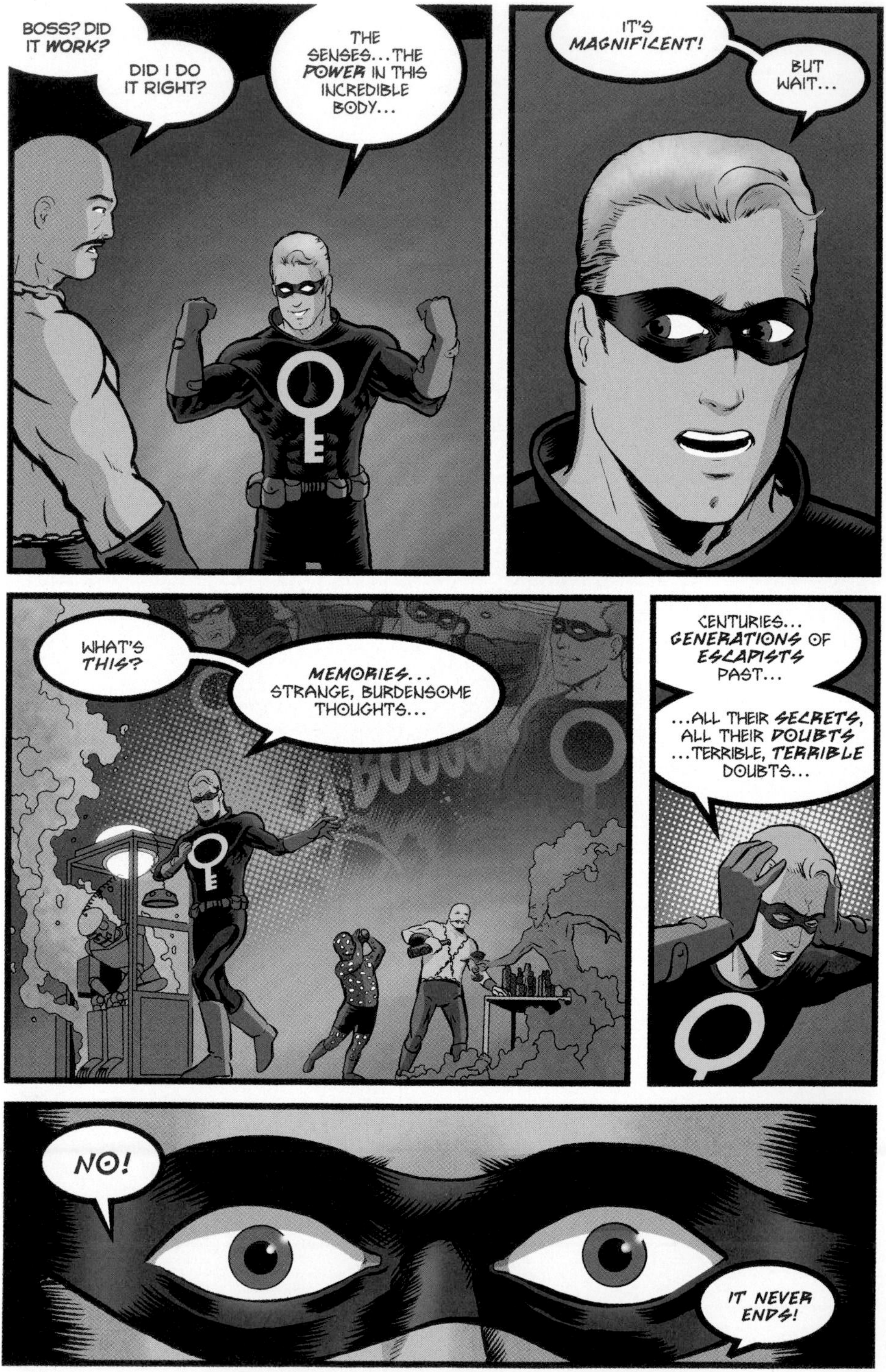
BOSS? DID IT WORK?
DID I DO IT RIGHT?
THE SENSES... THE POWER IN THIS INCREDIBLE BODY...
IT'S MAGNIFICENT!
BUT WAIT...
WHAT'S THIS?
MEMORIES... STRANGE, BURDENSOME THOUGHTS...
CENTURIES... GENERATIONS OF ESCAPISTS PAST...
...ALL THEIR SECRETS, ALL THEIR DOUBTS ...TERRIBLE, TERRIBLE DOUBTS...
NO!
IT NEVER ENDS!

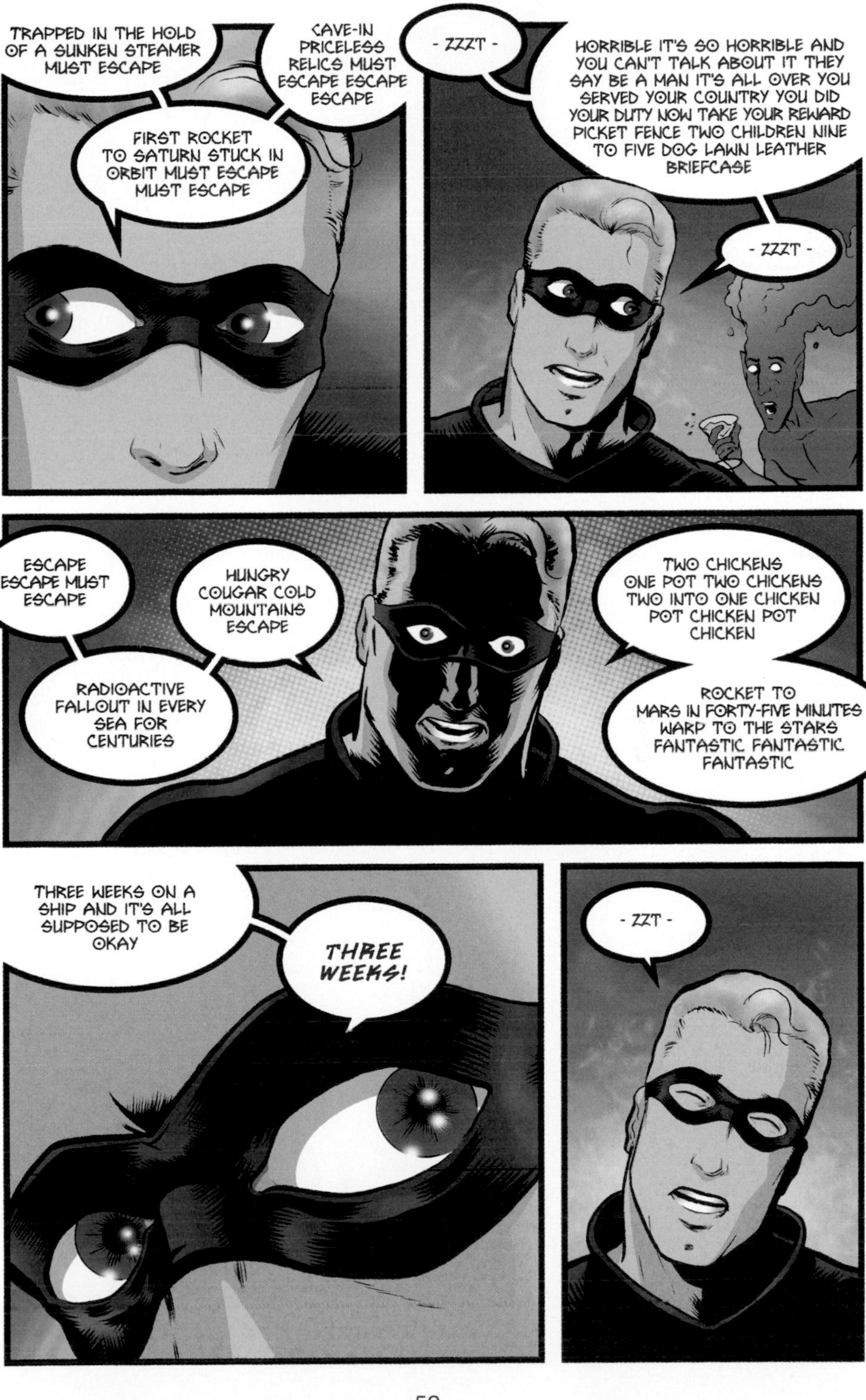
TRAPPED IN THE HOLD OF A SUNKEN STEAMER MUST ESCAPE
CAVE-IN PRICELESS RELICS MUST ESCAPE ESCAPE ESCAPE
FIRST ROCKET TO SATURN STUCK IN ORBIT MUST ESCAPE MUST ESCAPE
- ZZZT -
HORRIBLE IT'S SO HORRIBLE AND YOU CAN'T TALK ABOUT IT THEY SAY BE A MAN IT'S ALL OVER YOU SERVED YOUR COUNTRY YOU DID YOUR DUTY NOW TAKE YOUR REWARD PICKET FENCE TWO CHILDREN NINE TO FIVE DOG LAWN LEATHER BRIEFCASE
- ZZZT -
ESCAPE ESCAPE MUST ESCAPE
HUNGRY COUGAR COLD MOUNTAINS ESCAPE
RADIOACTIVE FALLOUT IN EVERY SEA FOR CENTURIES
TWO CHICKENS ONE POT TWO CHICKENS TWO INTO ONE CHICKEN POT CHICKEN POT CHICKEN
ROCKET TO MARS IN FORTY-FIVE MINUTES WARP TO THE STARS FANTASTIC FANTASTIC FANTASTIC
THREE WEEKS ON A SHIP AND IT'S ALL SUPPOSED TO BE OKAY
THREE WEEKS!
- ZZT -

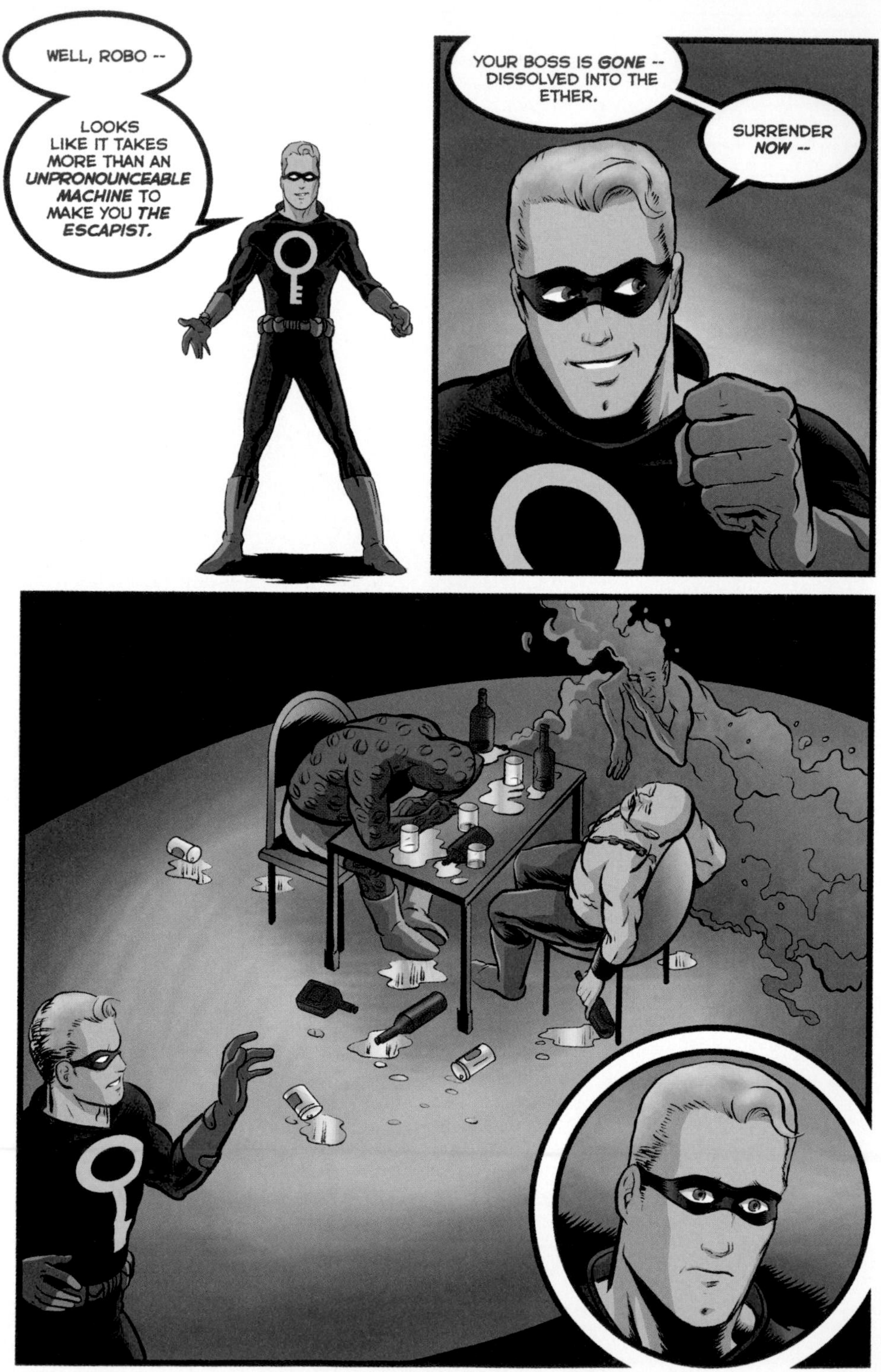
WELL, ROBO --
LOOKS LIKE IT TAKES MORE THAN AN *UNPRONOUNCEABLE MACHINE* TO MAKE YOU *THE ESCAPIST.*
YOUR BOSS IS *GONE* -- DISSOLVED INTO THE ETHER.
SURRENDER *NOW* --

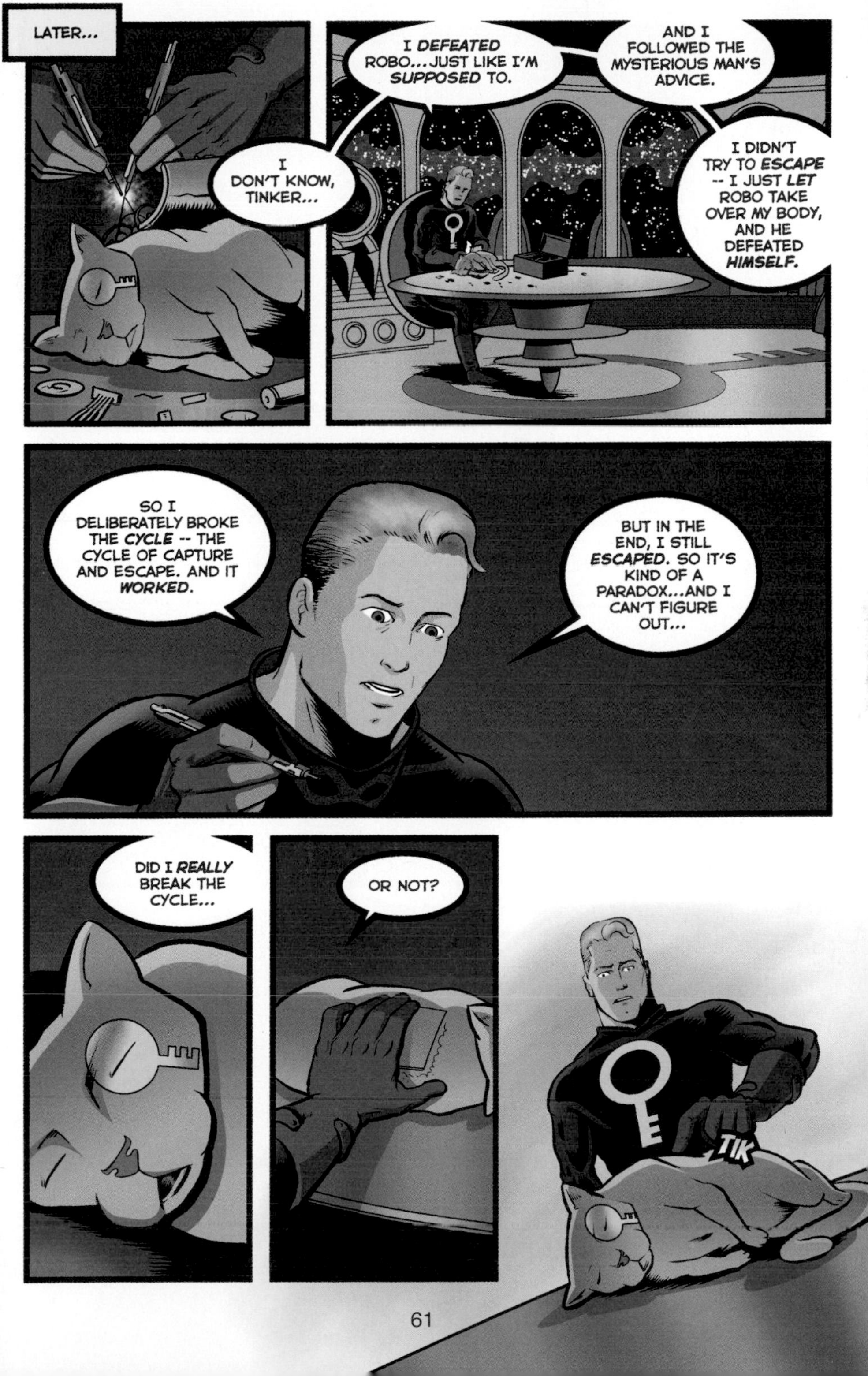
LATER...
I DON'T KNOW, TINKER...
I DEFEATED ROBO...JUST LIKE I'M SUPPOSED TO.
AND I FOLLOWED THE MYSTERIOUS MAN'S ADVICE.
I DIDN'T TRY TO ESCAPE -- I JUST LET ROBO TAKE OVER MY BODY, AND HE DEFEATED HIMSELF.
SO I DELIBERATELY BROKE THE CYCLE -- THE CYCLE OF CAPTURE AND ESCAPE. AND IT WORKED.
BUT IN THE END, I STILL ESCAPED. SO IT'S KIND OF A PARADOX...AND I CAN'T FIGURE OUT...
DID I REALLY BREAK THE CYCLE...
OR NOT?
TIK

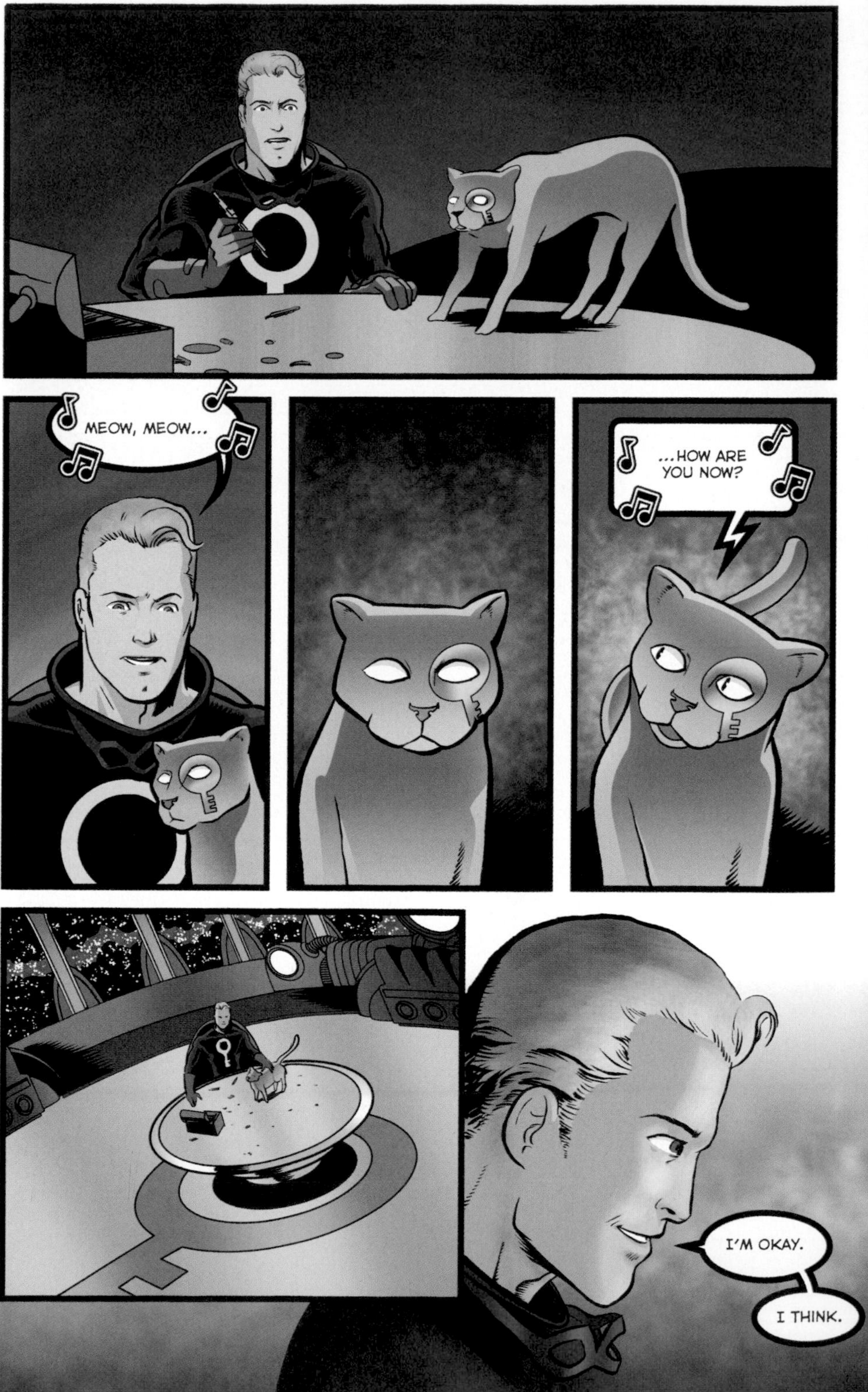
MEOW, MEOW...
...HOW ARE YOU NOW?
I'M OKAY.
I THINK.

Text: Panel 6: Closeup the Escapist, smiling softly now.
ESCAPIST: I'M OKAY.
ESCAPIST: I THINK.
Text: Panel 6:
smiling softly now.
ESCAPIST: I'M OKAY.
ESCAPIST: I THINK.
RRRIIP
THE ESCAPIST 2966
SCRIPT
Cyril M. Cutter
FAB COMICS
LOOK DEEP INTO THESE EYES!
IS IT LOVE, HATE OR MURDER?
THEY'RE THE EYES OF
BOGART
In A
Lonely Place
Gloria GRAHAME

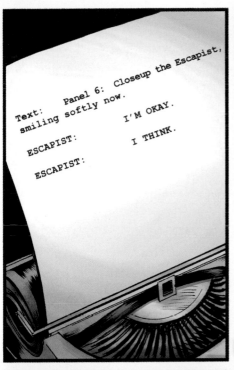

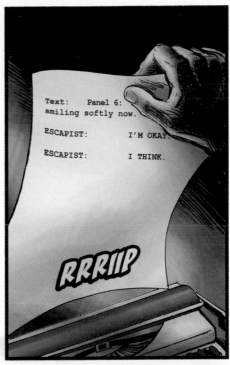

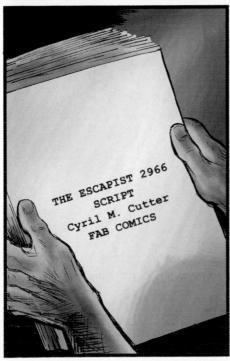

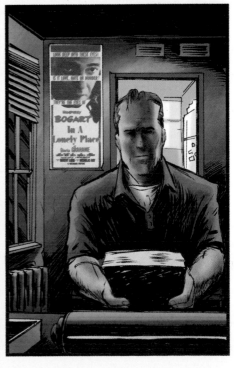

Writers Guild Award
CYRIL M. CUTTER
Best Teleplay - 1961
"The Fire on Main Street"
Series: The Inner Mind

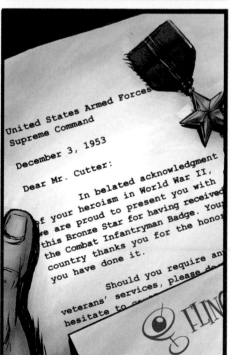

United States Armed Forces
Supreme Command

December 3, 1953

Dear Mr. Cutter:

In belated acknowledgment of your heroism in World War II, we are proud to present you with this Bronze Star for having received the Combat Infantryman Badge. You country thanks you for the honor you have done it.

Should you require an veterans' services, please d hesitate to

FLING!

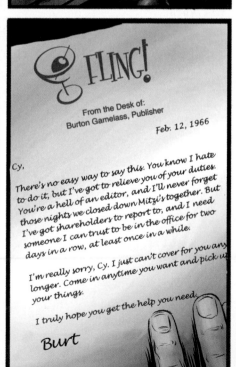

FLING!

From the Desk of:
Burton Gamelass, Publisher

Feb. 12, 1966

Cy,

There's no easy way to say this. You know I hate to do it, but I've got to relieve you of your duties. You're a hell of an editor, and I'll never forget those nights we closed down Mitzi's together. But I've got shareholders to report to, and I need someone I can trust to be in the office for two days in a row, at least once in a while.

I'm really sorry, Cy. I just can't cover for you any longer. Come in anytime you want and pick up your things.

I truly hope you get the help you need.

Burt

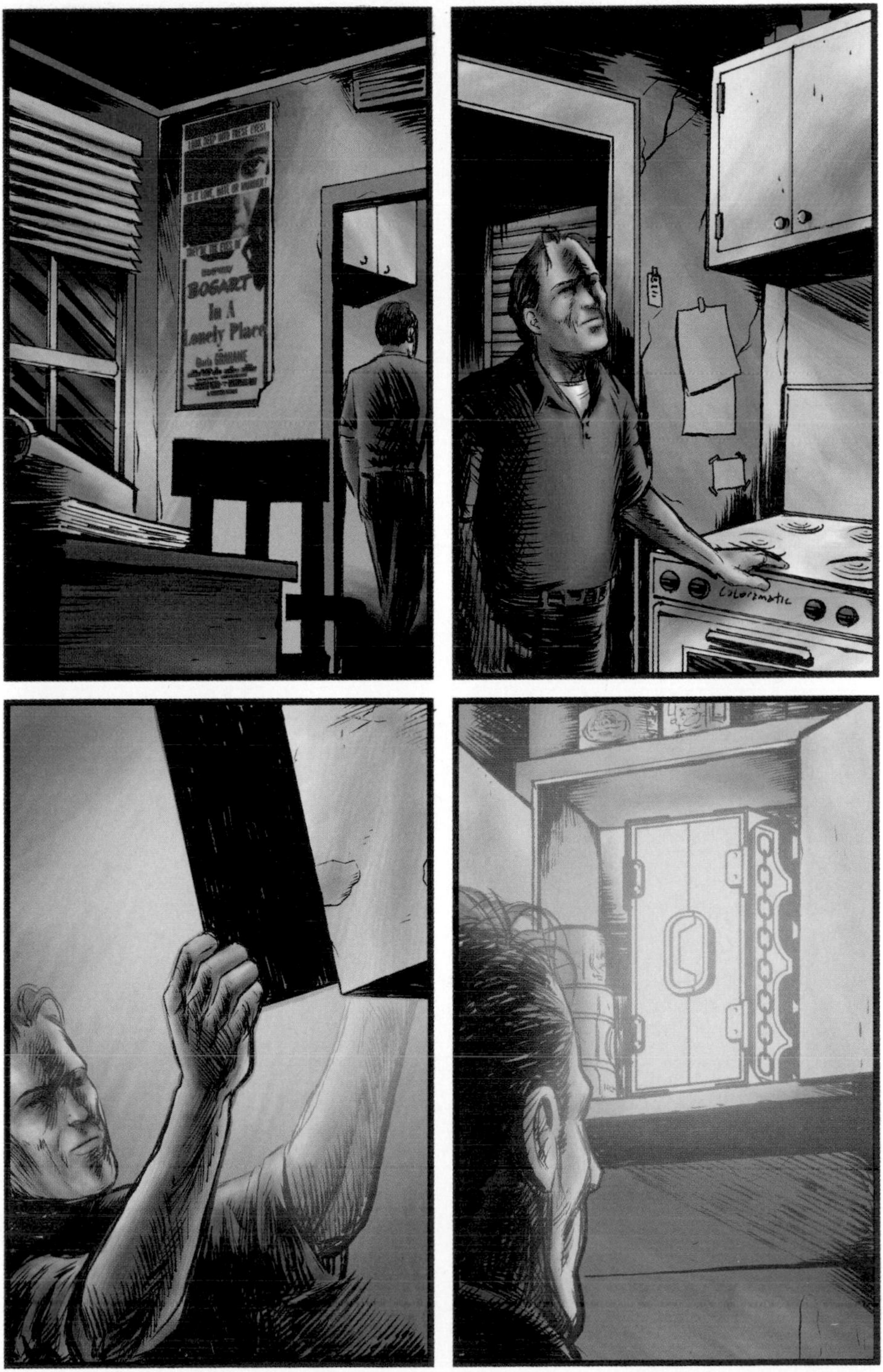

BOGART
In A
Lonely Place
Colorzmatic

KA-KLIK

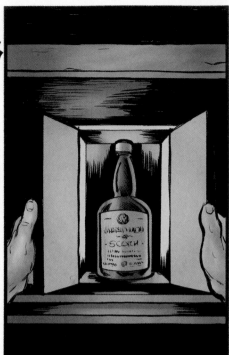

SCOTCH

"THAT CYCLE...

"IS WHAT YOU MUST ESCAPE."

THE END

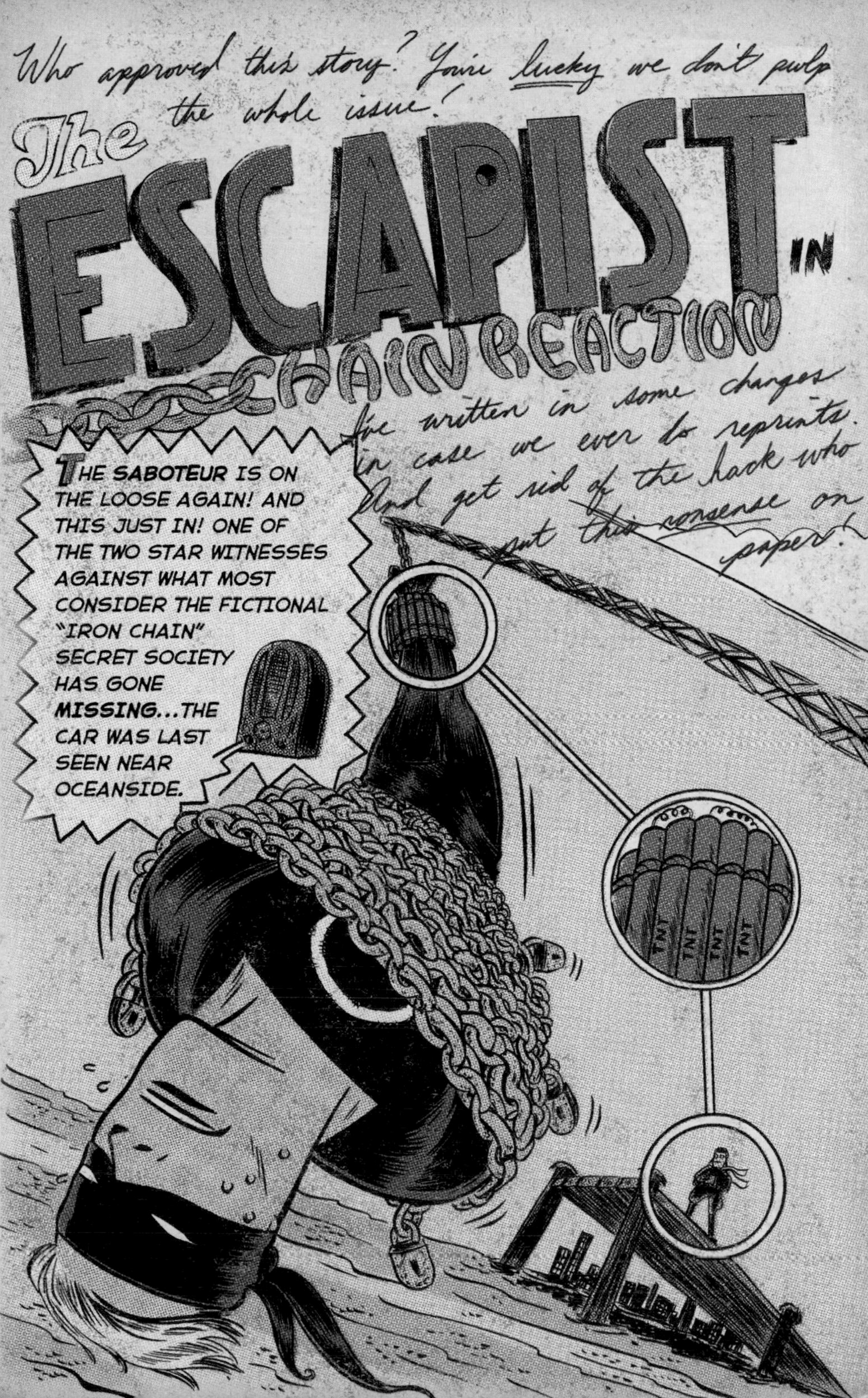
Who approved this story? You're lucky we don't pulp the whole issue!
The ESCAPIST in
CHAIN REACTION
I've written in some changes in case we ever do reprints. And get rid of the hack who put this nonsense on paper!
THE SABOTEUR IS ON THE LOOSE AGAIN! AND THIS JUST IN! ONE OF THE TWO STAR WITNESSES AGAINST WHAT MOST CONSIDER THE FICTIONAL "IRON CHAIN" SECRET SOCIETY HAS GONE MISSING... THE CAR WAS LAST SEEN NEAR OCEANSIDE.
TNT
TNT
TNT
TNT

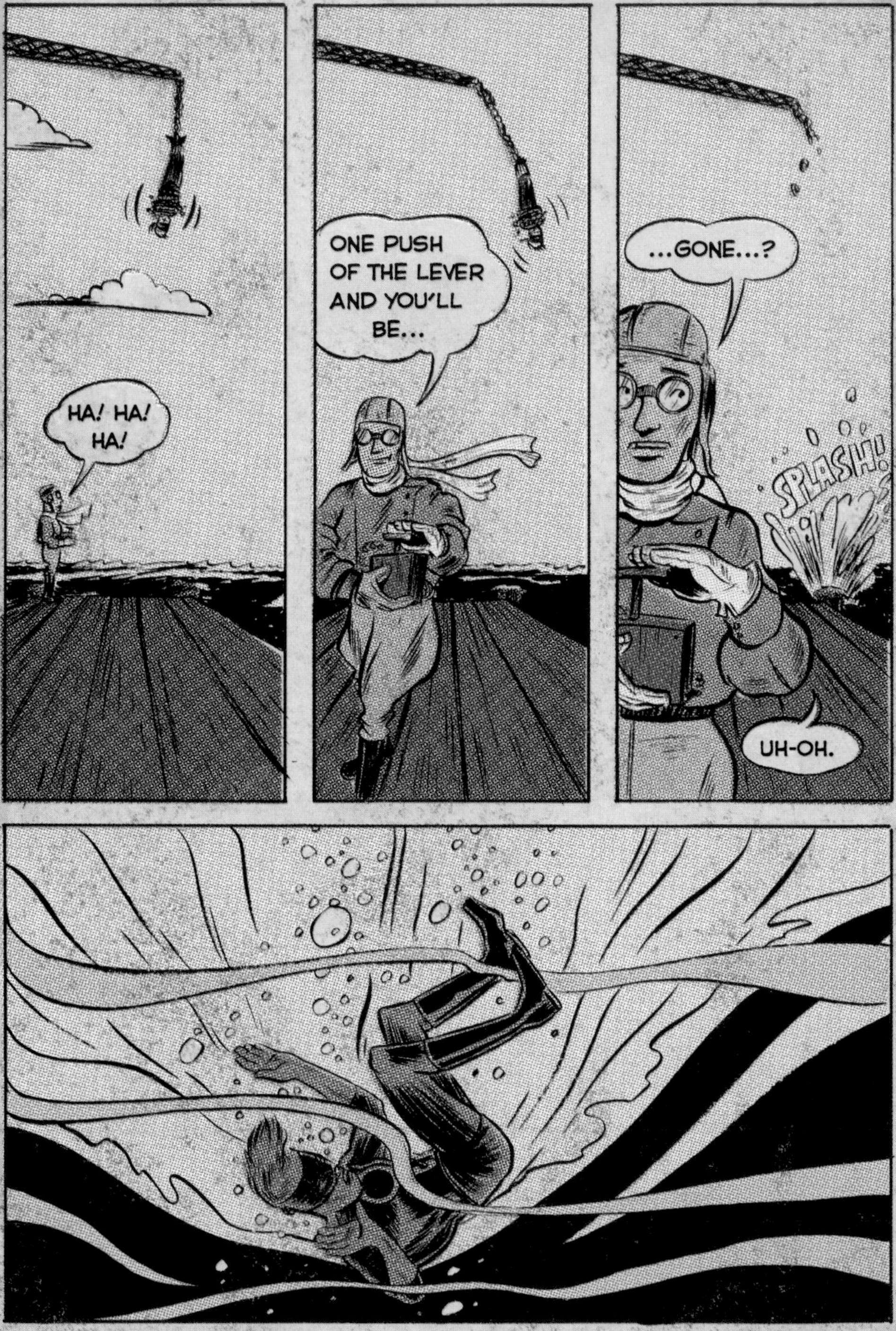
HA! HA! HA!
ONE PUSH OF THE LEVER AND YOU'LL BE...
...GONE...?
SPLASH!
UH-OH.

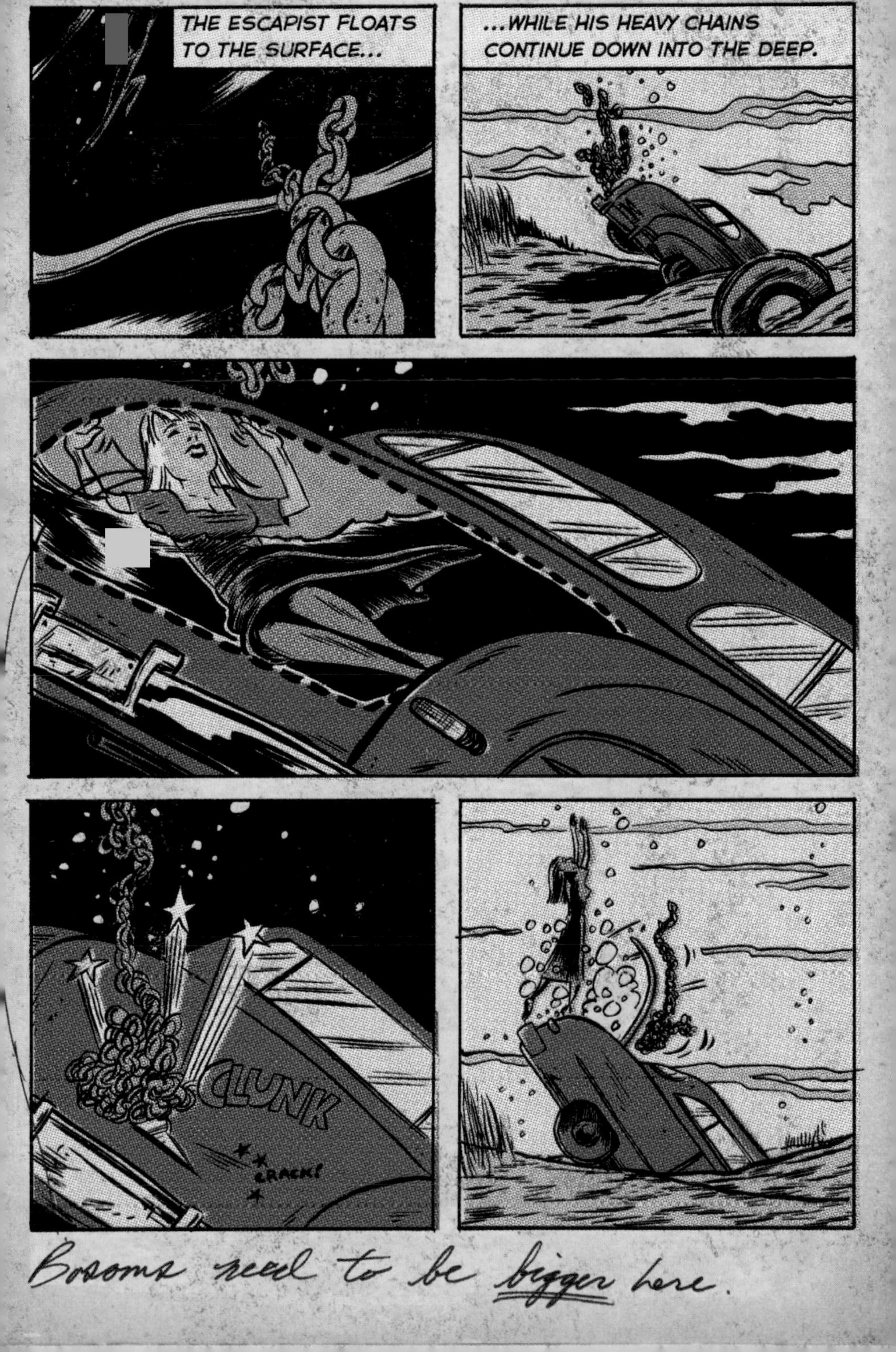
THE ESCAPIST FLOATS TO THE SURFACE...
...WHILE HIS HEAVY CHAINS CONTINUE DOWN INTO THE DEEP.
CLUNK
CRACK!

Bosoms need to be bigger here.

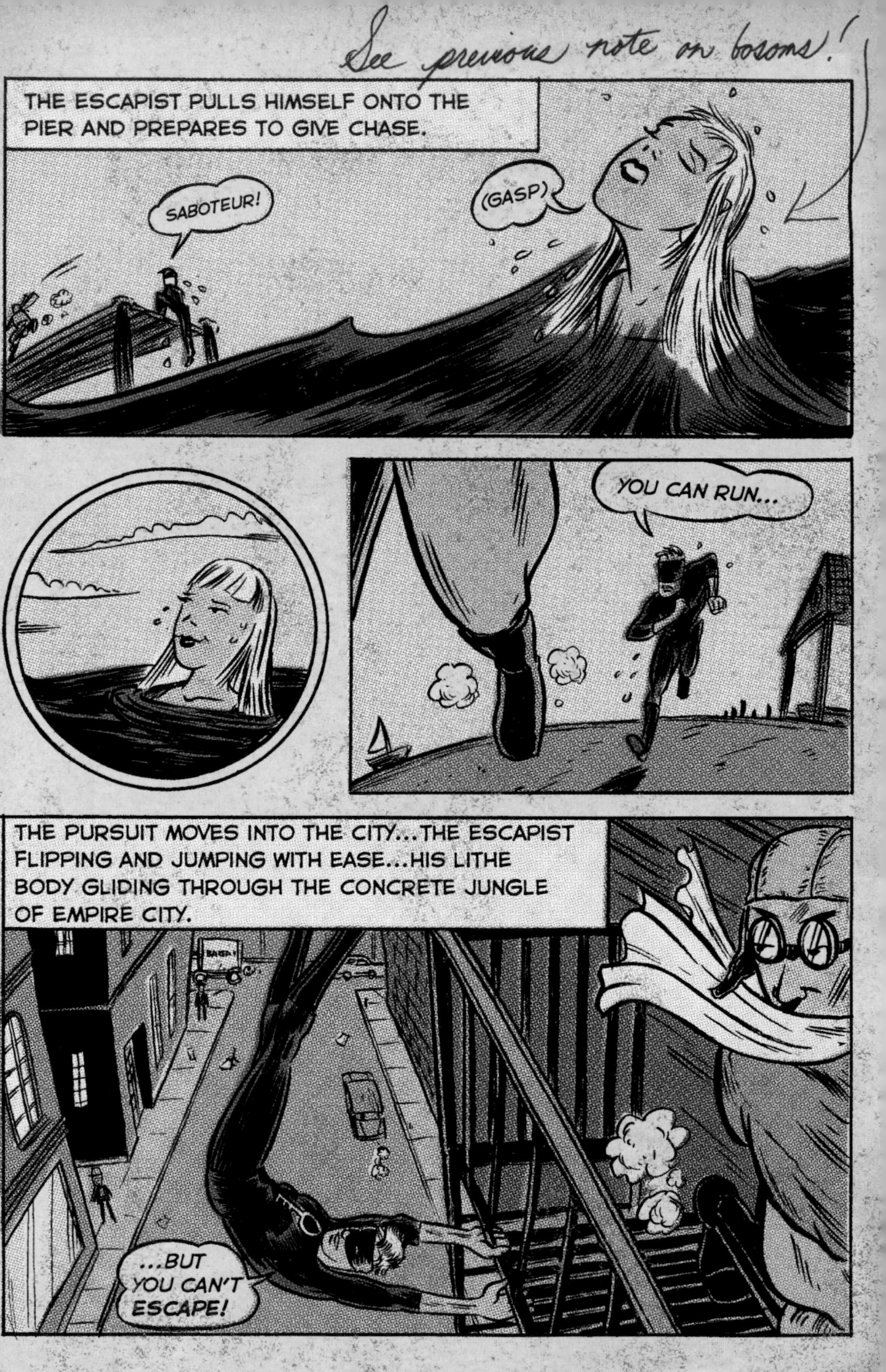
See previous note on bosoms!
THE ESCAPIST PULLS HIMSELF ONTO THE PIER AND PREPARES TO GIVE CHASE.
SABOTEUR!
(GASP)
YOU CAN RUN...
THE PURSUIT MOVES INTO THE CITY...THE ESCAPIST FLIPPING AND JUMPING WITH EASE...HIS LITHE BODY GLIDING THROUGH THE CONCRETE JUNGLE OF EMPIRE CITY.
...BUT YOU CAN'T ESCAPE!

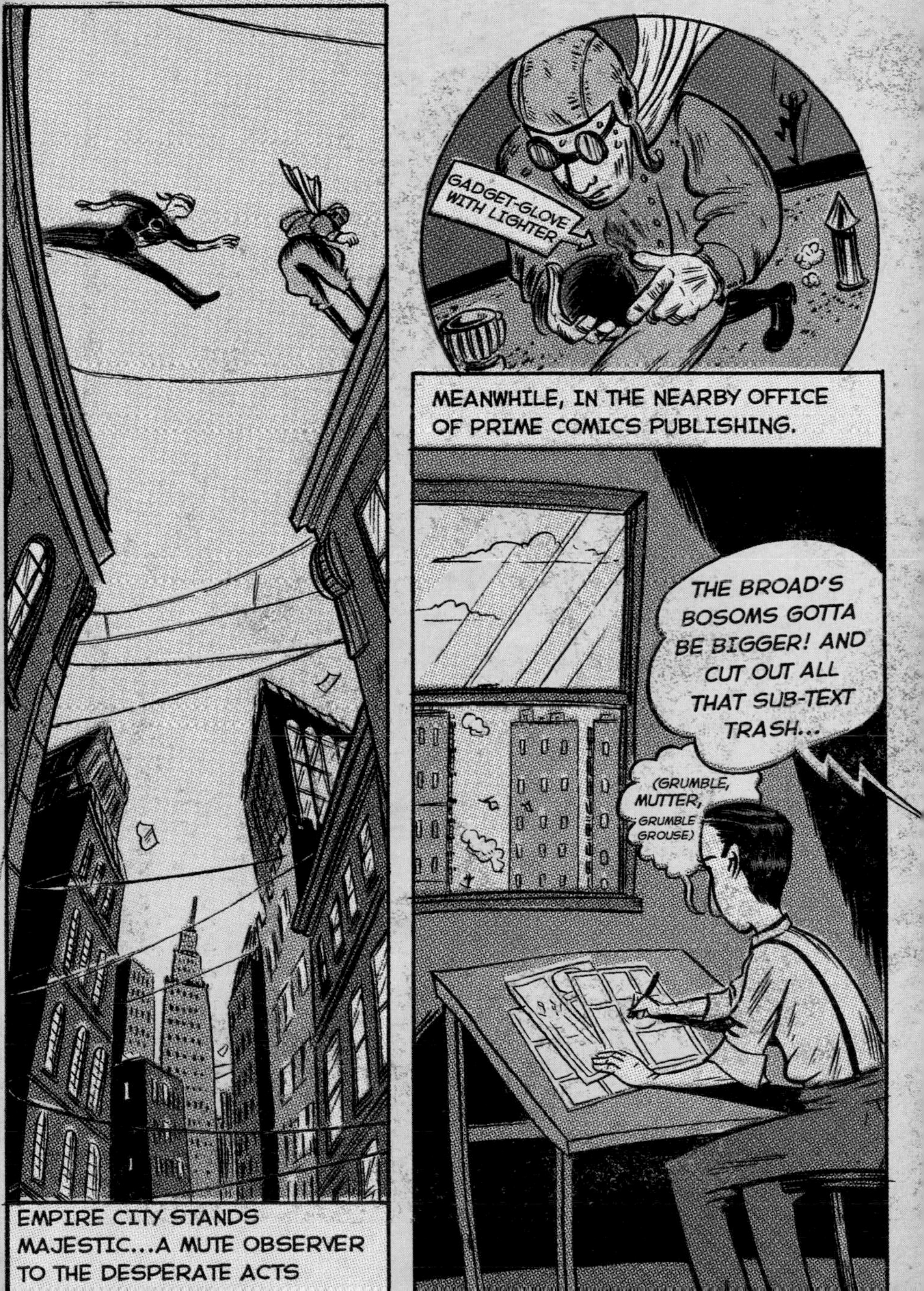
EMPIRE CITY STANDS MAJESTIC...A MUTE OBSERVER TO THE DESPERATE ACTS OF ITS INHABITANTS.
GADGET-GLOVE WITH LIGHTER
MEANWHILE, IN THE NEARBY OFFICE OF PRIME COMICS PUBLISHING.
THE BROAD'S BOSOMS GOTTA BE BIGGER! AND CUT OUT ALL THAT SUB-TEXT TRASH...
(GRUMBLE, MUTTER, GRUMBLE GROUSE)

NO GOOD, ROTTEN ...
THE READER WANTS ACTION! NOT "ART"!
MORE WORDS AND FEWER PICTURES.
Sigh
YA GOTTA BEAT THE READER OVER THE HEAD WITH IT!
NO! STOP!
WHAT DID YOU SAY?!?
?
BOOM!
I SAID "NO"! STOP GIVING ME THIS NON-SENSE DIRECTION! I'M SICK OF THE PANDERING AND THE TRITE, MORALISTIC ENDINGS!
I'M CREATING REAL ART HERE!

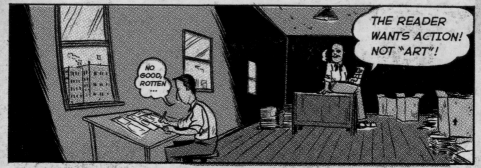

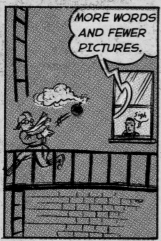

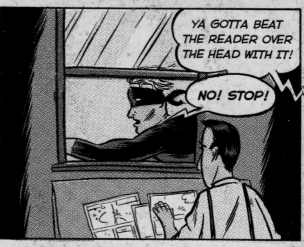

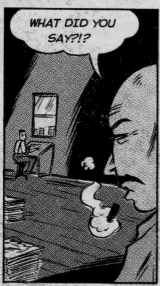

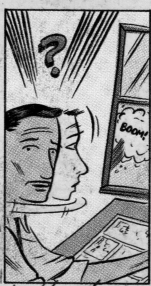

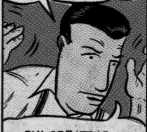

What happened to the chase scene through the bordello?

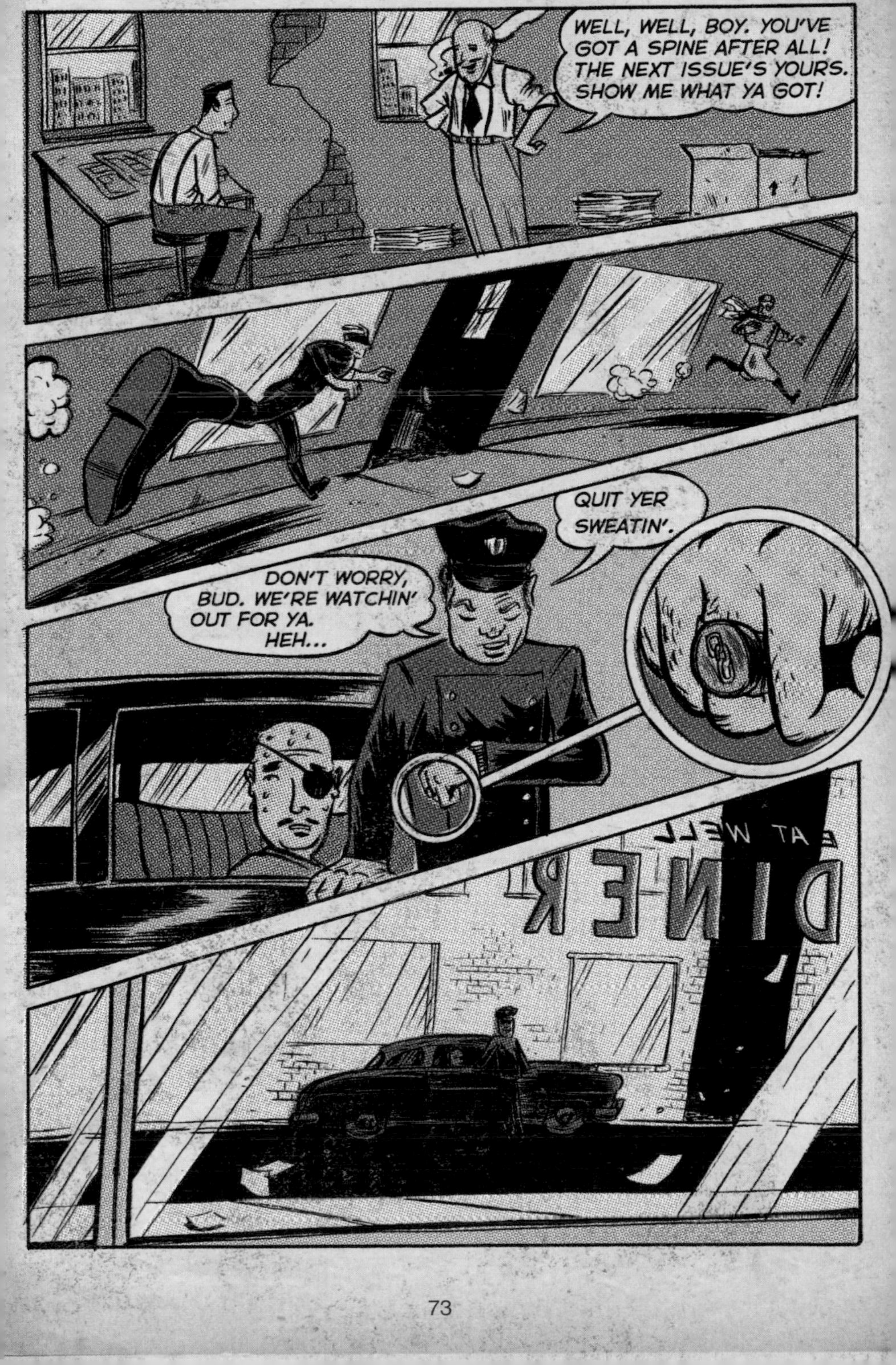
WELL, WELL, BOY. YOU'VE GOT A SPINE AFTER ALL! THE NEXT ISSUE'S YOURS. SHOW ME WHAT YA GOT!
QUIT YER SWEATIN'.
DON'T WORRY, BUD. WE'RE WATCHIN' OUT FOR YA. HEH...
EAT WELL
DINER

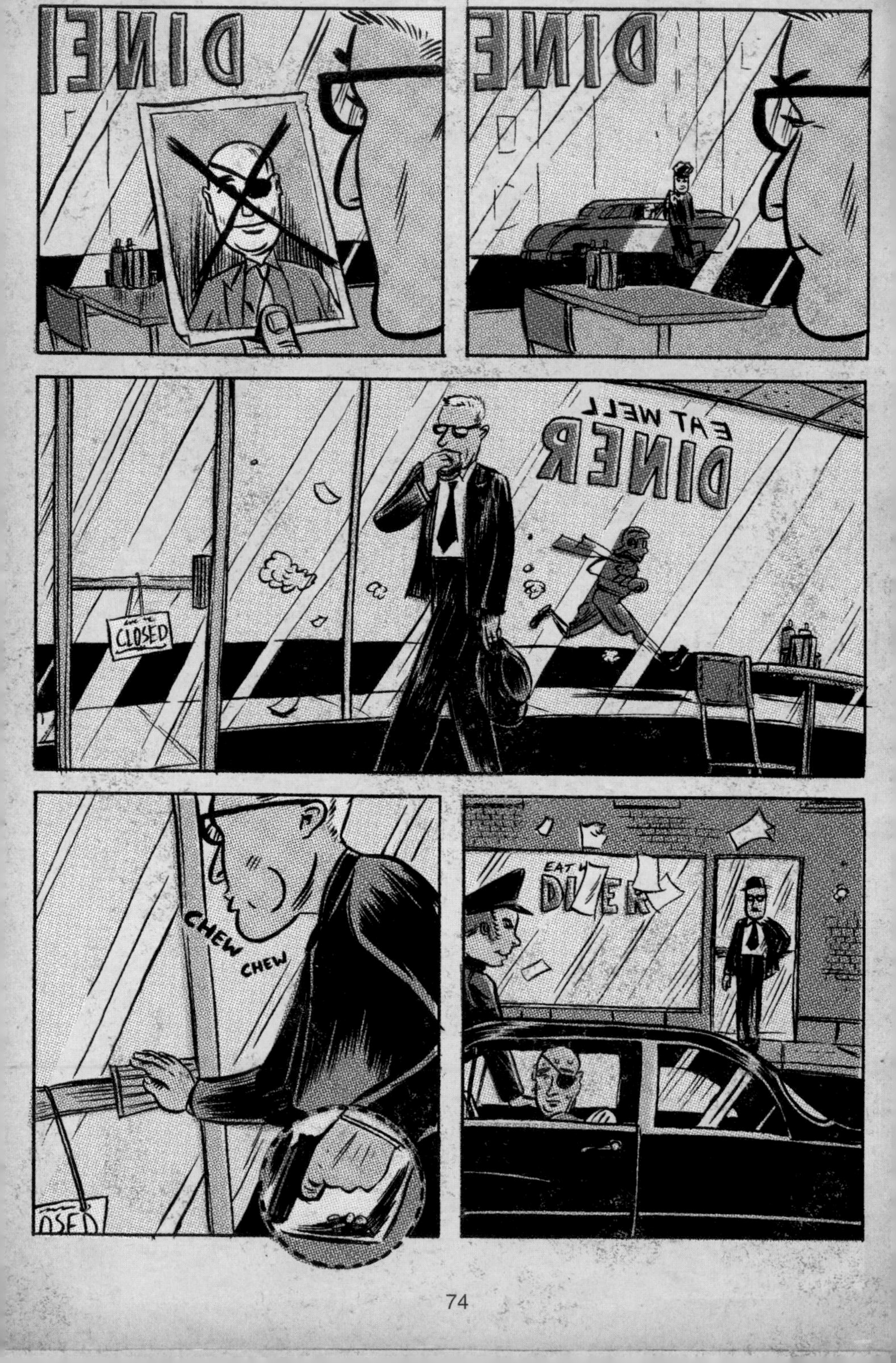
CLOSED
CHEW
CHEW

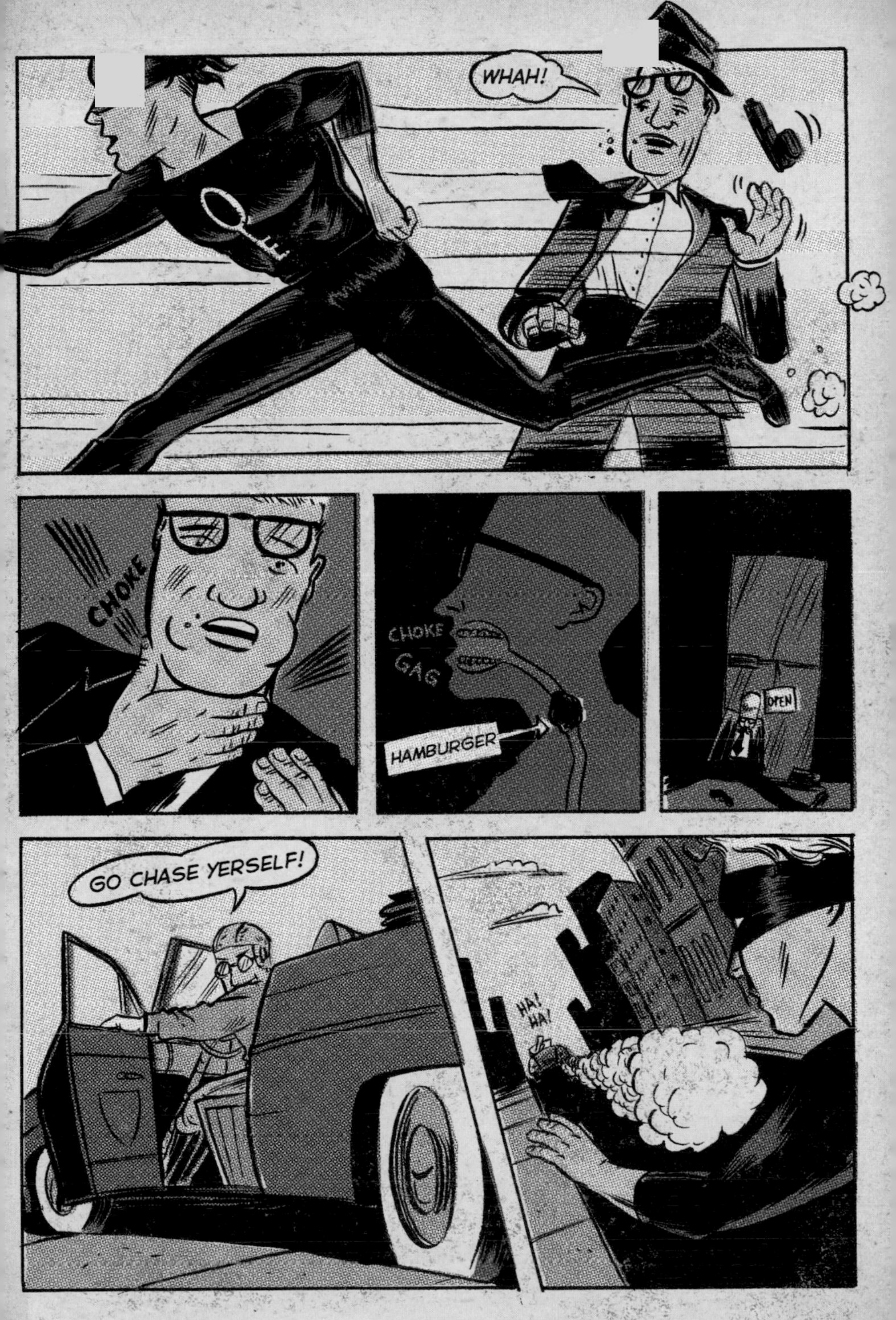
WHAH!
CHOKE
CHOKE
GAG
HAMBURGER
OPEN
GO CHASE YERSELF!
HA! HA!

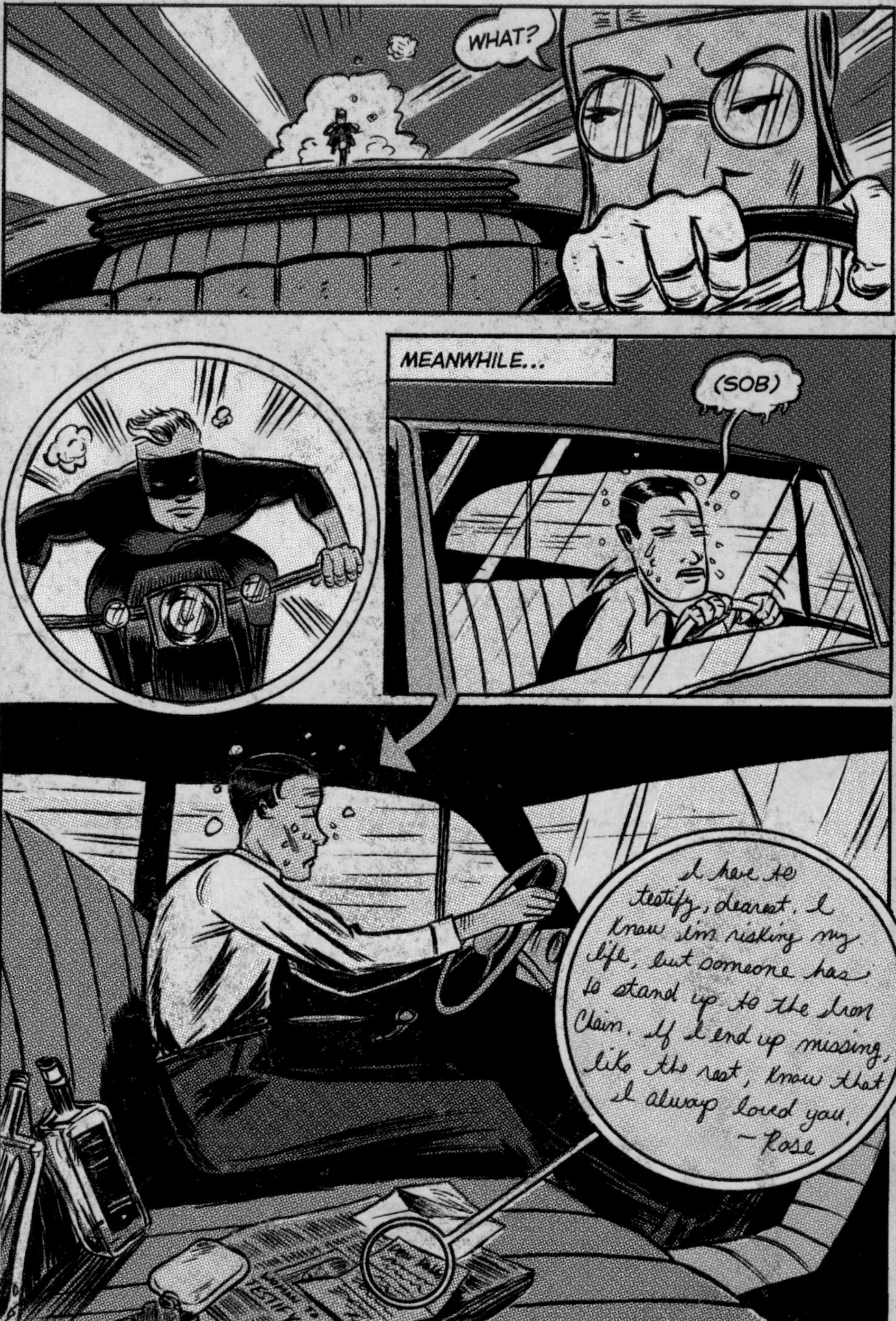
WHAT?
MEANWHILE...
(SOB)
I have to testify, dearest. I know I'm risking my life, but someone has to stand up to the Iron Chain. If I end up missing, like the rest, know that I always loved you.
—Rose

THE SABOTEUR SPEEDS BY —— UNNOTICED BY A YOUNG MOTORIST...

(SNIF)

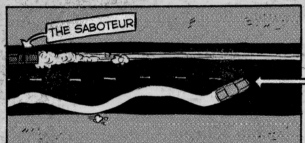

THE SABOTEUR

(SOB)

DANGER! CLIFFS!

(SOB)

THE ESCAPIST?!

BRAKE

SCREEECH!

Make the Escapist more heroic —

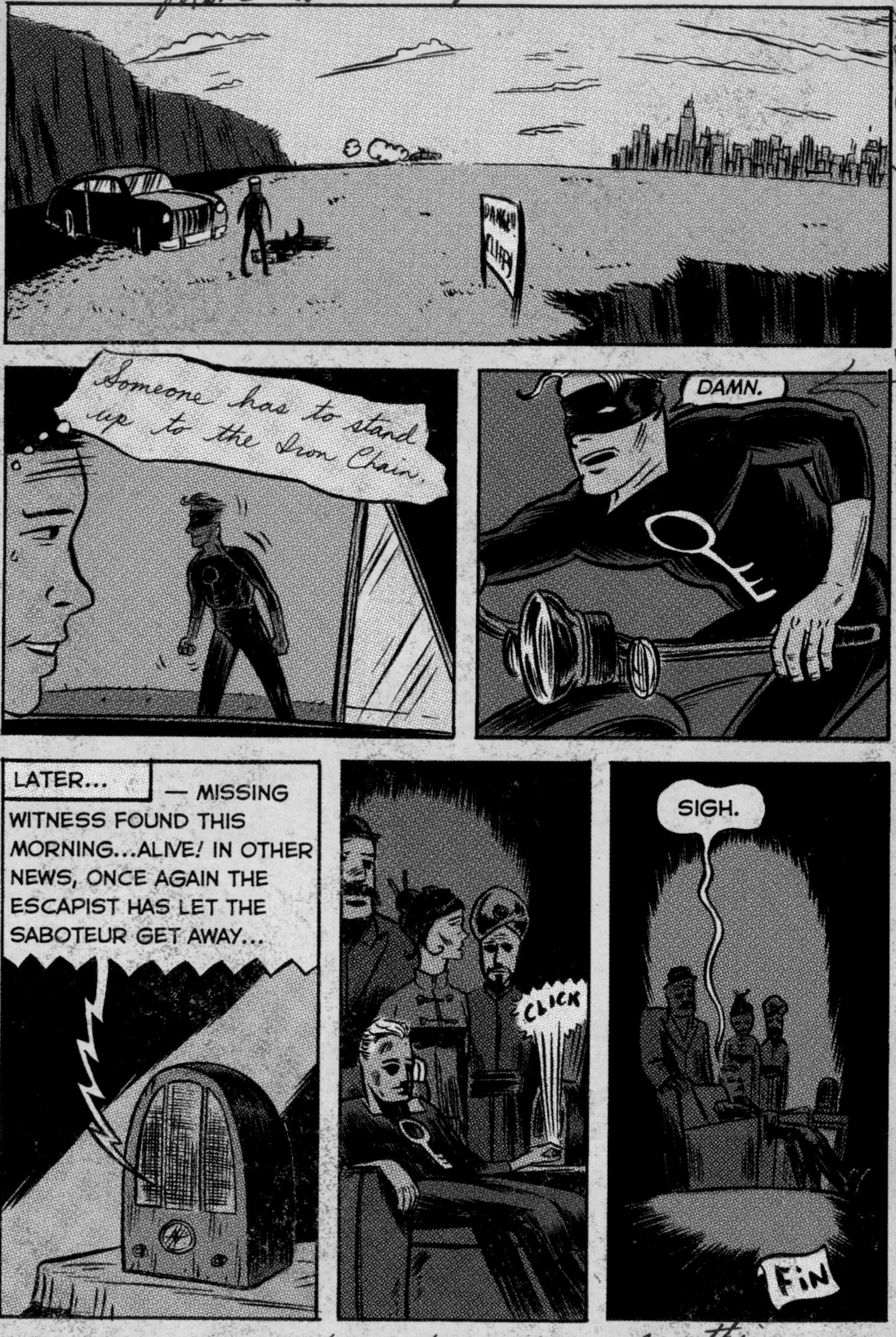
Someone has to stand up to the Iron Chain.
DAMN.
LATER...
— MISSING WITNESS FOUND THIS MORNING...ALIVE! IN OTHER NEWS, ONCE AGAIN THE ESCAPIST HAS LET THE SABOTEUR GET AWAY...
CLICK
SIGH.
FIN

and have him say something like "Can't win 'em all."

August 16, 2004 — Webster Groves Times

'Comic' Find is Nothing to Laugh At

A local man and avid collector of comic books recently made a fascinating find at a local estate sale. Louis Bartholomew was at the sale on Greeley Avenue last weekend, and in the basement of the two-bedroom house he found a musty box full of comic books. All together, he reported that there were approximately 20-25 comics dating from the late 1940s to the mid-1950s. In amongst the comic books were also various Empire Publishing souvenirs such as stationery, pens, and a small stack of *The Escapist* comic books.

Overall, Bartholomew rated the find as "not bad." However, the curious aspect of his find, which he would later learn, centered around issue #179 of *Radio Comics Featuring The Escapist*. The significance of this particular comic book is that there is no record of an issue #179 ever being published. The other oddity of this mystery issue is its content: six short stories all by the same writer/artist (a rarity at the time) — Matt Kindt, Sr. That didn't ring a bell with Bartholomew. Nor did it ring a bell with any of his collector friends, and the issue failed to appear in any price guides.

See COMIC FIND on next page

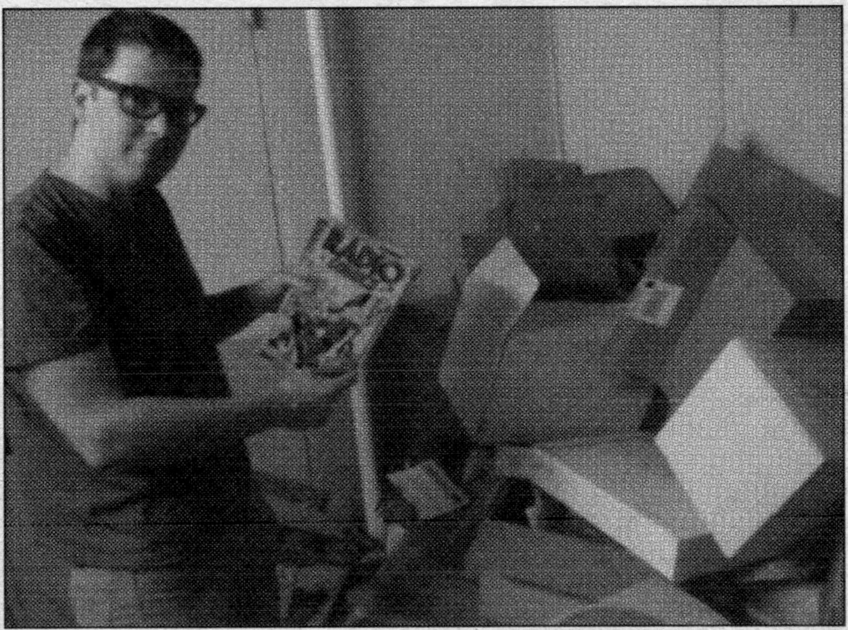

Louis Bartholomew in the basement where he found *Radio Comics Featuring The Escapist* #179.

COMIC FIND continued

Not to be stymied, Bartholomew took the issue in question to comic book historian Tony Rennick in New York. What he would find out was even more frustrating. No database or archive lists Kindt's name in connection with comic books. No surviving family or relatives exist to shed any light on his life, either. Only tax records tell the story. He had one tax return while living in New York, and his remaining 40 years were apparently spent in Missouri.

Rennick raises some interesting questions. Who was this artist? Clearly influenced by Eisner and his peers, how did he manage to get full creative control over such a popular character, albeit for only one issue? And how could only one printed copy remain? It is interesting to note that on this lone copy, there are handwritten notes in the margins. Perhaps from an editor? Rennick believes that the notes could be "Lucky" Lemberg's — the publisher of Score Comics, home of *The Escapist* from 1954 through 1959. Sadly, we will probably never know, but fortunately this one rare book was discovered. It is perhaps the rarest of all comic books — an 80-page testament to the skill and craftsmanship of the many comic book artists who once labored in obscurity for the sole reward of simply creating.

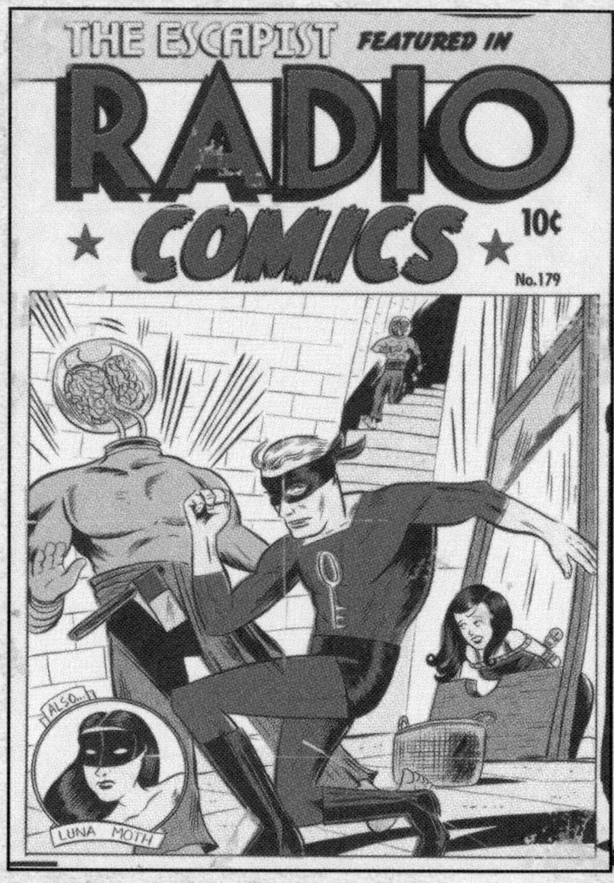
THE ESCAPIST FEATURED IN
RADIO
COMICS
10¢
No.179
ALSO...
LUNA MOTH

The famed issue #179 complete with cover art by an unknown artist.

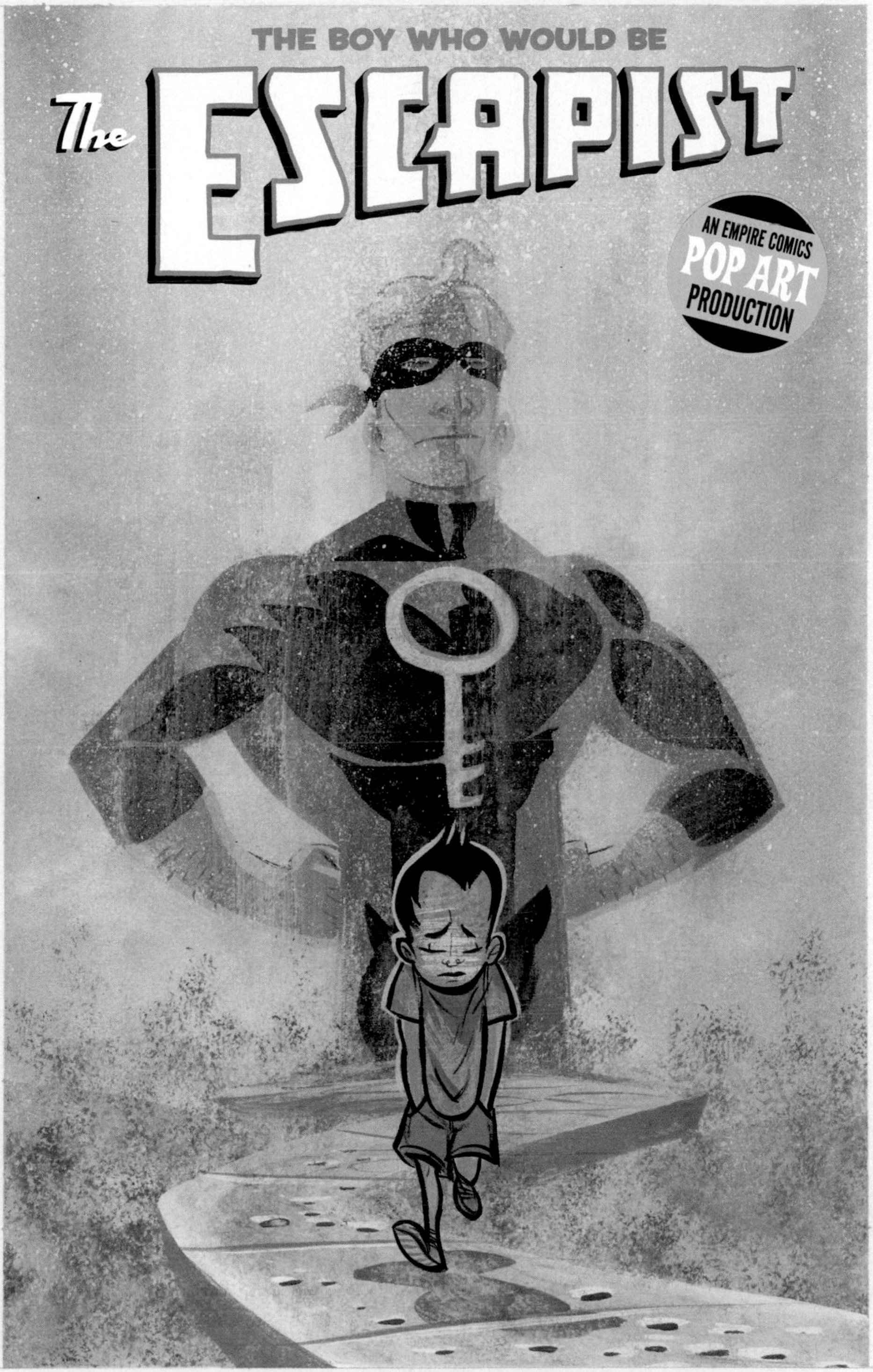
THE BOY WHO WOULD BE
The ESCAPIST™
AN EMPIRE COMICS
POP ART
PRODUCTION

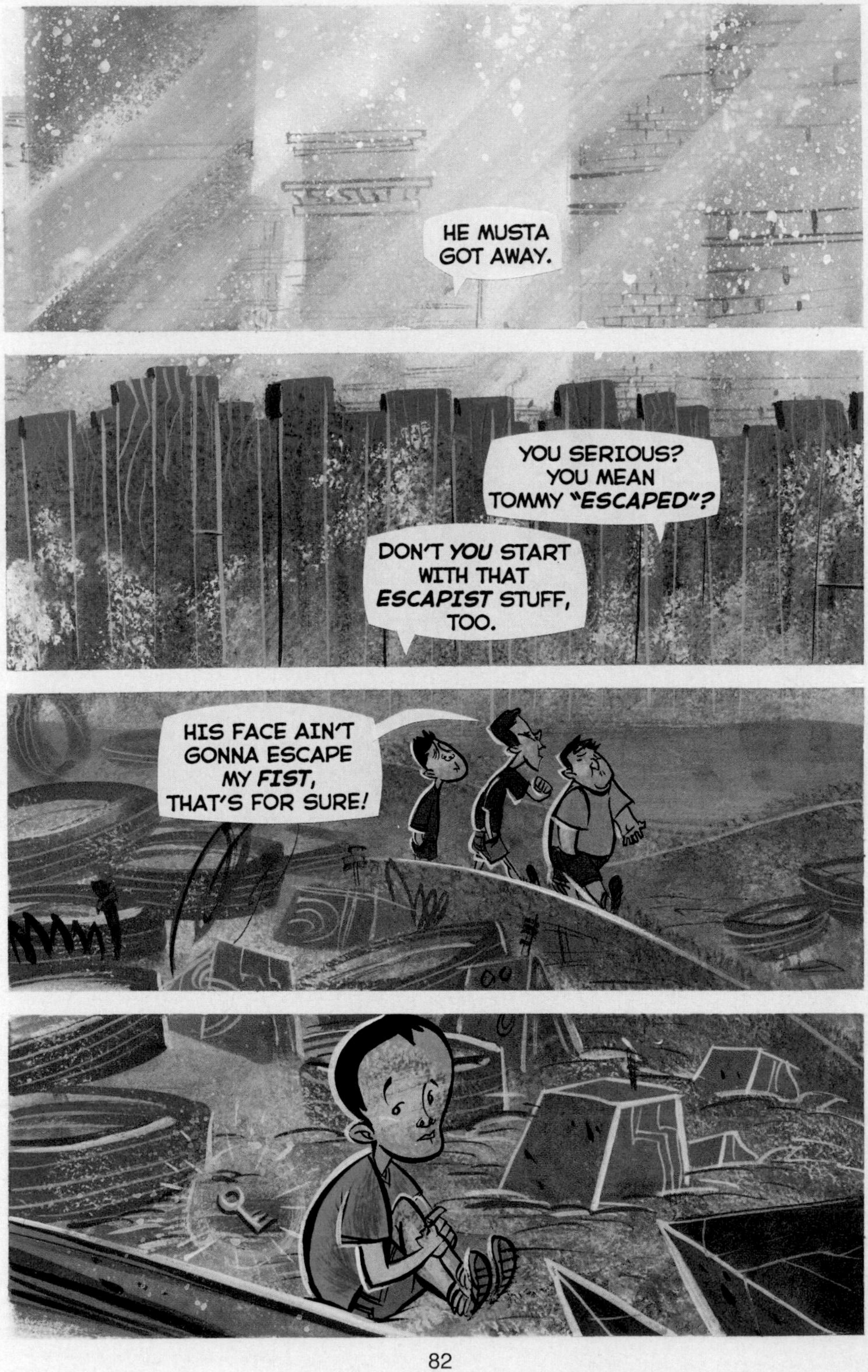
HE MUSTA GOT AWAY.
YOU SERIOUS? YOU MEAN TOMMY "ESCAPED"?
DON'T YOU START WITH THAT ESCAPIST STUFF, TOO.
HIS FACE AIN'T GONNA ESCAPE MY FIST, THAT'S FOR SURE!

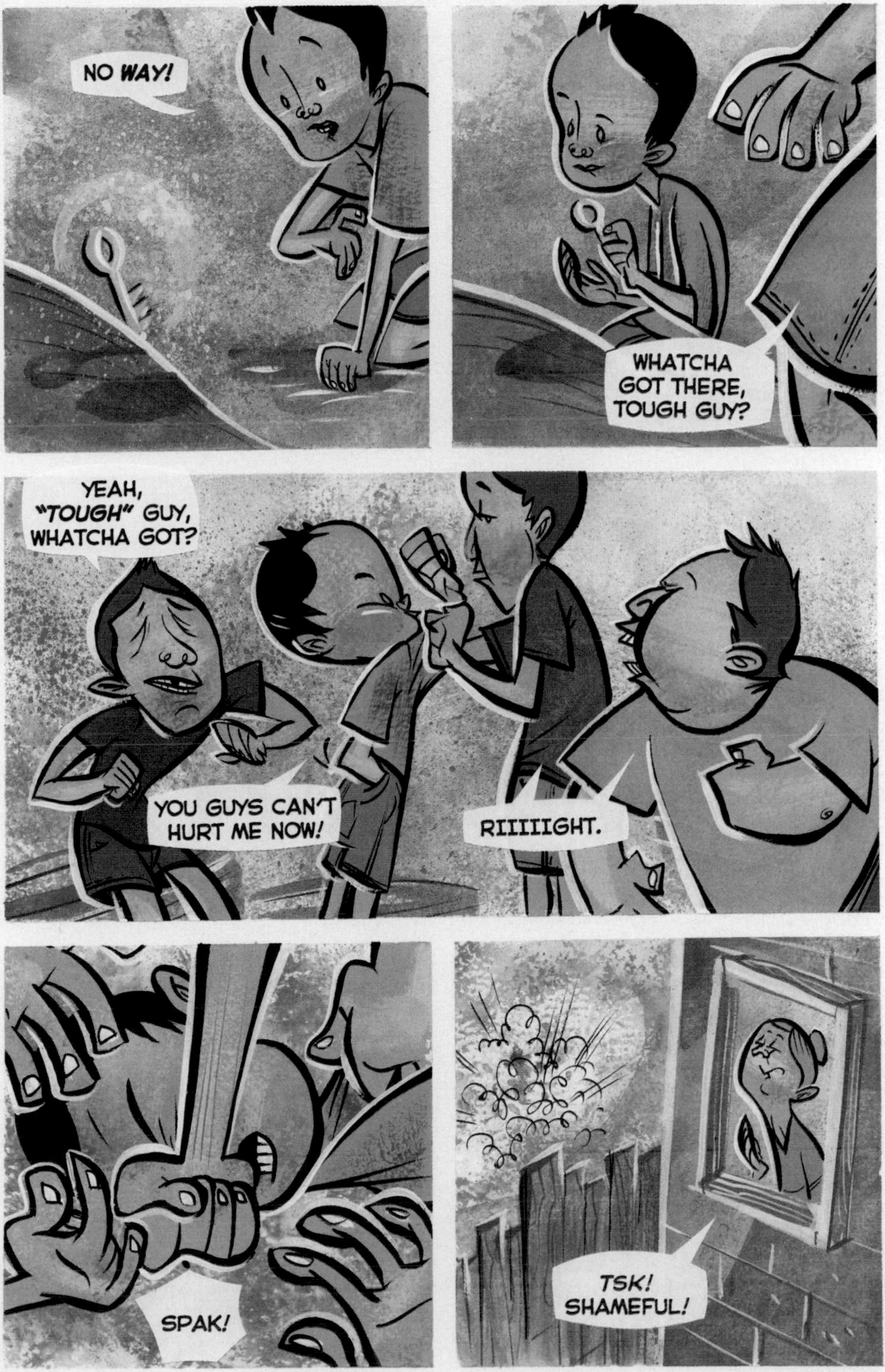
NO WAY!
WHATCHA GOT THERE, TOUGH GUY?
YEAH, "TOUGH" GUY, WHATCHA GOT?
YOU GUYS CAN'T HURT ME NOW!
RIIIIIGHT.
SPAK!
TSK! SHAMEFUL!

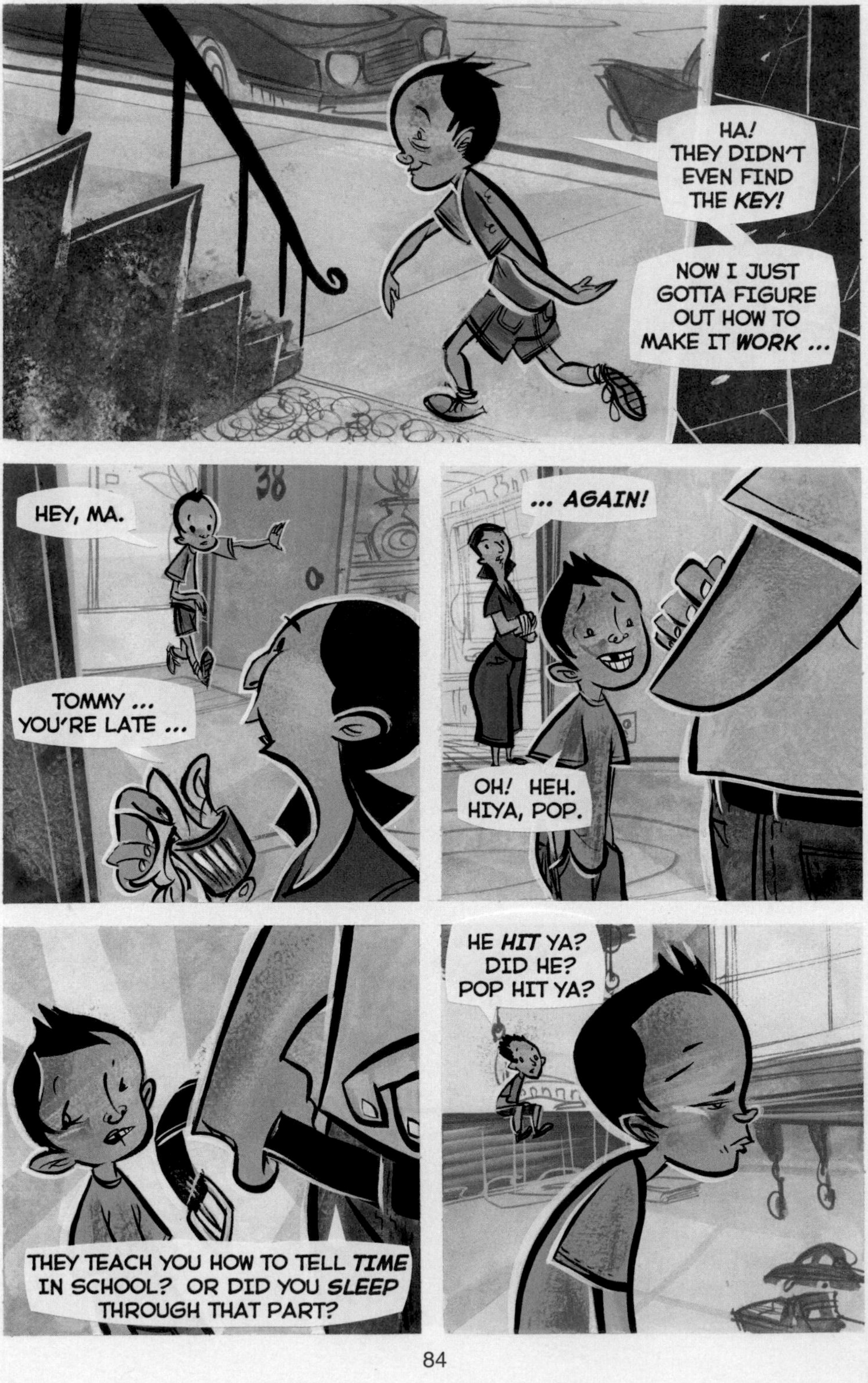
HA! THEY DIDN'T EVEN FIND THE KEY!
NOW I JUST GOTTA FIGURE OUT HOW TO MAKE IT WORK ...
HEY, MA.
TOMMY ... YOU'RE LATE ...
... AGAIN!
OH! HEH. HIYA, POP.
THEY TEACH YOU HOW TO TELL TIME IN SCHOOL? OR DID YOU SLEEP THROUGH THAT PART?
HE HIT YA? DID HE? POP HIT YA?

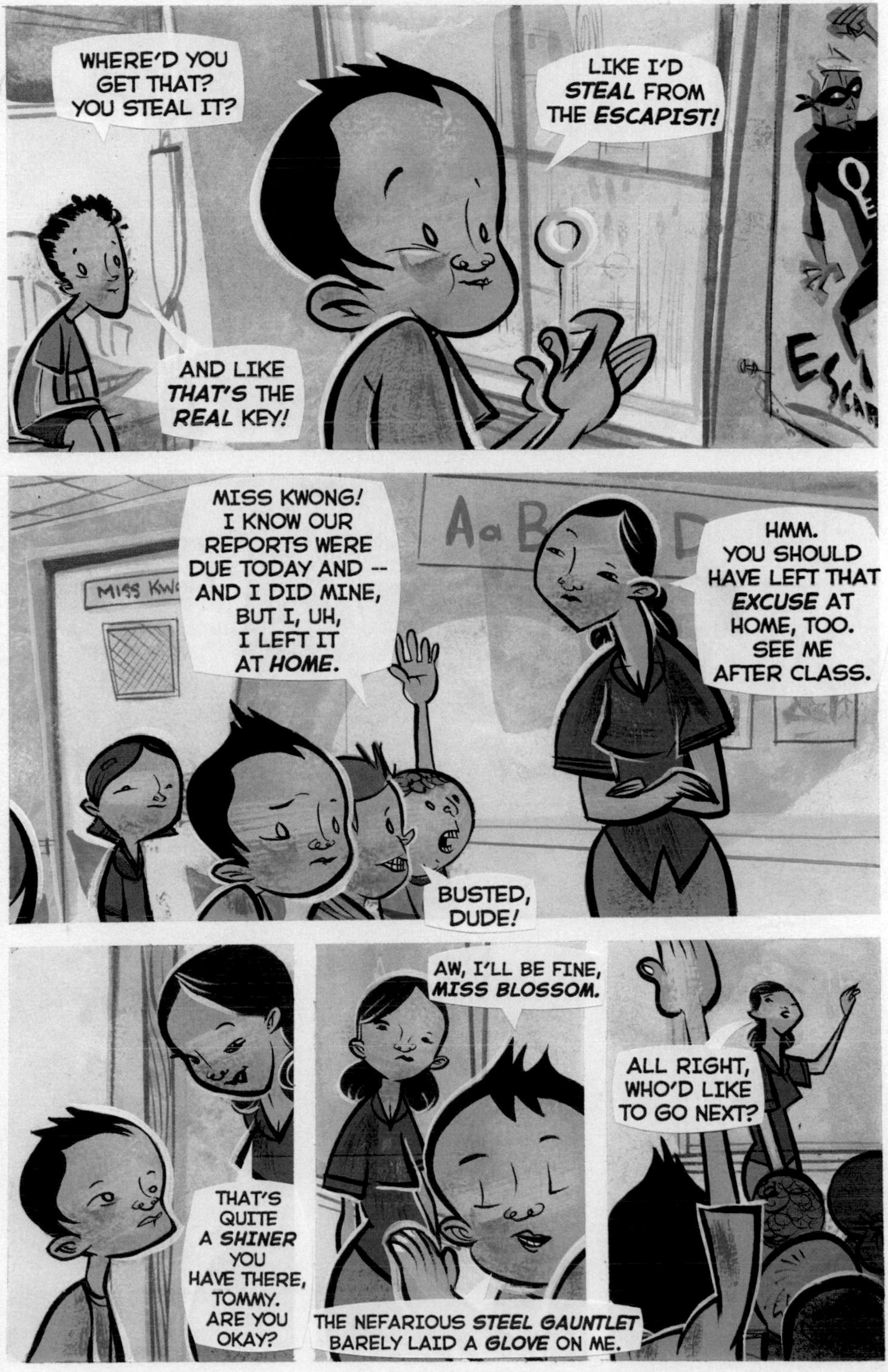
WHERE'D YOU GET THAT? YOU STEAL IT?
LIKE I'D STEAL FROM THE ESCAPIST!
AND LIKE THAT'S THE REAL KEY!
MISS KWONG! I KNOW OUR REPORTS WERE DUE TODAY AND -- AND I DID MINE, BUT I, UH, I LEFT IT AT HOME.
HMM. YOU SHOULD HAVE LEFT THAT EXCUSE AT HOME, TOO. SEE ME AFTER CLASS.
BUSTED, DUDE!
THAT'S QUITE A SHINER YOU HAVE THERE, TOMMY. ARE YOU OKAY?
AW, I'LL BE FINE, MISS BLOSSOM.
THE NEFARIOUS STEEL GAUNTLET BARELY LAID A GLOVE ON ME.
ALL RIGHT, WHO'D LIKE TO GO NEXT?

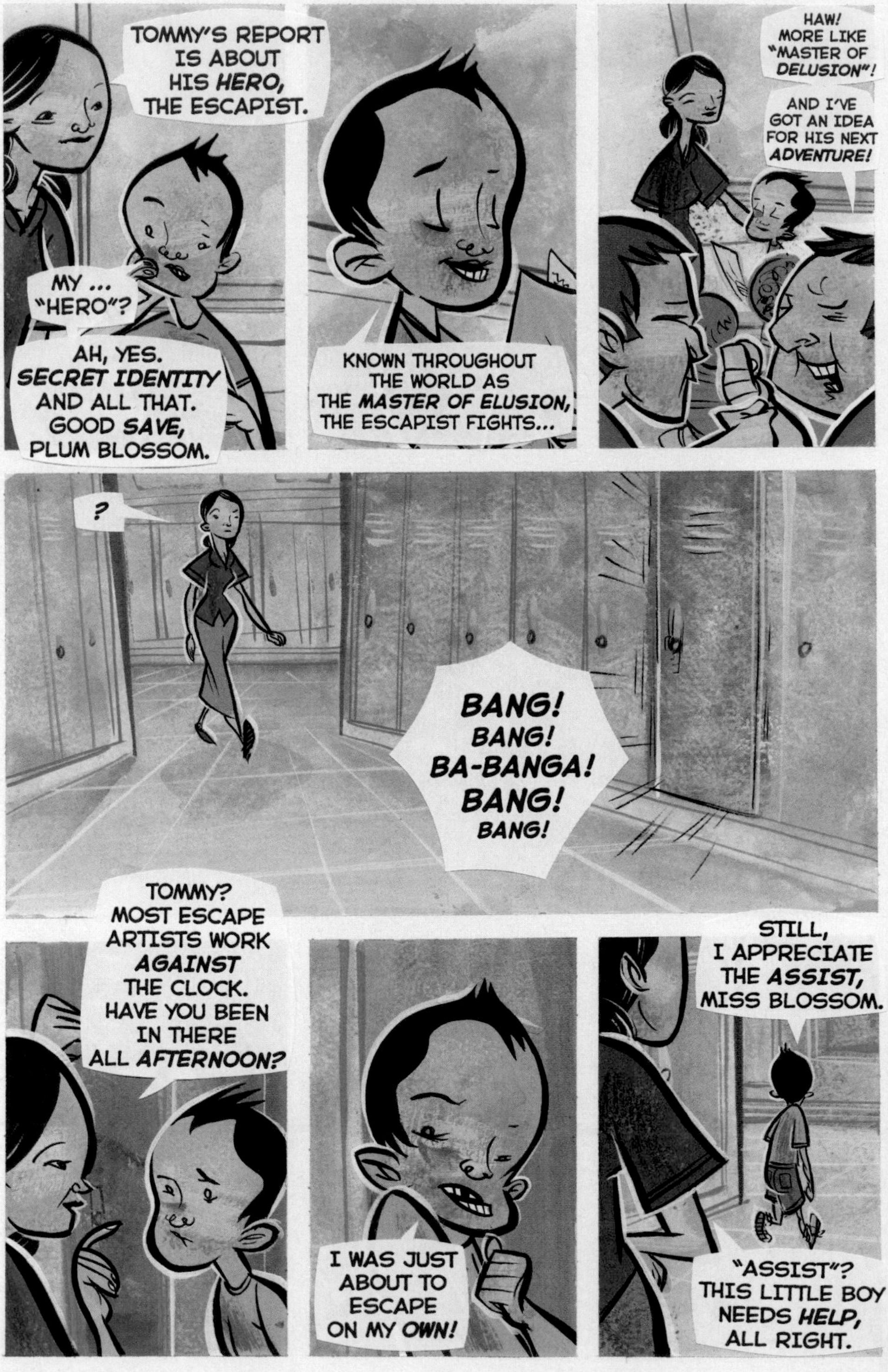
TOMMY'S REPORT IS ABOUT HIS HERO, THE ESCAPIST.
MY ... "HERO"?
AH, YES. SECRET IDENTITY AND ALL THAT. GOOD SAVE, PLUM BLOSSOM.
KNOWN THROUGHOUT THE WORLD AS THE MASTER OF ELUSION, THE ESCAPIST FIGHTS...
HAW! MORE LIKE "MASTER OF DELUSION"!
AND I'VE GOT AN IDEA FOR HIS NEXT ADVENTURE!
?
BANG! BANG! BA-BANGA! BANG! BANG!
TOMMY? MOST ESCAPE ARTISTS WORK AGAINST THE CLOCK. HAVE YOU BEEN IN THERE ALL AFTERNOON?
I WAS JUST ABOUT TO ESCAPE ON MY OWN!
STILL, I APPRECIATE THE ASSIST, MISS BLOSSOM.
"ASSIST"? THIS LITTLE BOY NEEDS HELP, ALL RIGHT.

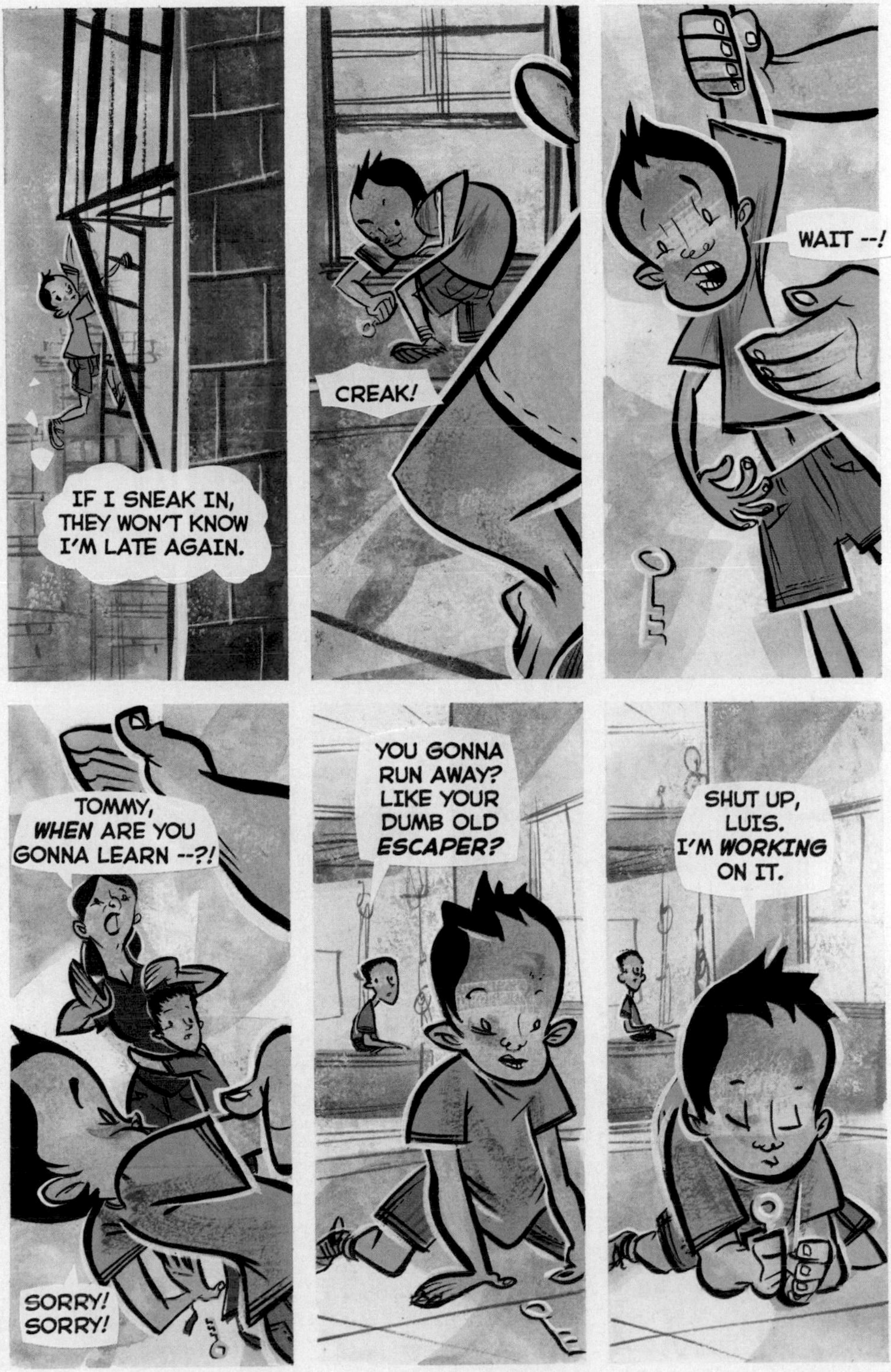
IF I SNEAK IN, THEY WON'T KNOW I'M LATE AGAIN.
CREAK!
WAIT --!
TOMMY, *WHEN* ARE YOU GONNA LEARN --?!
SORRY! SORRY!
YOU GONNA RUN AWAY? LIKE YOUR DUMB OLD *ESCAPER?*
SHUT UP, LUIS. I'M *WORKING* ON IT.

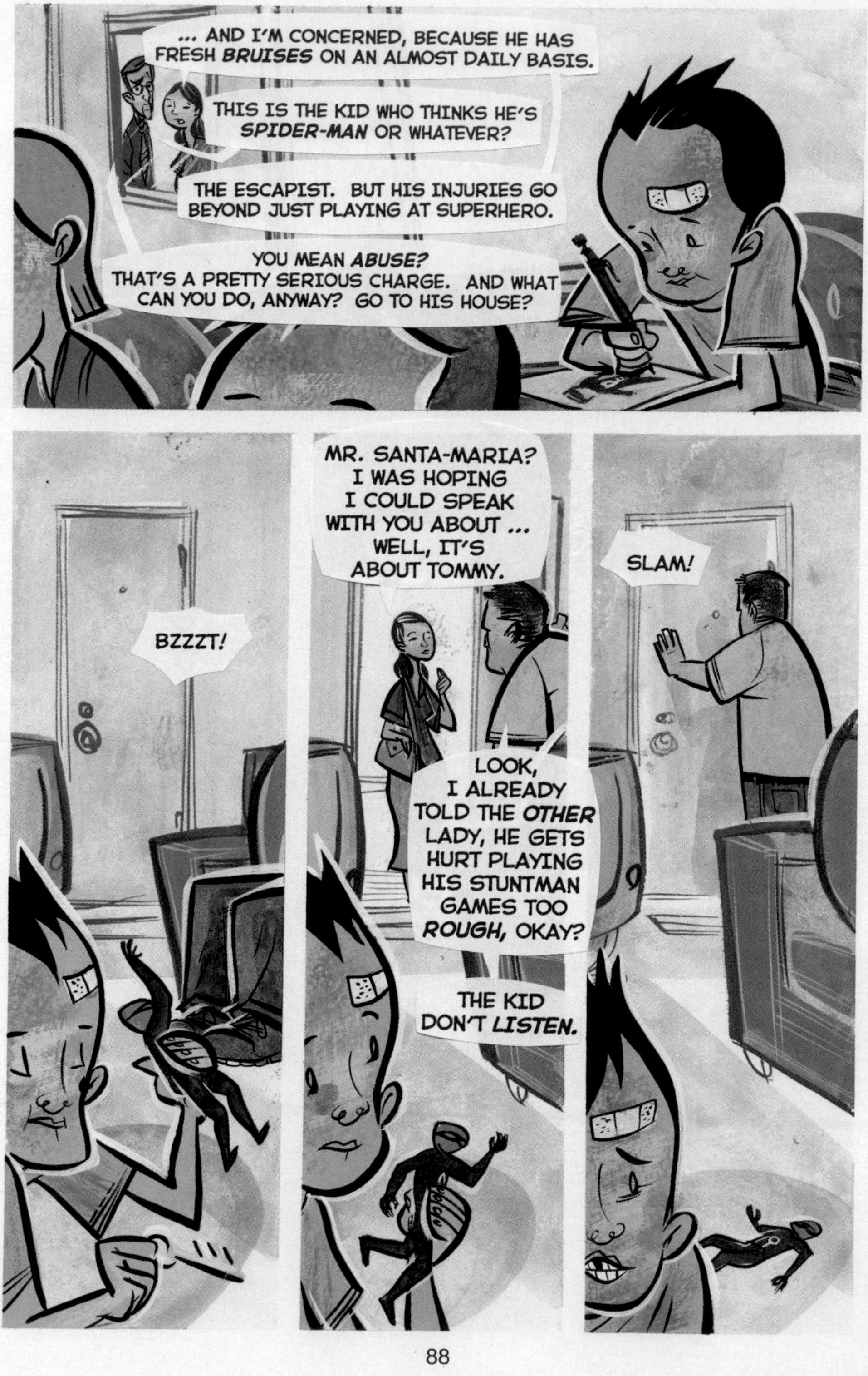
... AND I'M CONCERNED, BECAUSE HE HAS FRESH BRUISES ON AN ALMOST DAILY BASIS.
THIS IS THE KID WHO THINKS HE'S SPIDER-MAN OR WHATEVER?
THE ESCAPIST. BUT HIS INJURIES GO BEYOND JUST PLAYING AT SUPERHERO.
YOU MEAN ABUSE? THAT'S A PRETTY SERIOUS CHARGE. AND WHAT CAN YOU DO, ANYWAY? GO TO HIS HOUSE?
BZZZT!
MR. SANTA-MARIA? I WAS HOPING I COULD SPEAK WITH YOU ABOUT ... WELL, IT'S ABOUT TOMMY.
LOOK, I ALREADY TOLD THE OTHER LADY, HE GETS HURT PLAYING HIS STUNTMAN GAMES TOO ROUGH, OKAY?
THE KID DON'T LISTEN.
SLAM!

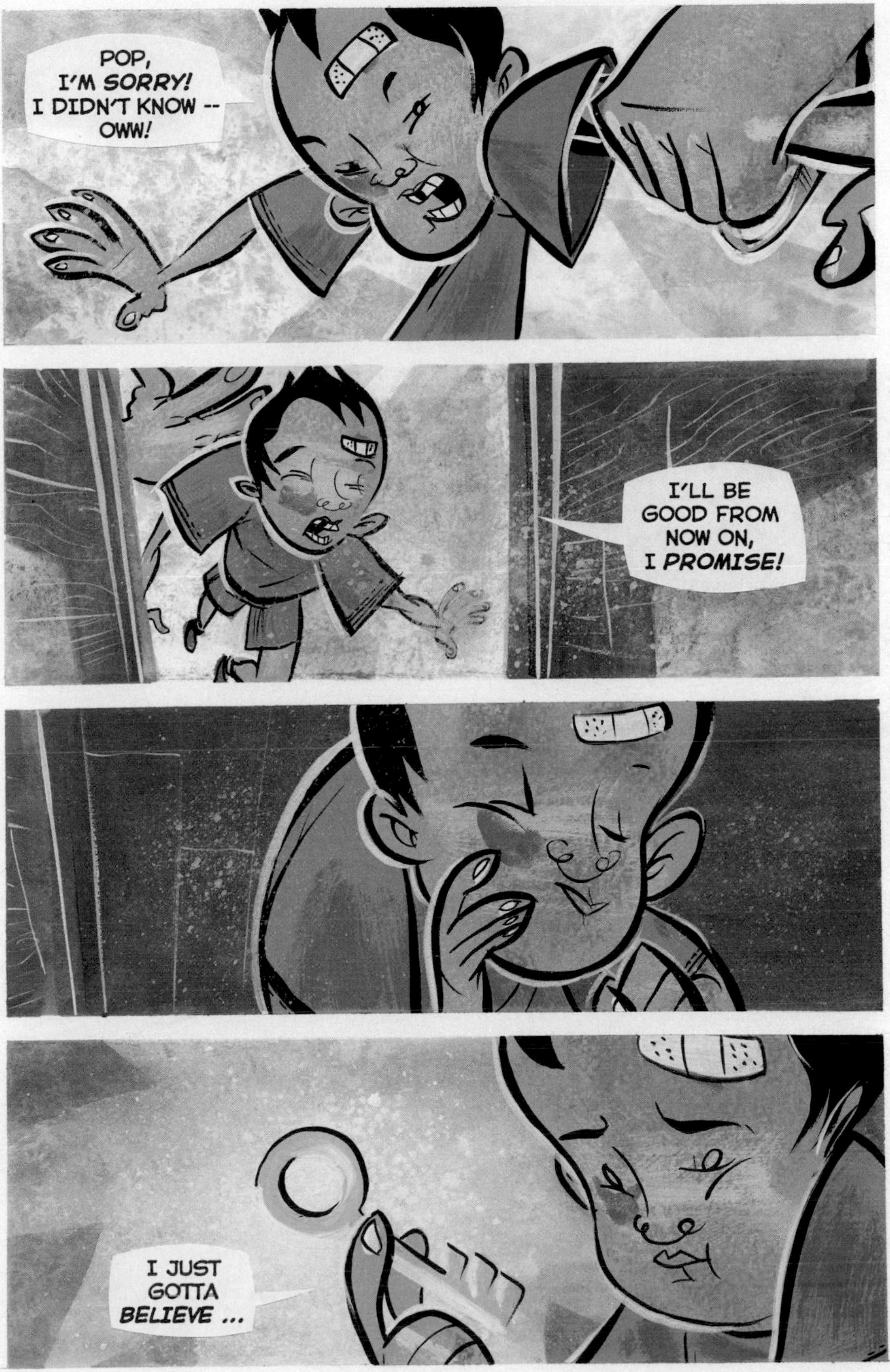
POP, I'M *SORRY!* I DIDN'T KNOW -- OWW!
I'LL BE GOOD FROM NOW ON, I *PROMISE!*
I JUST GOTTA *BELIEVE ...*

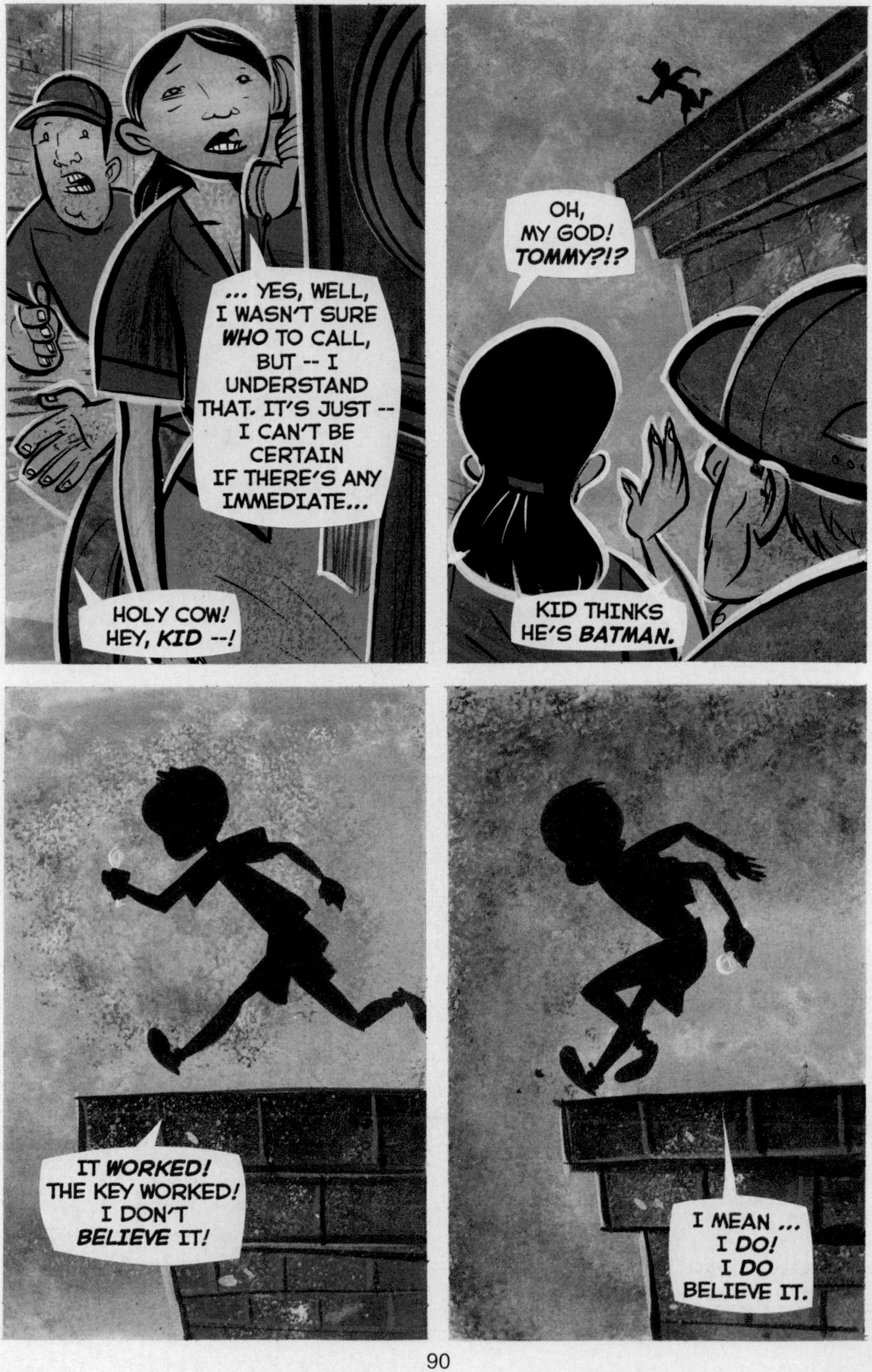
... YES, WELL, I WASN'T SURE WHO TO CALL, BUT -- I UNDERSTAND THAT. IT'S JUST -- I CAN'T BE CERTAIN IF THERE'S ANY IMMEDIATE...
HOLY COW! HEY, KID --!
OH, MY GOD! TOMMY?!?
KID THINKS HE'S BATMAN.
IT WORKED! THE KEY WORKED! I DON'T BELIEVE IT!
I MEAN ... I DO! I DO BELIEVE IT.

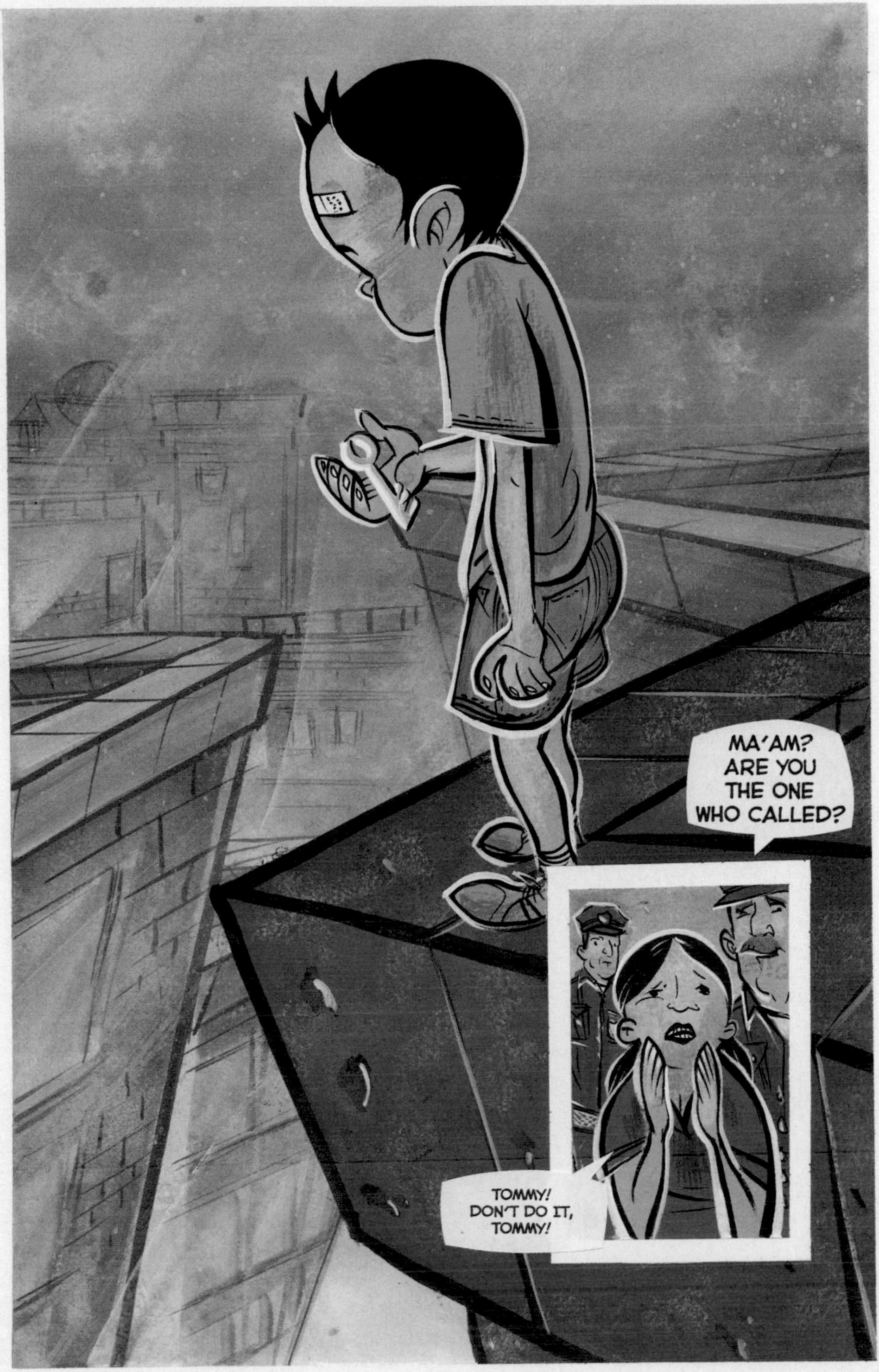
MA'AM? ARE YOU THE ONE WHO CALLED?
TOMMY! DON'T DO IT, TOMMY!

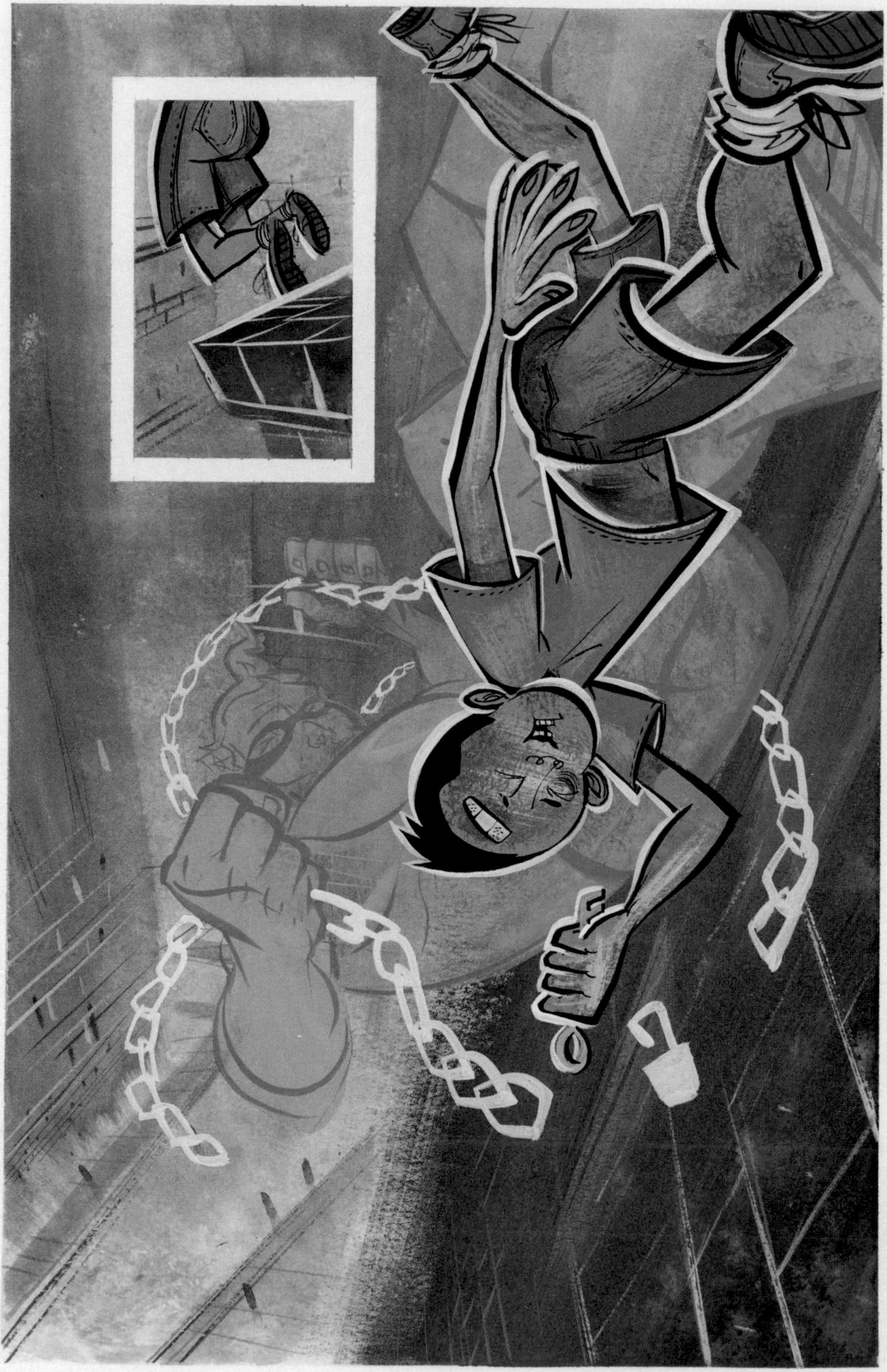

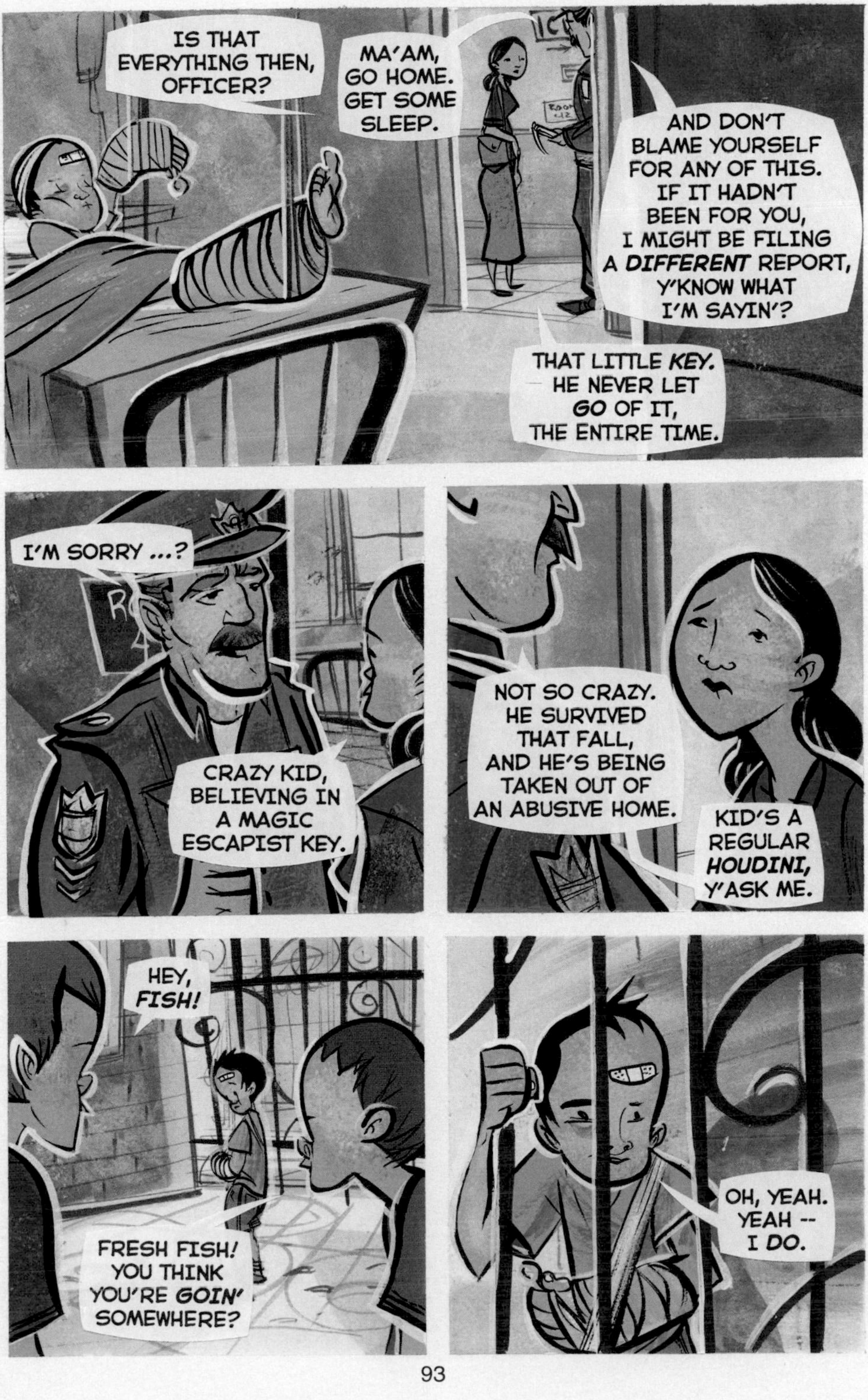
IS THAT EVERYTHING THEN, OFFICER?
MA'AM, GO HOME. GET SOME SLEEP.
AND DON'T BLAME YOURSELF FOR ANY OF THIS. IF IT HADN'T BEEN FOR YOU, I MIGHT BE FILING A *DIFFERENT* REPORT, Y'KNOW WHAT I'M SAYIN'?
THAT LITTLE *KEY.* HE NEVER LET *GO* OF IT, THE ENTIRE TIME.
I'M SORRY ...?
CRAZY KID, BELIEVING IN A MAGIC ESCAPIST KEY.
NOT SO CRAZY. HE SURVIVED THAT FALL, AND HE'S BEING TAKEN OUT OF AN ABUSIVE HOME.
KID'S A REGULAR *HOUDINI,* Y'ASK ME.
HEY, *FISH!*
FRESH FISH! YOU THINK YOU'RE *GOIN'* SOMEWHERE?
OH, YEAH. YEAH -- I *DO.*

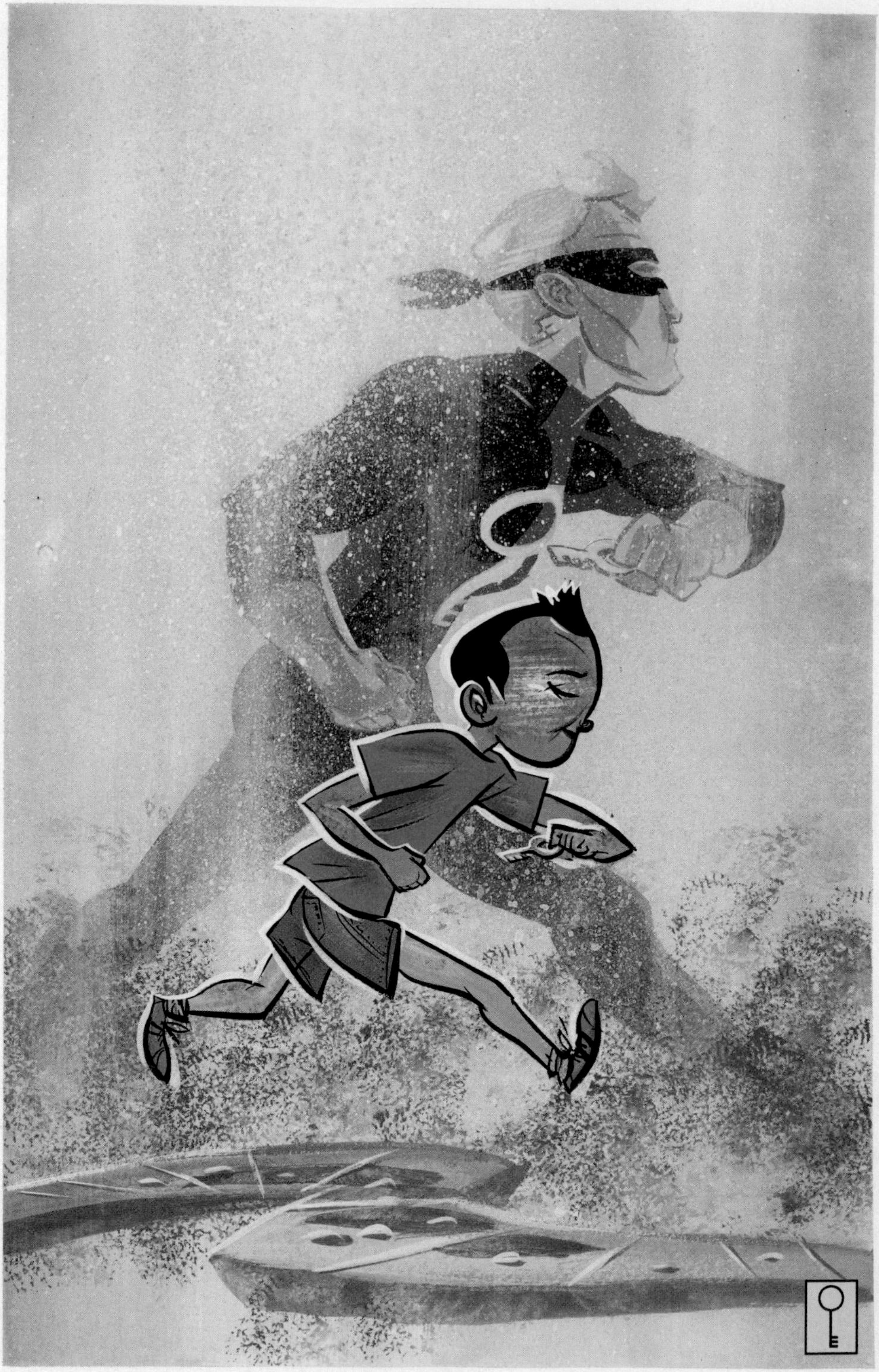

"ABSOLUTELY *FAB*-ULOUS!"

A Personal and Idiosyncratic Look at the Fab Comics Group (1965-1968)

by Roy Thomas

The following article was scheduled to appear in Roy Thomas's fanzine Alter Ego, but got squeezed out by special issues on Julie Schwartz and Jerry Robinson. Roy agreed to let it appear here instead, with the benefit of color reproduction.

Alter Ego name and logo
™ © 2004 Roy and Dann Thomas

"They're 'fab' — and all the rest of the pimply hyperboles!"

With that line of dialogue, a smarmy marketing executive in the 1964 Beatles film *A Hard Day's Night* snidely dismisses his own firm's trendy line of shirts — and, by inference, the Beatles themselves, the "Fab Four" who that year had taken western popular culture by storm.

Those of us who were around during the latter 1960s, however, couldn't afford to be quite so blasé about the Fab *comics* line, which surged briefly onto the scene in late 1965 and blazed like Bill Haley's Comets across the sky before falling to Earth.

It always seemed to me like a four-color monkey wrench tossed into the middle of an otherwise simple situation. Having moved to New York in mid-1965 to work for DC Comics, then jumping ship after two weeks to begin a 15-year stint as Stan Lee's right-hand man at smaller Marvel, I was all geared up to play my part in the David-and-Goliath battle between the upstart Marvel Comics Group and National/DC (the reigning champs ever since 1938) — when, in late '65, a wild card was suddenly tossed onto the table.

I'm talking about ... Fab Comics!

Fab Comics was Jerry Glovsky's big chance. Never really one of the big stars in the comic book heavens, even in the glory days of Empire Comics and *The Escapist* back in the early 1940s, he had contented himself with writing and drawing minor heroes like The Snowman. Eventually, with the decline of superhero sales after World War II, he had drawn crime and later horror comics. He'd never quite been able to storm the gates at Lev Gleason's outfit (for one thing, Charlie Biro said he used too many "blacks" in his inking, and Biro's motto was: "Blacks are cheating"); and his luck was no better at Bill Gaines's EC (though there were rumors he'd once helped Al Williamson, Frank Frazetta, and Roy G. Krenkel on a tight deadline on one particularly exquisite story in *Weird Science*). Eventually he had wangled a staff job in the fabled Marvel (then Timely) bullpen, just in time to be canned along with everybody else during what fans now call the "Implosion" of 1957, when American News went under and sucked companies down with it like a whirlpool.

Now, at fifty, Glovsky suddenly found himself hired as editor by a new company, Fab Comics. Like the other minor players at that time — Tower and Harvey and Charlton and Archie — Fab wanted to take advantage of the sudden surge in publicity garnered by the growing popularity of Marvel Comics and the tide of nostalgia for old comics, as epitomized in the Feb. 15, 1965, *Newsweek* article. (Nobody could have dreamt, just then, that the phenomenal success of the 1966 *Batman* TV show would soon dwarf what had come before.)

The only problem was that, at that point, Fab was nothing but a hopefully attention-getting name and a ravening desire for huge profits. It was left to Glovsky to figure out what to put in the comics. Looking back to his relationship with Sammy Clay and Joe Kavalier and Empire, it apparently occurred to Glovsky that, in light of what Malachi B. Cohen (in *The Comics Journal*) has called "a gray-lit realm of uncertain ownership," the Escapist and the rest of the old Empire *oeuvre* might well be up for grabs. So he grabbed it.

He sold his bosses on initially publishing a single comic called *The League of the Golden K.E.Y.*, a name which would be trademarkable (which *The Escapist*, at that point, might not be). The "League" part, of course, echoed *Justice League of America*, one of DC's top sellers and the mag that had inspired Marvel's flagship title *Fantastic Four*. "K.E.Y.," which stood for "Keepers of the Enigmas of Yesteryear," was a blatant attempt to latch onto the acronymical craze launched by James Bond's S.P.E.C.T.R.E. and TV's *The Man from U.N.C.L.E.* Hey, if Tower and Marvel could do it, why couldn't Fab?

Glovsky's main problem was talent. Many of his old comic book buddies had long since left the field for commercial art and advertising, and were hardly eager to return to the comic book ghetto. Nor could he expect to lure anyone away from DC, which paid the best rates in the industry. Even those venturesome souls like Gene Colan, Mike Esposito, and Frank Giacoia who yielded to Stan Lee's siren call to moonlight for Marvel did so under pseudonyms,* lest they be retaliated against by the turf-protective DC editors.

So Glovsky went after a bunch of newcomers —and struck gold:

Neal Adams, after selling a few pages of gag art to *Archie's Joke Book* and working at Johnstone and Cushing Art Service, had been tapped in 1962 to draw the *Ben Casey* daily comic strip based on the popular TV-doctor series; yet somehow he found time to draw a Luna Moth exploit for *League of the Golden K.E.Y.* #1. She had never looked sexier, nor had her curves been rendered more realistically and voluptuously, even though the published strip had to be printed from Neal's pencils and a bit of the delicate linework was thus lost.

Jim Steranko, up from Reading, Pennsylvania, hadn't quite been able to crack Marvel that summer when he journeyed to New York for the first "full-service" comics convention, held at the decrepit Broadway Central Hotel. But he somehow managed to turn his newest sample story — which featured a motorcyle-riding hero reminiscent of scenes in an old Simon & Kirby *Captain America* — into an Escapist escapade. Jim had the added advantage that he wanted to write his own stories.

And Steve Ditko, fresh from his departure from Marvel at the end of '65, would soon be aboard, as well. But not in time for the first issue.

---

* Rumor has it that Jack Kirby may have been lured away from Marvel by Glovsky to pseudonymously draw one story, a Luna Moth tale entitled "The Trial of Judy Dark," which is reprinted in this very volume. The story is credited to a "Dean Haspiel," his single story credit until the mid-1990s, when an artist of the same name surfaced in small-press indie comics. It's interesting to note that the story in question served as precursor to Fab's popular *If/Then* series of stories, which later inspired the *What If?* series at Marvel. — Bubbles LaTour

Fab had at least one false start, as well.

During the first half of the 1960s, Gil Kane's star had risen at DC because of his work as the original penciller of editor Julius Schwartz's two popular titles, *Green Lantern* and *The Atom*. By 1965, though, Gil was chafing at the bit to branch out to other companies. He had already pencilled part of a Menthor story for *T.H.U.N.D.E.R. Agents* #1, which hit the stands that autumn; but rumor had it that Fab Comics was paying better page rates than either Tower or Marvel (which wasn't hard — Marvel's rates were roughly half DC's at that stage), so Gil stopped by to talk to his old lunch buddy, Jerry Glovsky.

Glovsky was so eager to get Gil on board that he danced around the subject of rates and persuaded Gil to draw up a few pencil sketches of the Escapist and Luna Moth. Gil even tossed in his own take on Kommandant X (who in the 1950s had switched from Nazi to Commie, and now was about to head the League's acronymical enemy group). As seen for the first time ever on these pages, courtesy of Mrs. Elaine Kane, the artist did fabulous renditions of the characters. For Gil, who felt confined by DC's staid editorial standards, it was a chance to develop the Jack Kirby-influenced side of his style; after all, one of his first jobs had been as assistant/ghost to Simon & Kirby back in the early '40s. Indeed, one of Gil's major complaints about DC was its attitude toward action. As he told me after we began working together in 1969 on Marvel's *Captain Marvel*: "I had to fight Julie [Schwartz] to get him to let me have Green Lantern throw one goddam punch!"

Gil also admitted that he got a bit annoyed when, without consulting him, Glovsky had a novice named Bucky Gomez ink his sample figures. Not that Gomez hadn't done a stellar job, but another of Gil's motives for going to Fab was that Schwartz wouldn't let him ink his own pencils at DC.

But the real sticking point was money. Fab's publisher had decided he couldn't afford the rates he had originally empowered Glovsky to bruit about, and had retreated to even less than Marvel was currently

In late 1966/early 1967, Silver Age great Gil Kane pencilled sketches of his own version of The Escapist, Luna Moth, and even a new Kommandant X for the editor of the Fab Comics Group. Inking by Bucky Gomez. *Artwork courtesy of Elaine Kane.*

paying. So Gil stomped out of Fab and strode over to Marvel, where Stan Lee promptly assigned him to pencil an Incredible Hulk story — but over Kirby layouts, and to be inked by Mike Esposito as "Mickey Demeo." Both Gil and Stan were dissatisfied with the resulting art in *Tales to Astonish* #76 (Feb. 1966), and Gil contented himself with drawing for DC, with an occasional foray at Tower, for another year or two.

Glovsky couldn't count on having top established artists come through his door, however, so he put out the word that Fab would be a great place for new talent to make a name for itself.

One early bright spot was Herbert William (Herb) Trimpe. A graduate of the School of Visual Arts, Herb had been inker/assistant to veteran Tom Gill in 1960-'62 and had drawn a spot of Archie in '64, and was eager to get back into the field. His friend John Verpoorten, who was still assisting Gill on *The Owl* and other features for Western, heard about Fab and suggested Herb give it a shot. Herb talked to Jerry Glovsky and was immediately given a rush job, a cover for *League of the Golden K.E.Y. #2*, which showed the hero in battle with the deadly Snapping Turtle, horrific henchman of Kommandant X.

Herb did several more Escapist stories for Fab until, when Glovsky held back one of his checks during a cash-flow shortage (while Adams, Steranko, and Ditko got paid), the young artist decided that even operating a photostat machine was preferable to working for Fab, so he took that position at Marvel. There, he soon graduated to doing artwork — and later got Verpoorten a staff job, as well.

With Adams, Steranko, Ditko, Trimpe, and others — even without Gil Kane — Fab Comics quickly attracted the attention of Stan Lee, who said to me one day out of the blue: "Why aren't these guys working for *us*?" (He didn't mean Ditko, of course — he'd long since given up trying to understand Steve, or, probably, vice versa.) I had to remind Stan that Steranko, at least, had come up to Marvel looking for work and had been turned down as "not quite ready yet." "Well, next time he comes up," Stan said, "let's grab him."

And, in summer of '66, we did.

A major player in early comics fandom, Roy Thomas co-created Alter Ego *in 1961, went to work at Marvel Comics in 1965 as Stan Lee's assistant editor, and by 1972 became Marvel's editor-in-chief. He's written comics extensively over the years, for both Marvel and DC, and although in "semi-retirement," he still continues to shepherd each monthly issue of* Alter Ego, *now published by TwoMorrows.*

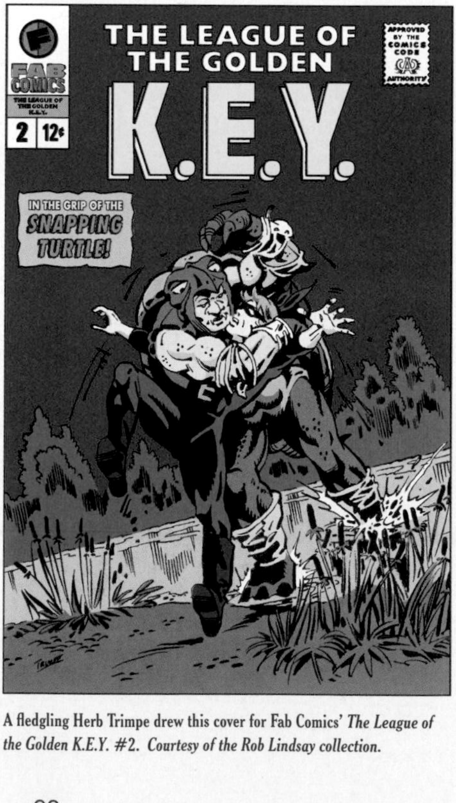
FAB COMICS
2 12¢
THE LEAGUE OF THE GOLDEN
K.E.Y.
APPROVED BY THE COMICS CODE AUTHORITY
IN THE GRIP OF THE SNAPPING TURTLE!

A fledgling Herb Trimpe drew this cover for Fab Comics' *The League of the Golden K.E.Y. #2*. *Courtesy of the Rob Lindsay collection.*

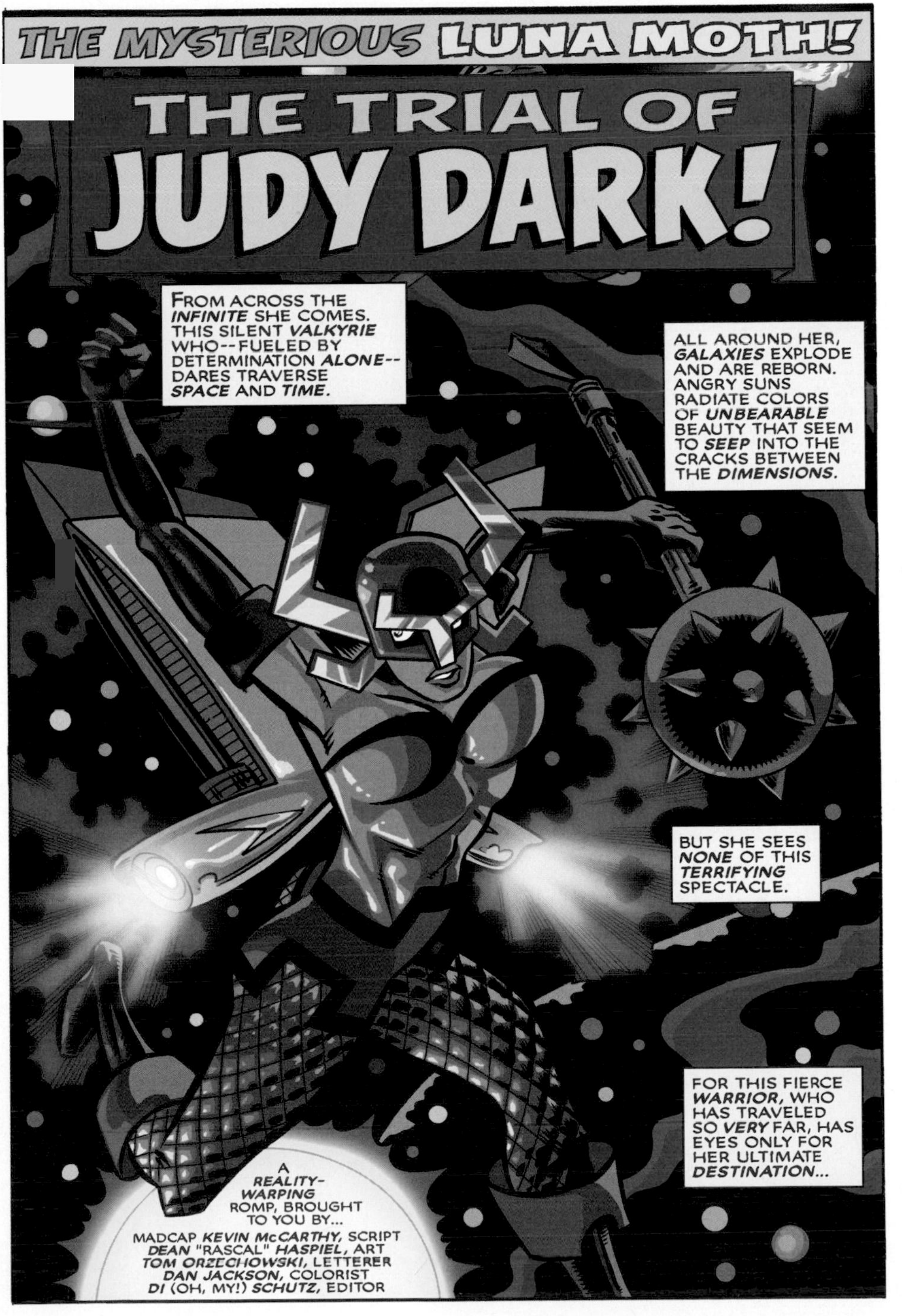
THE MYSTERIOUS LUNA MOTH!
THE TRIAL OF JUDY DARK!
FROM ACROSS THE INFINITE SHE COMES. THIS SILENT VALKYRIE WHO--FUELED BY DETERMINATION ALONE--DARES TRAVERSE SPACE AND TIME.
ALL AROUND HER, GALAXIES EXPLODE AND ARE REBORN. ANGRY SUNS RADIATE COLORS OF UNBEARABLE BEAUTY THAT SEEM TO SEEP INTO THE CRACKS BETWEEN THE DIMENSIONS.
BUT SHE SEES NONE OF THIS TERRIFYING SPECTACLE.
FOR THIS FIERCE WARRIOR, WHO HAS TRAVELED SO VERY FAR, HAS EYES ONLY FOR HER ULTIMATE DESTINATION...
A REALITY-WARPING ROMP, BROUGHT TO YOU BY...
MADCAP KEVIN McCARTHY, SCRIPT
DEAN "RASCAL" HASPIEL, ART
TOM ORZECHOWSKI, LETTERER
DAN JACKSON, COLORIST
DI (OH, MY!) SCHUTZ, EDITOR

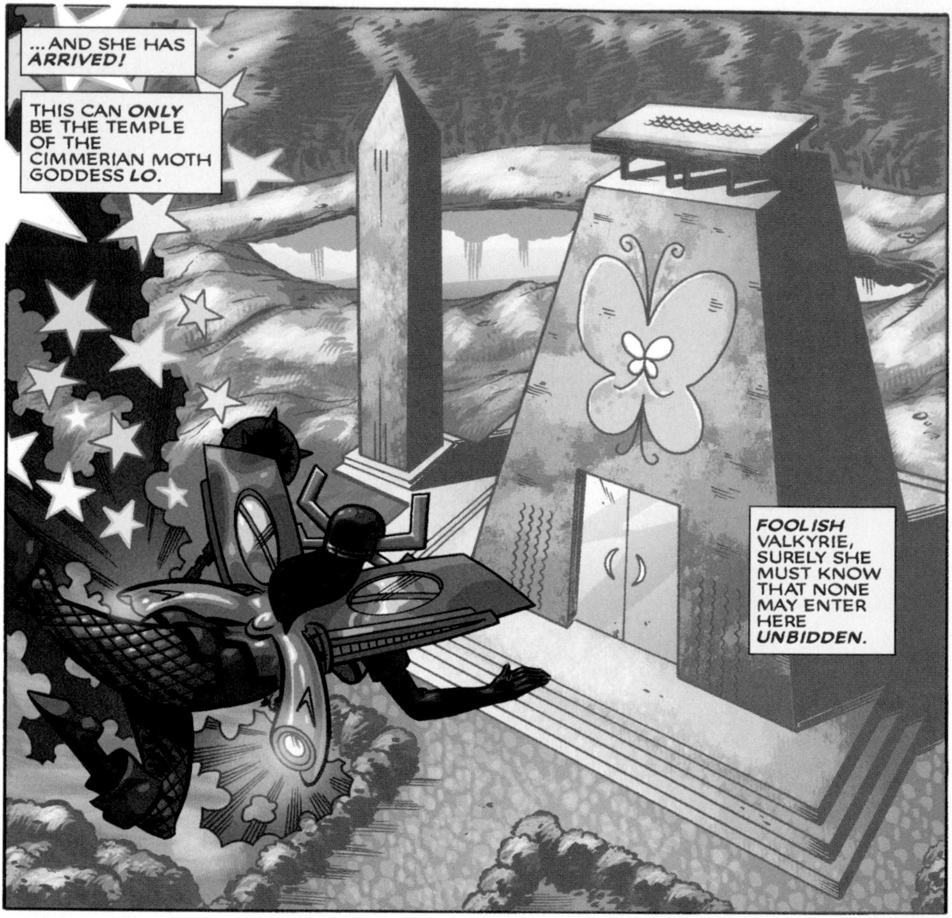
...AND SHE HAS ARRIVED!
THIS CAN ONLY BE THE TEMPLE OF THE CIMMERIAN MOTH GODDESS LO.
FOOLISH VALKYRIE, SURELY SHE MUST KNOW THAT NONE MAY ENTER HERE UNBIDDEN.

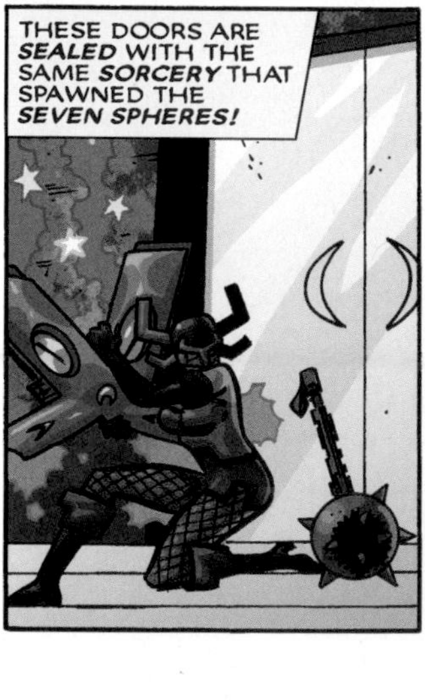
THESE DOORS ARE SEALED WITH THE SAME SORCERY THAT SPAWNED THE SEVEN SPHERES!

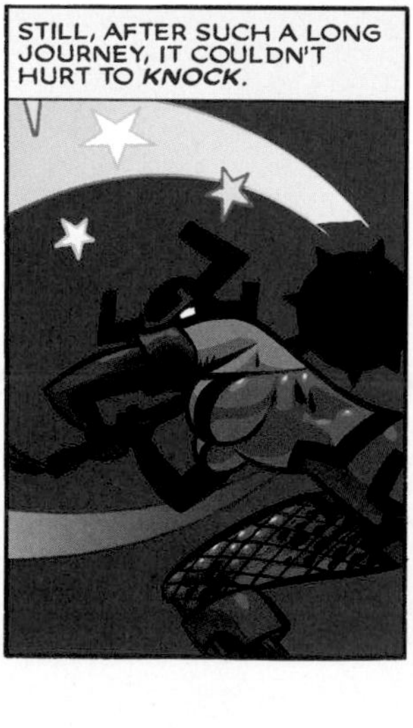
STILL, AFTER SUCH A LONG JOURNEY, IT COULDN'T HURT TO KNOCK.

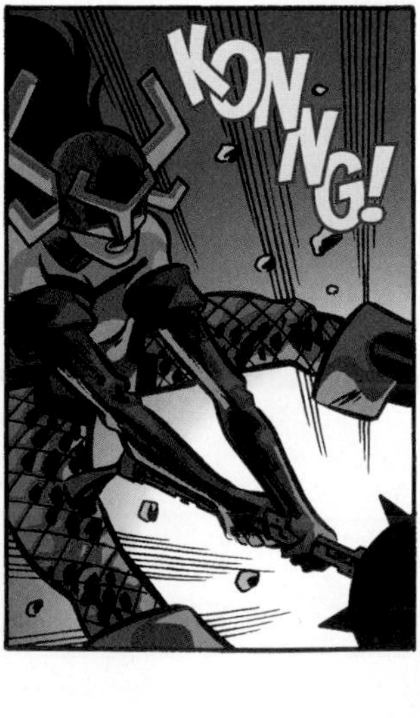
KONNNG!

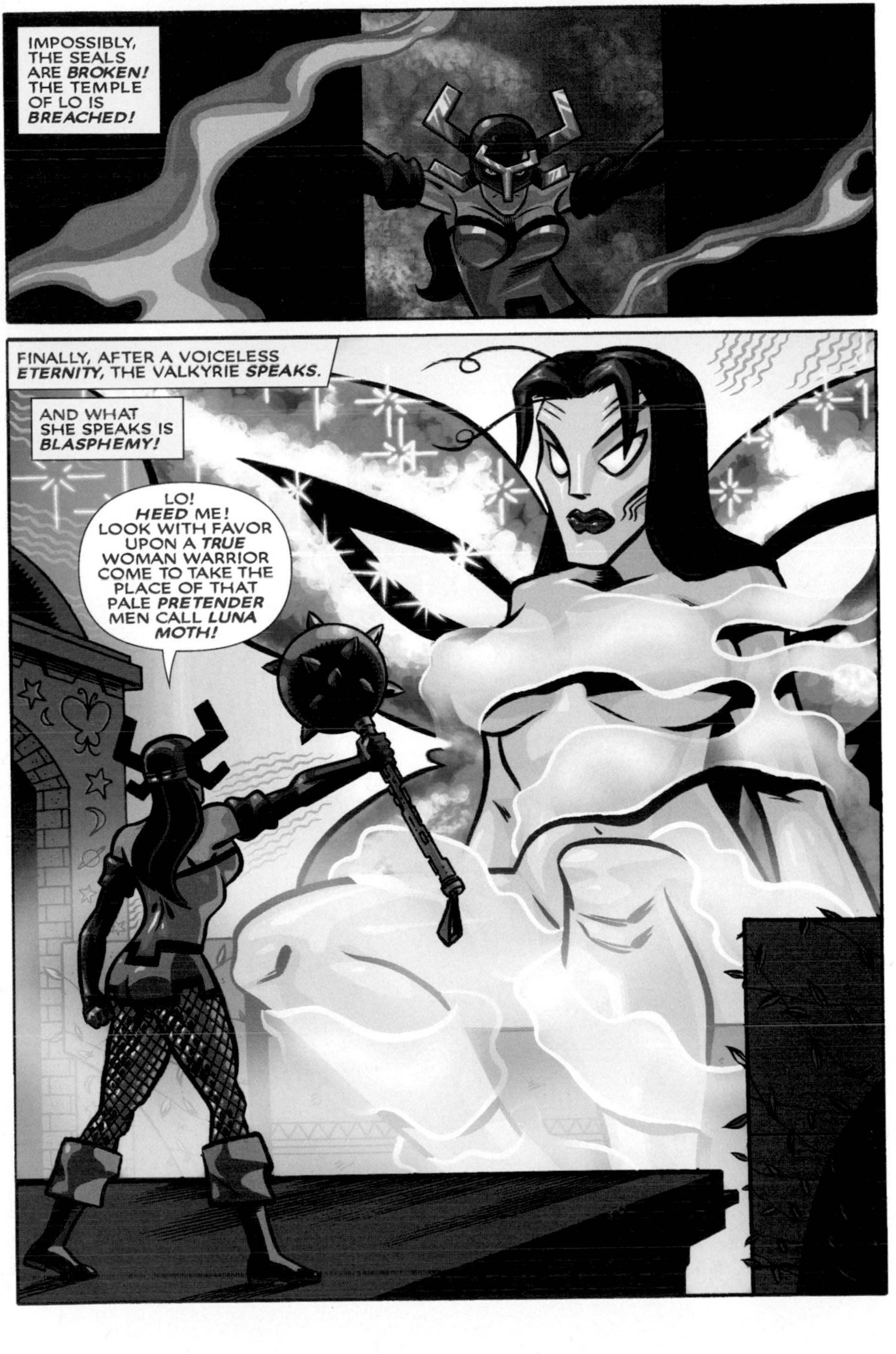
IMPOSSIBLY, THE SEALS ARE *BROKEN!* THE TEMPLE OF LO IS *BREACHED!*
FINALLY, AFTER A VOICELESS *ETERNITY,* THE VALKYRIE *SPEAKS.*
AND WHAT SHE SPEAKS IS *BLASPHEMY!*
LO! *HEED* ME! LOOK WITH FAVOR UPON A *TRUE* WOMAN WARRIOR COME TO TAKE THE PLACE OF THAT PALE *PRETENDER* MEN CALL *LUNA MOTH!*

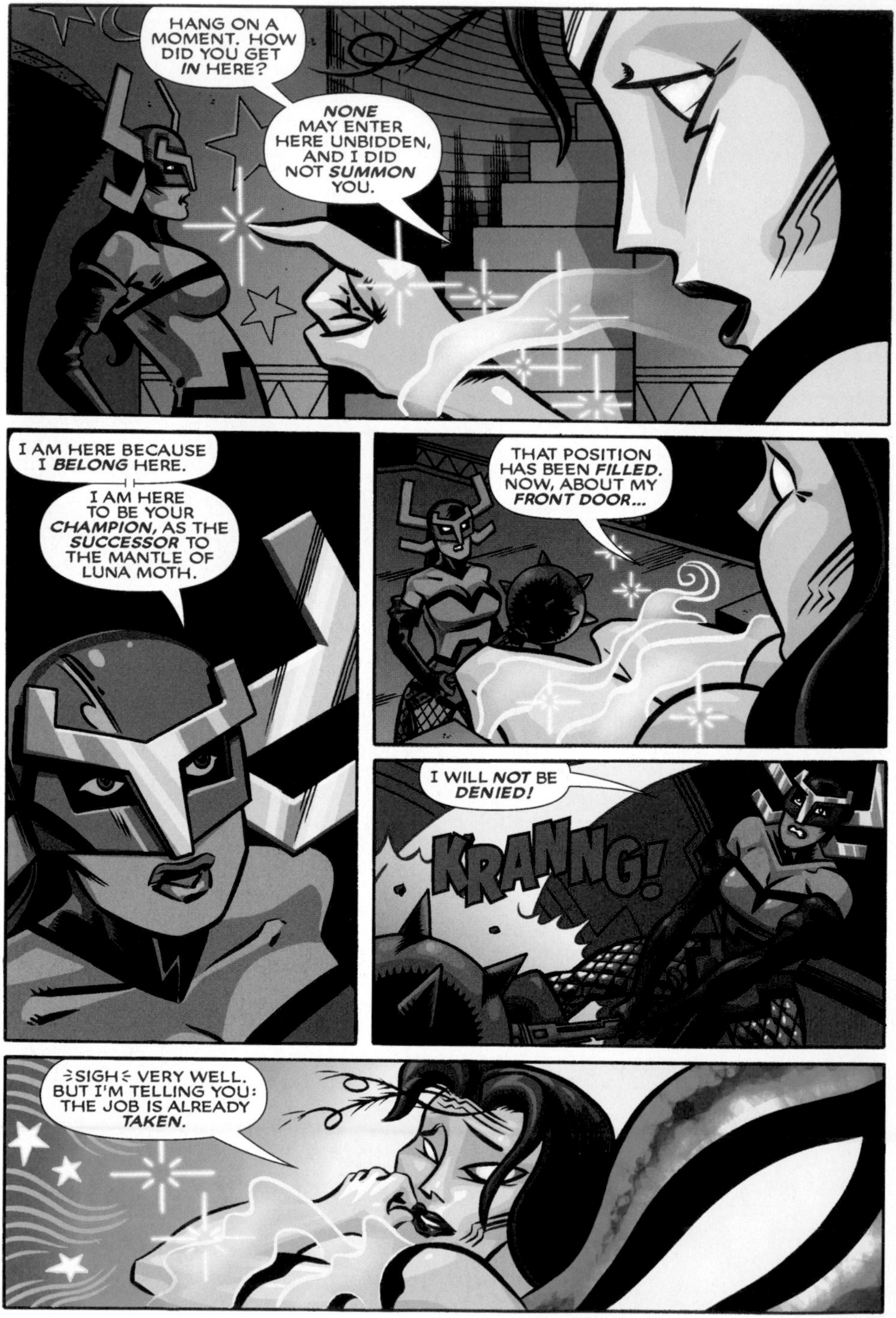
HANG ON A MOMENT. HOW DID YOU GET *IN* HERE?
NONE MAY ENTER HERE UNBIDDEN, AND I DID NOT *SUMMON* YOU.
I AM HERE BECAUSE I *BELONG* HERE.
I AM HERE TO BE YOUR *CHAMPION,* AS THE *SUCCESSOR* TO THE MANTLE OF LUNA MOTH.
THAT POSITION HAS BEEN *FILLED.* NOW, ABOUT MY *FRONT DOOR...*
I WILL *NOT* BE *DENIED!*
KRANNG!
SIGH VERY WELL. BUT I'M TELLING YOU: THE JOB IS ALREADY *TAKEN.*

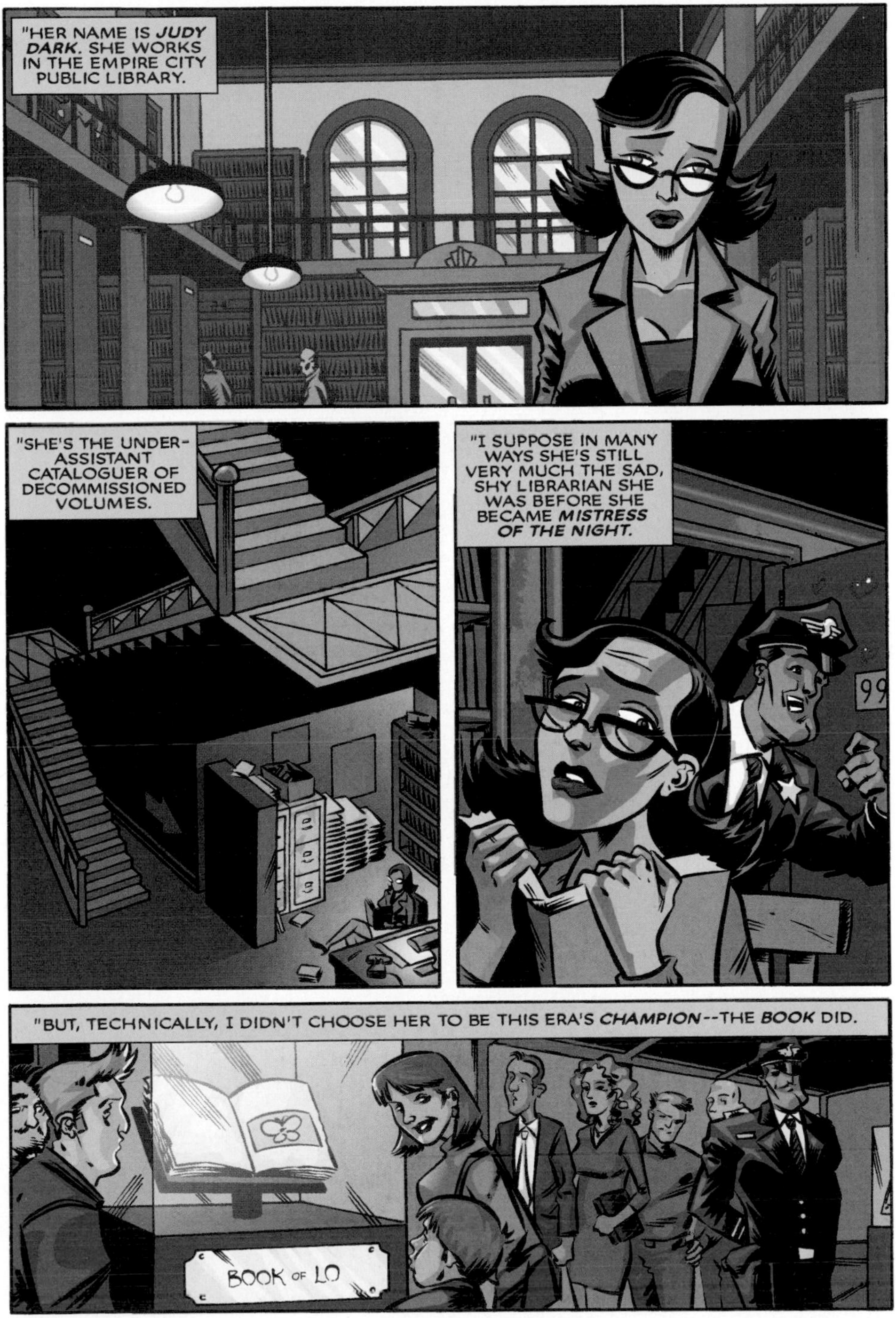
"HER NAME IS JUDY DARK. SHE WORKS IN THE EMPIRE CITY PUBLIC LIBRARY.
"SHE'S THE UNDER-ASSISTANT CATALOGUER OF DECOMMISSIONED VOLUMES.
"I SUPPOSE IN MANY WAYS SHE'S STILL VERY MUCH THE SAD, SHY LIBRARIAN SHE WAS BEFORE SHE BECAME MISTRESS OF THE NIGHT.
99
"BUT, TECHNICALLY, I DIDN'T CHOOSE HER TO BE THIS ERA'S CHAMPION--THE BOOK DID.
BOOK OF LO

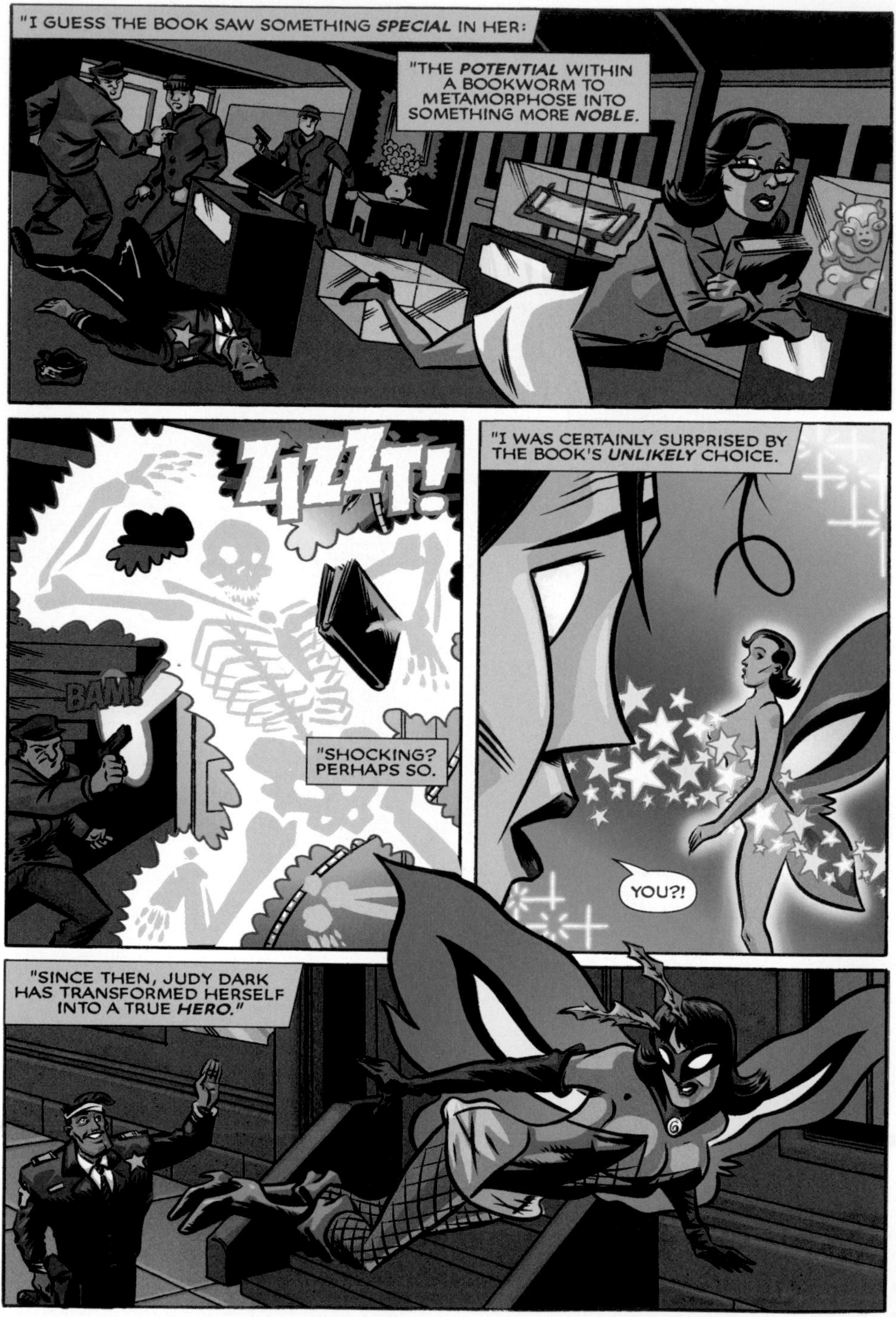
"I GUESS THE BOOK SAW SOMETHING *SPECIAL* IN HER:
"THE *POTENTIAL* WITHIN A BOOKWORM TO METAMORPHOSE INTO SOMETHING MORE *NOBLE*.
ZIZZT!
BAM!
"SHOCKING? PERHAPS SO.
"I WAS CERTAINLY SURPRISED BY THE BOOK'S *UNLIKELY* CHOICE.
YOU?!
"SINCE THEN, JUDY DARK HAS TRANSFORMED HERSELF INTO A TRUE *HERO*."

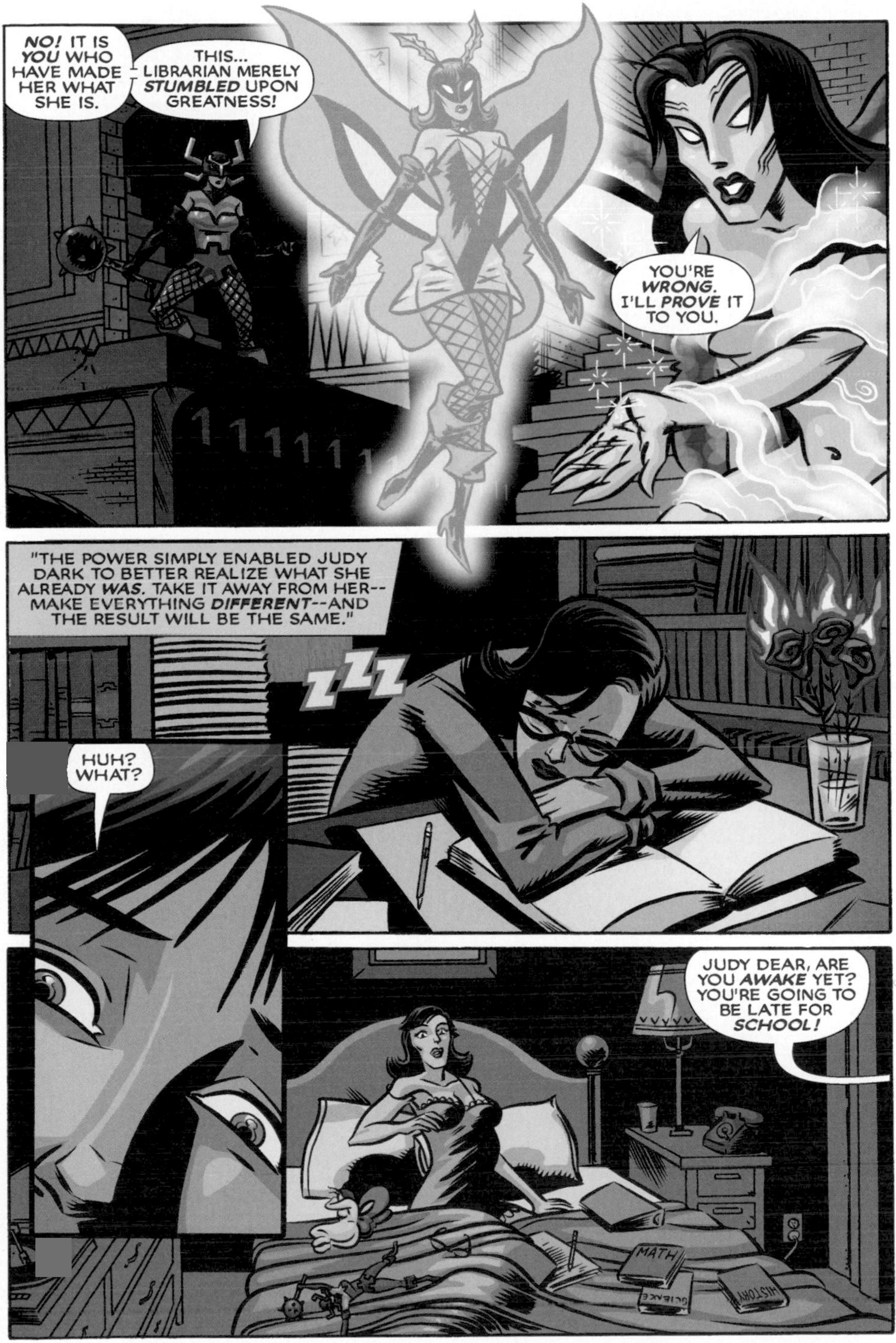
NO! IT IS YOU WHO HAVE MADE HER WHAT SHE IS.
THIS... LIBRARIAN MERELY STUMBLED UPON GREATNESS!
YOU'RE WRONG. I'LL PROVE IT TO YOU.
"THE POWER SIMPLY ENABLED JUDY DARK TO BETTER REALIZE WHAT SHE ALREADY WAS. TAKE IT AWAY FROM HER--MAKE EVERYTHING DIFFERENT--AND THE RESULT WILL BE THE SAME."
ZZZ
HUH? WHAT?
JUDY DEAR, ARE YOU AWAKE YET? YOU'RE GOING TO BE LATE FOR SCHOOL!
MATH
HISTORY

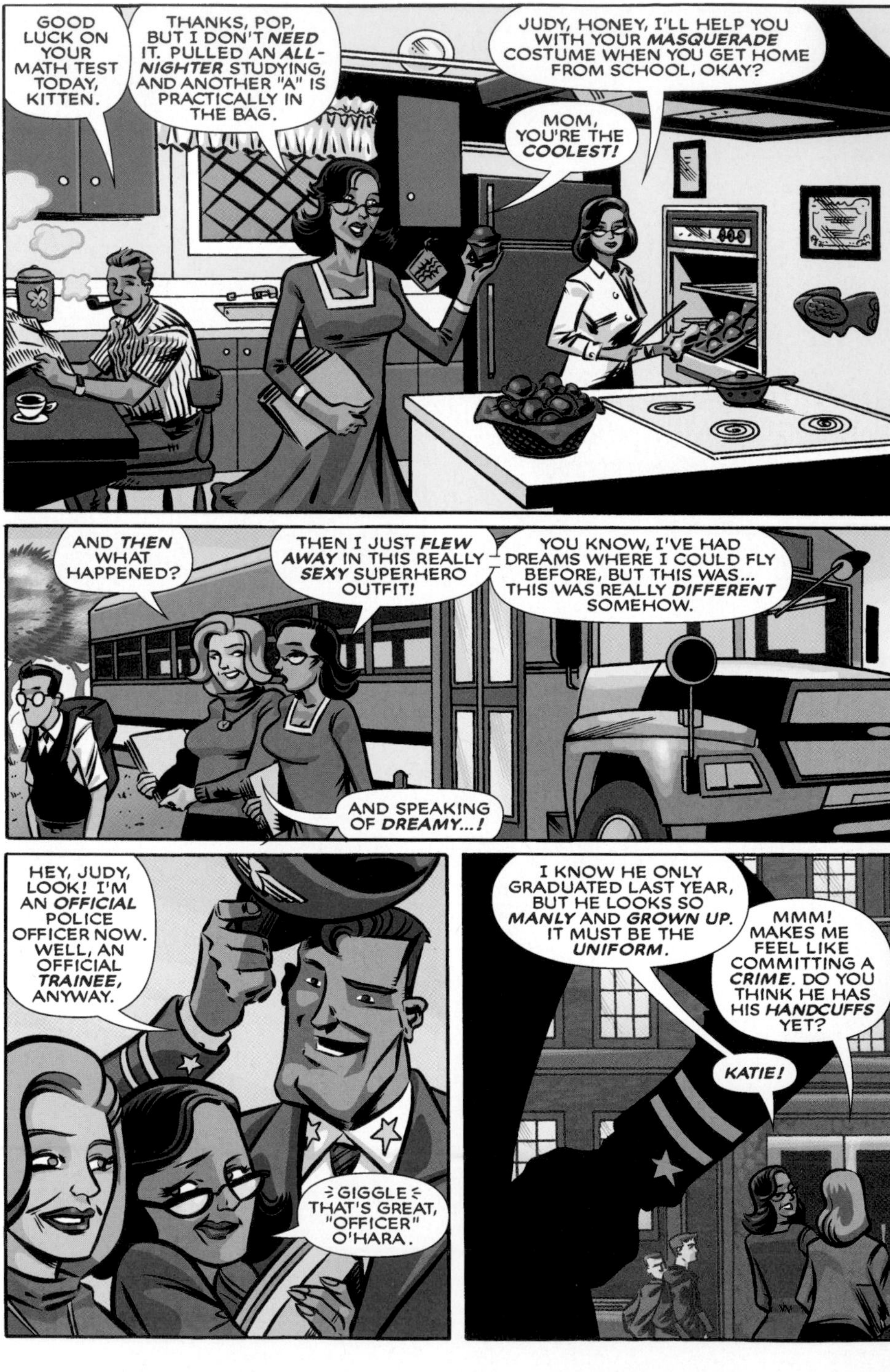
GOOD LUCK ON YOUR MATH TEST TODAY, KITTEN.
THANKS, POP, BUT I DON'T NEED IT. PULLED AN ALL-NIGHTER STUDYING, AND ANOTHER "A" IS PRACTICALLY IN THE BAG.
JUDY, HONEY, I'LL HELP YOU WITH YOUR MASQUERADE COSTUME WHEN YOU GET HOME FROM SCHOOL, OKAY?
MOM, YOU'RE THE COOLEST!
AND THEN WHAT HAPPENED?
THEN I JUST FLEW AWAY IN THIS REALLY SEXY SUPERHERO OUTFIT!
YOU KNOW, I'VE HAD DREAMS WHERE I COULD FLY BEFORE, BUT THIS WAS... THIS WAS REALLY DIFFERENT SOMEHOW.
AND SPEAKING OF DREAMY...!
HEY, JUDY, LOOK! I'M AN OFFICIAL POLICE OFFICER NOW. WELL, AN OFFICIAL TRAINEE, ANYWAY.
GIGGLE THAT'S GREAT, "OFFICER" O'HARA.
I KNOW HE ONLY GRADUATED LAST YEAR, BUT HE LOOKS SO MANLY AND GROWN UP. IT MUST BE THE UNIFORM.
MMM! MAKES ME FEEL LIKE COMMITTING A CRIME. DO YOU THINK HE HAS HIS HANDCUFFS YET?
KATIE!

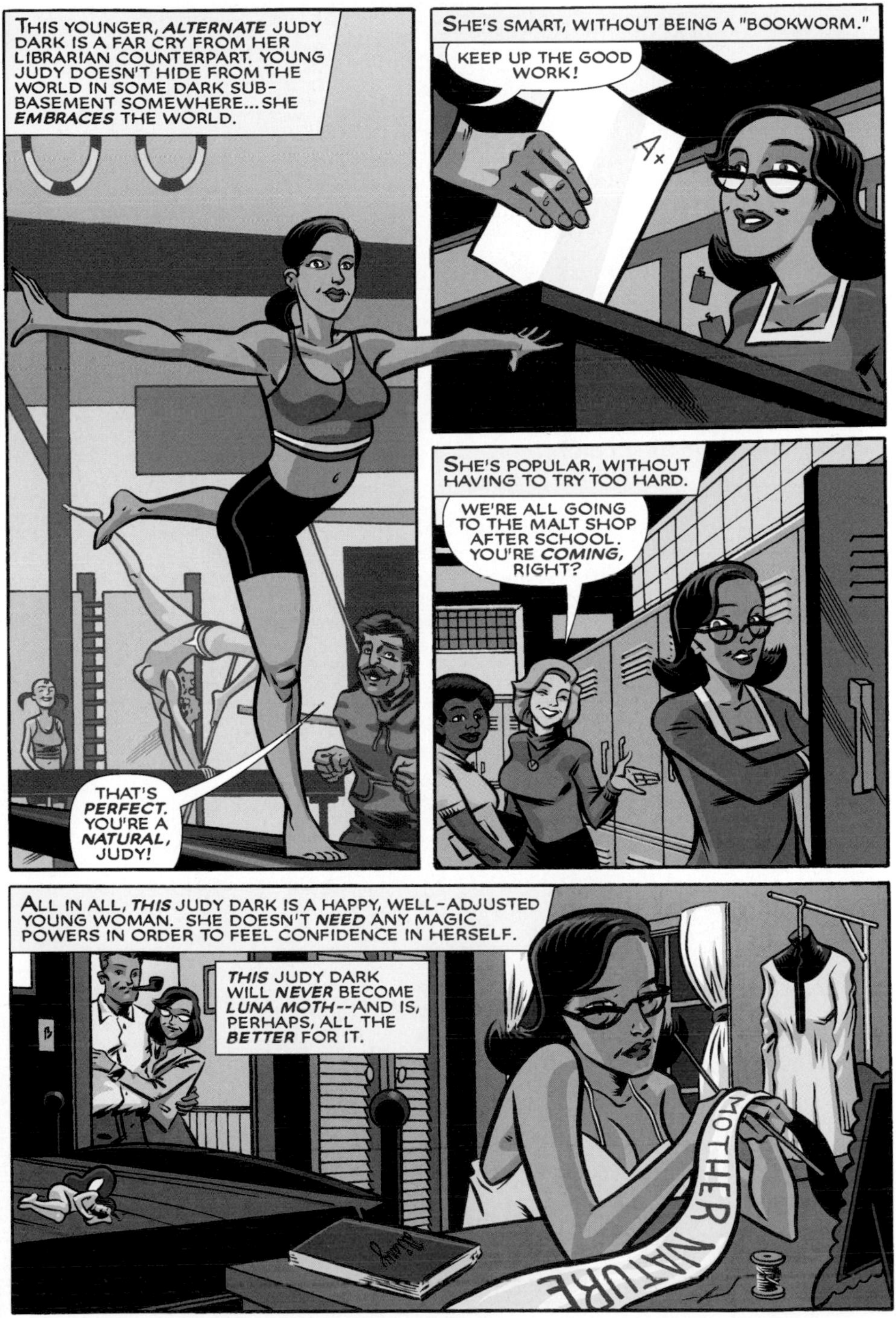
THIS YOUNGER, ALTERNATE JUDY DARK IS A FAR CRY FROM HER LIBRARIAN COUNTERPART. YOUNG JUDY DOESN'T HIDE FROM THE WORLD IN SOME DARK SUB-BASEMENT SOMEWHERE... SHE EMBRACES THE WORLD.
THAT'S PERFECT. YOU'RE A NATURAL, JUDY!
SHE'S SMART, WITHOUT BEING A "BOOKWORM."
KEEP UP THE GOOD WORK!
SHE'S POPULAR, WITHOUT HAVING TO TRY TOO HARD.
WE'RE ALL GOING TO THE MALT SHOP AFTER SCHOOL. YOU'RE COMING, RIGHT?
ALL IN ALL, THIS JUDY DARK IS A HAPPY, WELL-ADJUSTED YOUNG WOMAN. SHE DOESN'T NEED ANY MAGIC POWERS IN ORDER TO FEEL CONFIDENCE IN HERSELF.
THIS JUDY DARK WILL NEVER BECOME LUNA MOTH--AND IS, PERHAPS, ALL THE BETTER FOR IT.
MOTHER NATURE

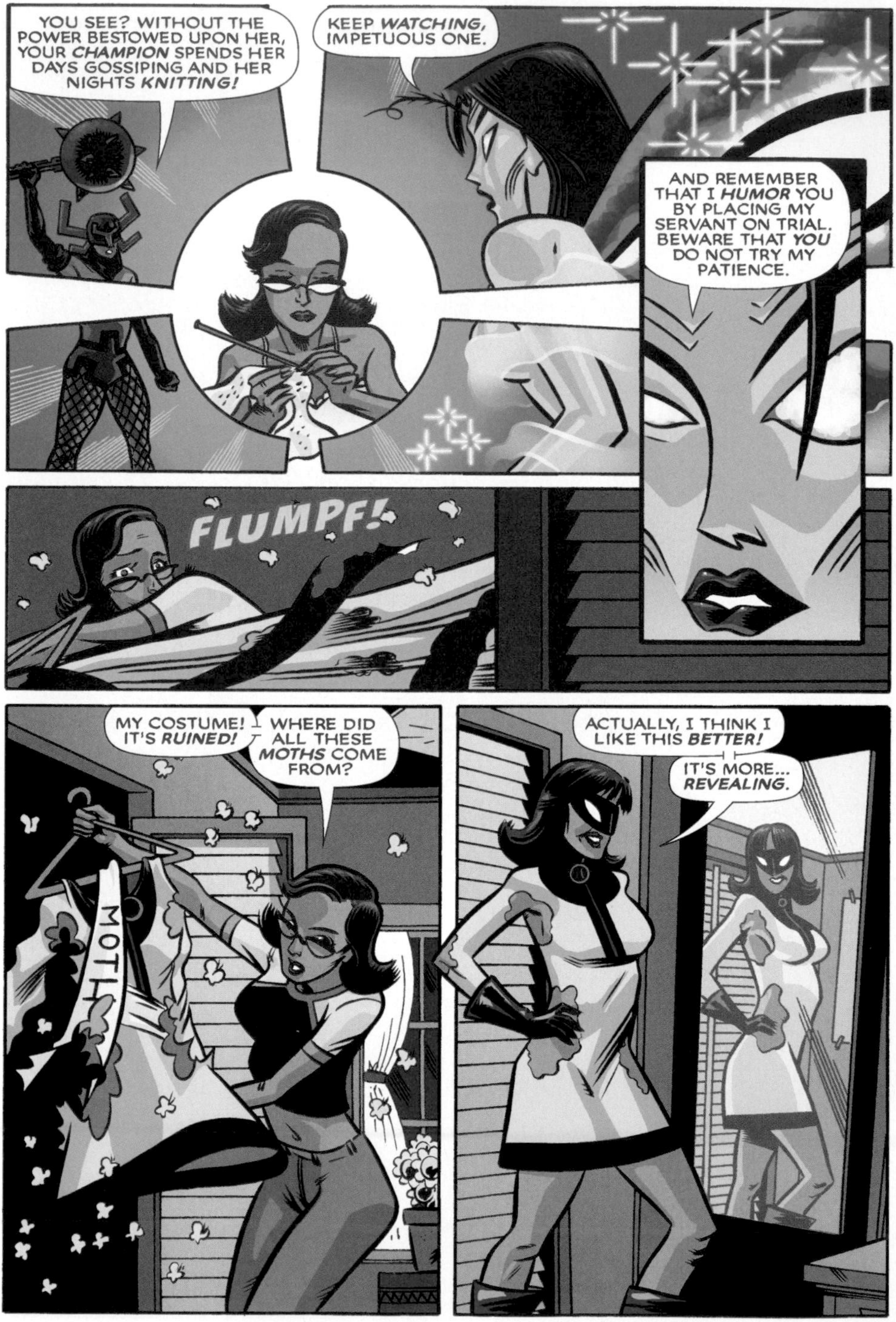
YOU SEE? WITHOUT THE POWER BESTOWED UPON HER, YOUR CHAMPION SPENDS HER DAYS GOSSIPING AND HER NIGHTS KNITTING!
KEEP WATCHING, IMPETUOUS ONE.
AND REMEMBER THAT I HUMOR YOU BY PLACING MY SERVANT ON TRIAL. BEWARE THAT YOU DO NOT TRY MY PATIENCE.
FLUMPF!
MY COSTUME! IT'S RUINED!
WHERE DID ALL THESE MOTHS COME FROM?
MOTH
ACTUALLY, I THINK I LIKE THIS BETTER!
IT'S MORE... REVEALING.

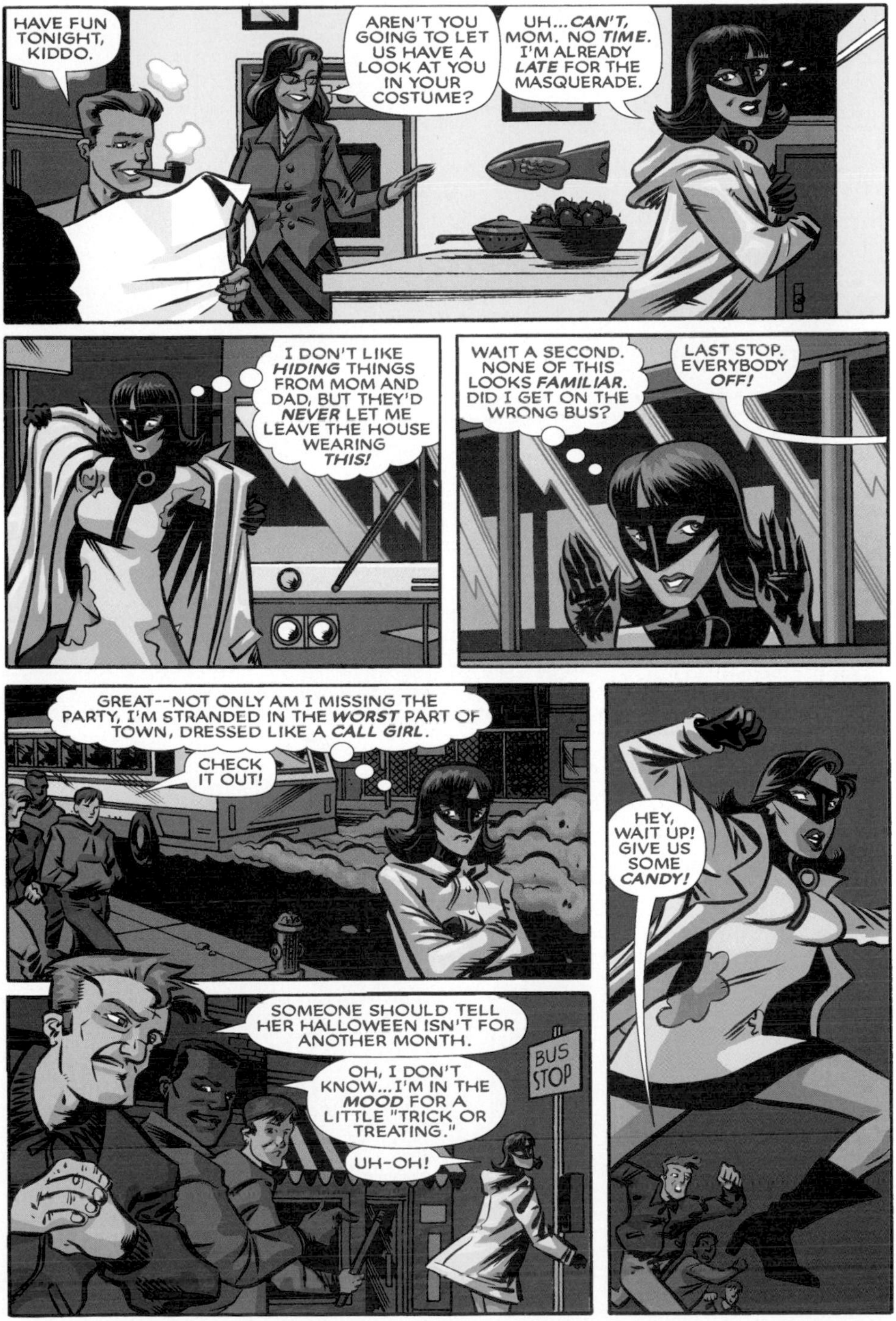
HAVE FUN TONIGHT, KIDDO.
AREN'T YOU GOING TO LET US HAVE A LOOK AT YOU IN YOUR COSTUME?
UH... CAN'T, MOM. NO TIME. I'M ALREADY LATE FOR THE MASQUERADE.
I DON'T LIKE HIDING THINGS FROM MOM AND DAD, BUT THEY'D NEVER LET ME LEAVE THE HOUSE WEARING THIS!
WAIT A SECOND. NONE OF THIS LOOKS FAMILIAR. DID I GET ON THE WRONG BUS?
LAST STOP. EVERYBODY OFF!
GREAT--NOT ONLY AM I MISSING THE PARTY, I'M STRANDED IN THE WORST PART OF TOWN, DRESSED LIKE A CALL GIRL.
CHECK IT OUT!
SOMEONE SHOULD TELL HER HALLOWEEN ISN'T FOR ANOTHER MONTH.
OH, I DON'T KNOW... I'M IN THE MOOD FOR A LITTLE "TRICK OR TREATING."
BUS STOP
UH-OH!
HEY, WAIT UP! GIVE US SOME CANDY!

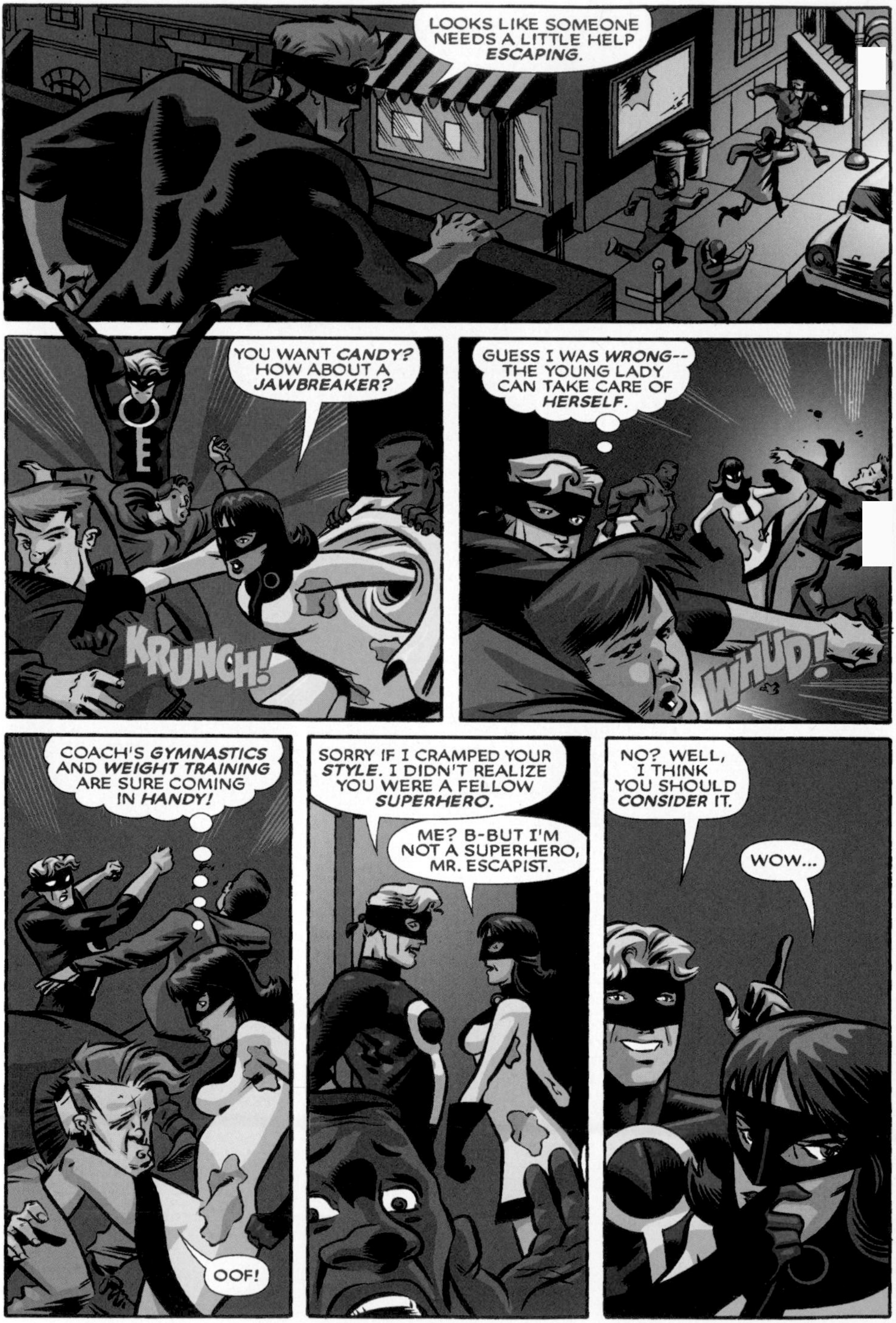
LOOKS LIKE SOMEONE NEEDS A LITTLE HELP ESCAPING.
YOU WANT CANDY? HOW ABOUT A JAWBREAKER?
KRUNCH!
GUESS I WAS WRONG-- THE YOUNG LADY CAN TAKE CARE OF HERSELF.
WHUD!
COACH'S GYMNASTICS AND WEIGHT TRAINING ARE SURE COMING IN HANDY!
OOF!
SORRY IF I CRAMPED YOUR STYLE. I DIDN'T REALIZE YOU WERE A FELLOW SUPERHERO.
ME? B-BUT I'M NOT A SUPERHERO, MR. ESCAPIST.
NO? WELL, I THINK YOU SHOULD CONSIDER IT.
WOW...

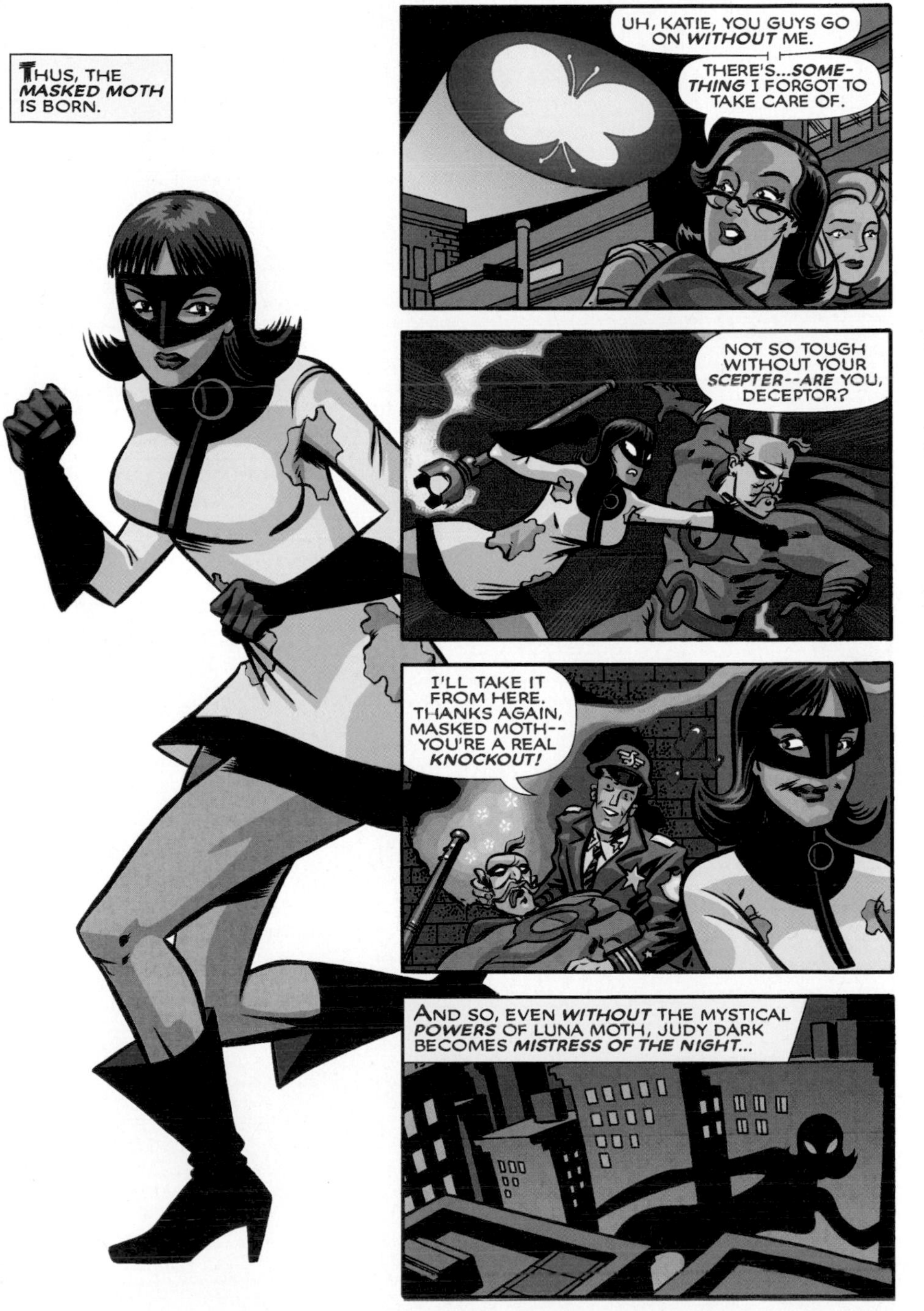
THUS, THE MASKED MOTH IS BORN.
UH, KATIE, YOU GUYS GO ON WITHOUT ME.
THERE'S...SOMETHING I FORGOT TO TAKE CARE OF.
NOT SO TOUGH WITHOUT YOUR SCEPTER--ARE YOU, DECEPTOR?
I'LL TAKE IT FROM HERE. THANKS AGAIN, MASKED MOTH--YOU'RE A REAL KNOCKOUT!
AND SO, EVEN WITHOUT THE MYSTICAL POWERS OF LUNA MOTH, JUDY DARK BECOMES MISTRESS OF THE NIGHT...

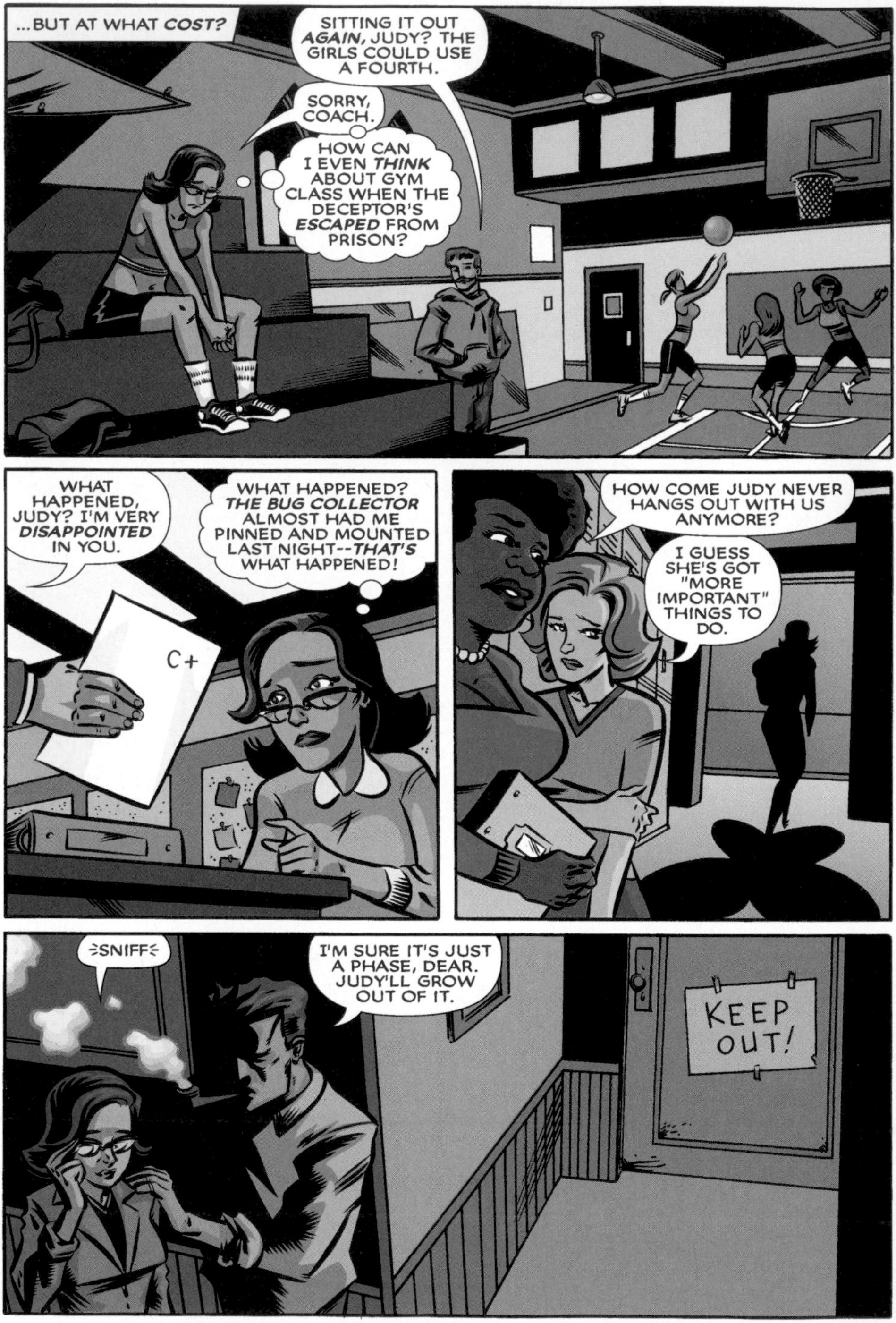
...BUT AT WHAT COST?
SITTING IT OUT AGAIN, JUDY? THE GIRLS COULD USE A FOURTH.
SORRY, COACH.
HOW CAN I EVEN THINK ABOUT GYM CLASS WHEN THE DECEPTOR'S ESCAPED FROM PRISON?
WHAT HAPPENED, JUDY? I'M VERY DISAPPOINTED IN YOU.
WHAT HAPPENED? THE BUG COLLECTOR ALMOST HAD ME PINNED AND MOUNTED LAST NIGHT--THAT'S WHAT HAPPENED!
C+
HOW COME JUDY NEVER HANGS OUT WITH US ANYMORE?
I GUESS SHE'S GOT "MORE IMPORTANT" THINGS TO DO.
SNIFF
I'M SURE IT'S JUST A PHASE, DEAR. JUDY'LL GROW OUT OF IT.
KEEP OUT!

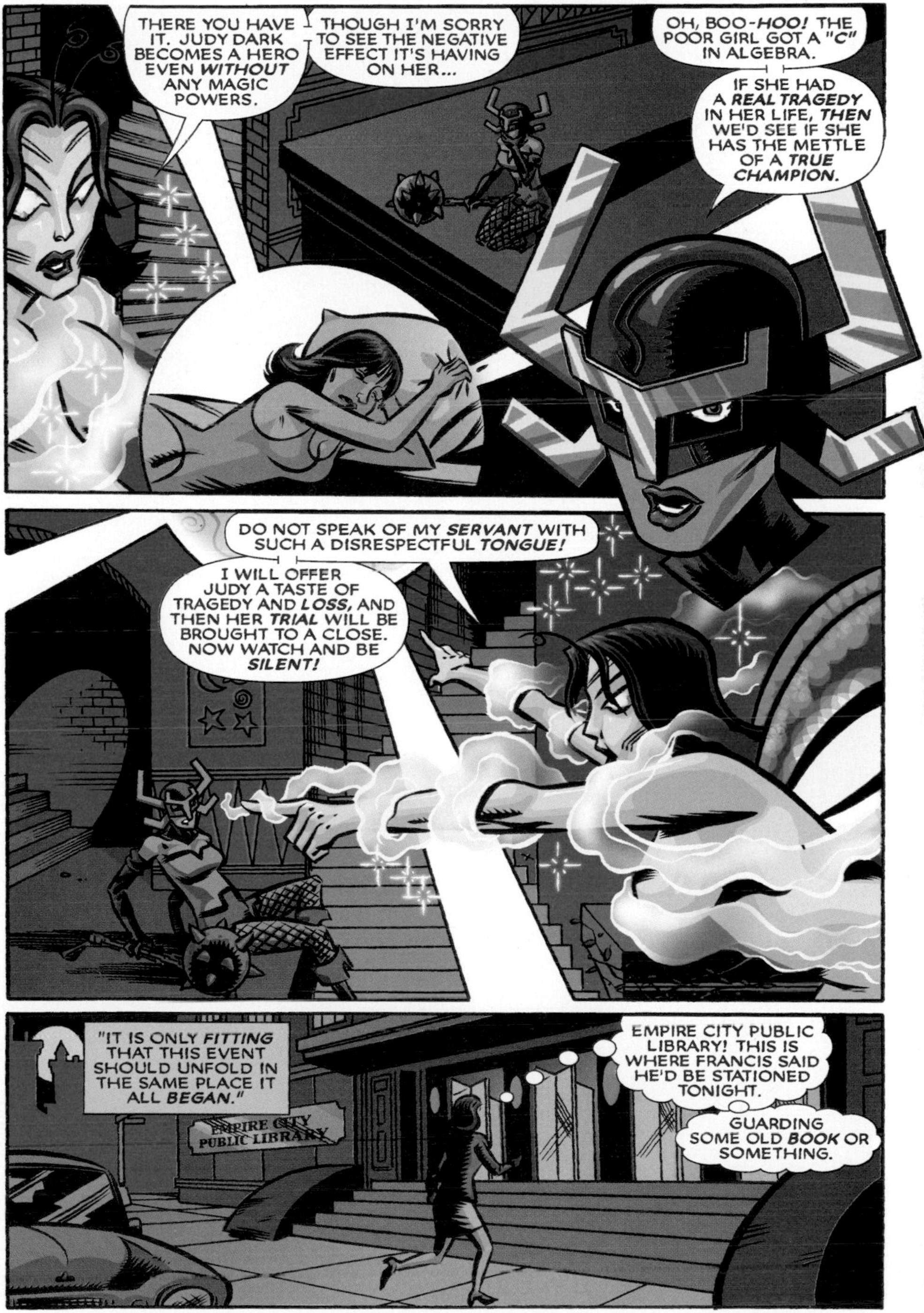
THERE YOU HAVE IT. JUDY DARK BECOMES A HERO EVEN *WITHOUT* ANY MAGIC POWERS.
THOUGH I'M SORRY TO SEE THE NEGATIVE EFFECT IT'S HAVING ON HER...
OH, BOO-*HOO!* THE POOR GIRL GOT A *"C"* IN ALGEBRA.
IF SHE HAD A *REAL TRAGEDY* IN HER LIFE, *THEN* WE'D SEE IF SHE HAS THE METTLE OF A *TRUE CHAMPION.*
DO NOT SPEAK OF MY *SERVANT* WITH SUCH A DISRESPECTFUL *TONGUE!*
I WILL OFFER JUDY A TASTE OF TRAGEDY AND *LOSS,* AND THEN HER *TRIAL* WILL BE BROUGHT TO A CLOSE. NOW WATCH AND BE *SILENT!*
"IT IS ONLY *FITTING* THAT THIS EVENT SHOULD UNFOLD IN THE SAME PLACE IT ALL *BEGAN.*"
EMPIRE CITY PUBLIC LIBRARY
EMPIRE CITY PUBLIC LIBRARY! THIS IS WHERE FRANCIS SAID HE'D BE STATIONED TONIGHT.
GUARDING SOME OLD *BOOK* OR SOMETHING.

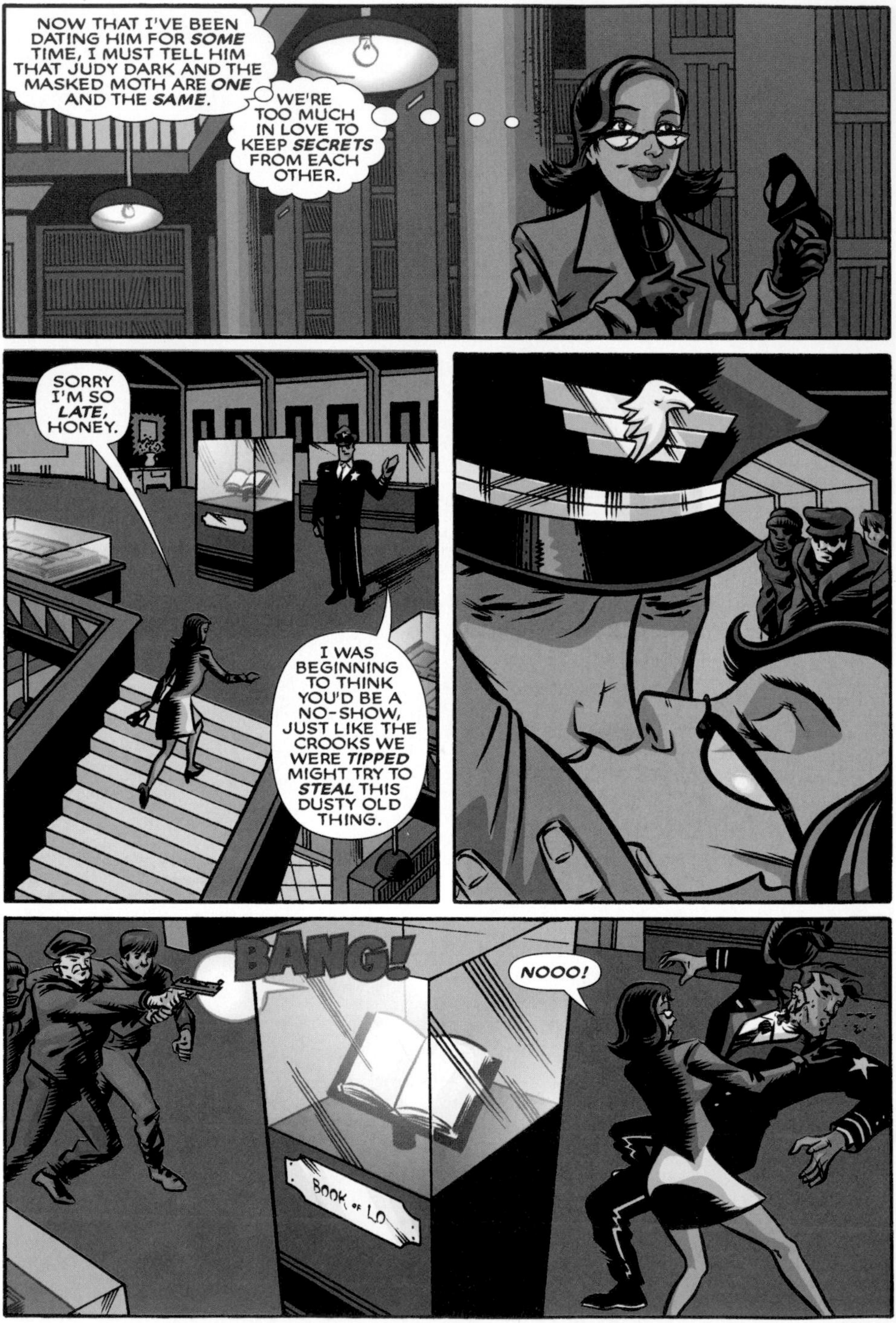
NOW THAT I'VE BEEN DATING HIM FOR SOME TIME, I MUST TELL HIM THAT JUDY DARK AND THE MASKED MOTH ARE ONE AND THE SAME.
WE'RE TOO MUCH IN LOVE TO KEEP SECRETS FROM EACH OTHER.
SORRY I'M SO LATE, HONEY.
I WAS BEGINNING TO THINK YOU'D BE A NO-SHOW, JUST LIKE THE CROOKS WE WERE TIPPED MIGHT TRY TO STEAL THIS DUSTY OLD THING.
BANG!
NOOO!
BOOK OF LO

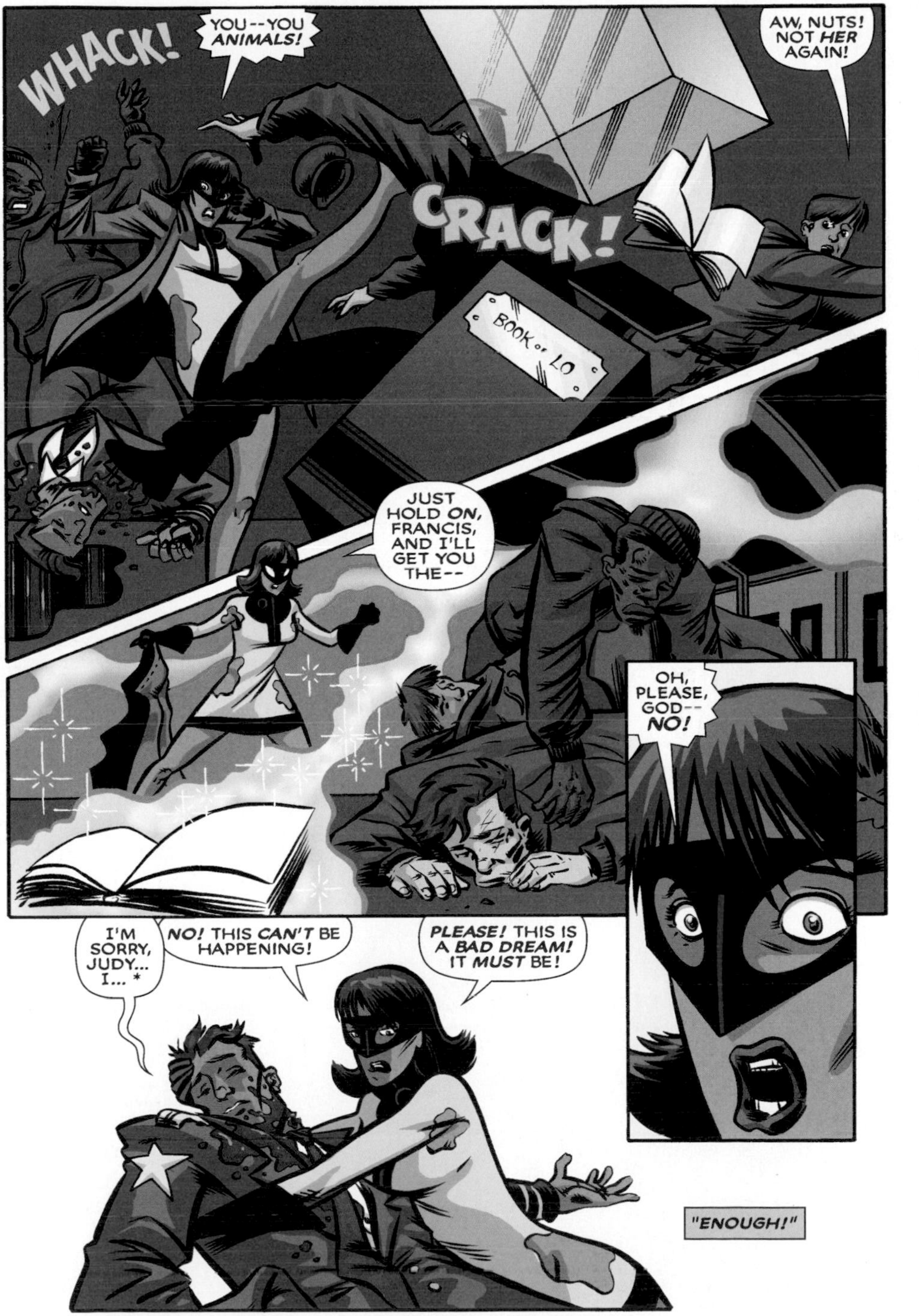
WHACK!
YOU--YOU ANIMALS!
AW, NUTS! NOT HER AGAIN!
CRACK!
BOOK OF LO
JUST HOLD ON, FRANCIS, AND I'LL GET YOU THE--
OH, PLEASE, GOD-- NO!
I'M SORRY, JUDY... I... *
NO! THIS CAN'T BE HAPPENING!
PLEASE! THIS IS A BAD DREAM! IT MUST BE!
"ENOUGH!"

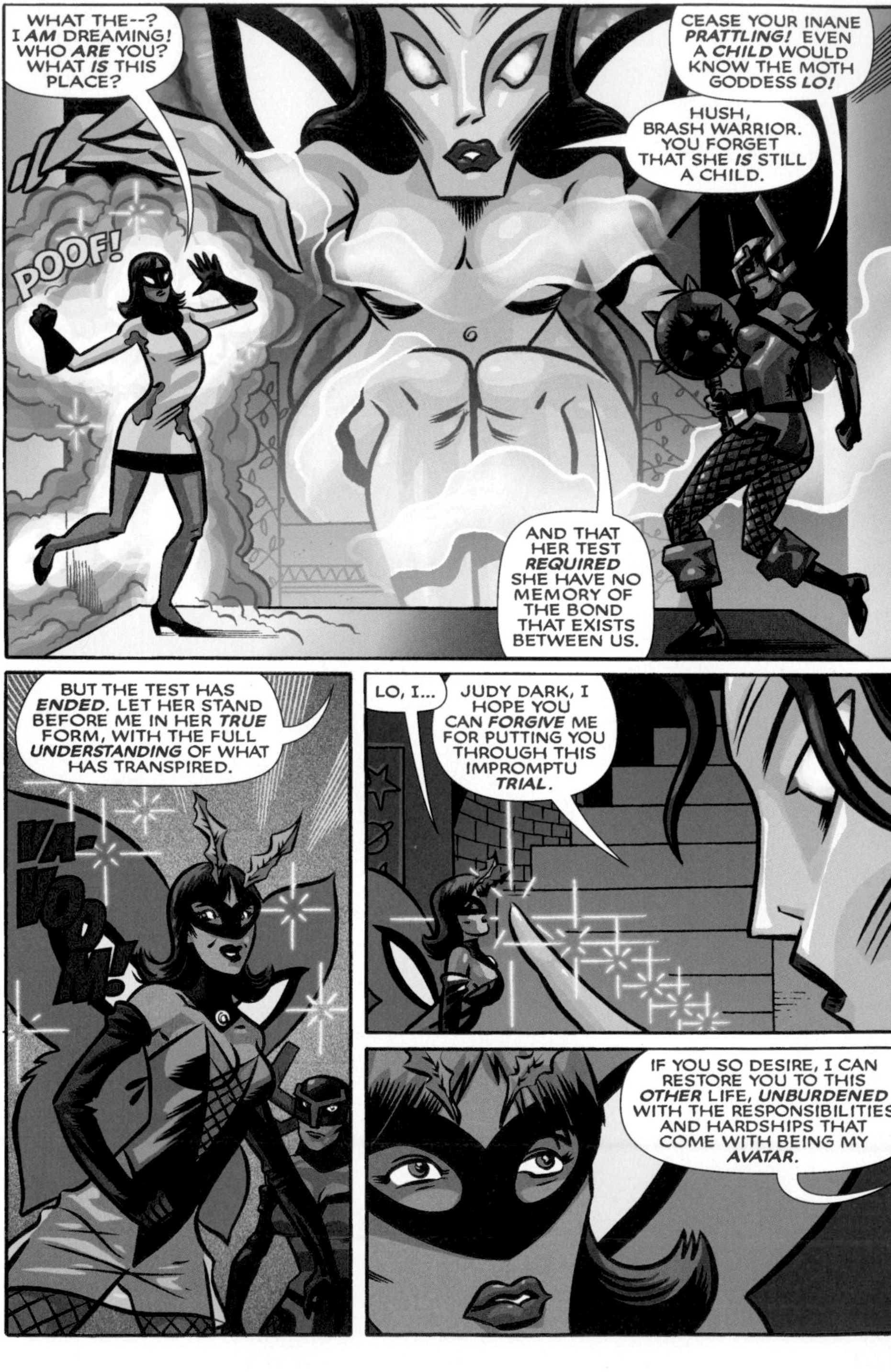
WHAT THE--? I AM DREAMING! WHO ARE YOU? WHAT IS THIS PLACE?
CEASE YOUR INANE PRATTLING! EVEN A CHILD WOULD KNOW THE MOTH GODDESS LO!
HUSH, BRASH WARRIOR. YOU FORGET THAT SHE IS STILL A CHILD.
POOF!
AND THAT HER TEST REQUIRED SHE HAVE NO MEMORY OF THE BOND THAT EXISTS BETWEEN US.
BUT THE TEST HAS ENDED. LET HER STAND BEFORE ME IN HER TRUE FORM, WITH THE FULL UNDERSTANDING OF WHAT HAS TRANSPIRED.
VA-VOOM!
LO, I...
JUDY DARK, I HOPE YOU CAN FORGIVE ME FOR PUTTING YOU THROUGH THIS IMPROMPTU TRIAL.
IF YOU SO DESIRE, I CAN RESTORE YOU TO THIS OTHER LIFE, UNBURDENED WITH THE RESPONSIBILITIES AND HARDSHIPS THAT COME WITH BEING MY AVATAR.

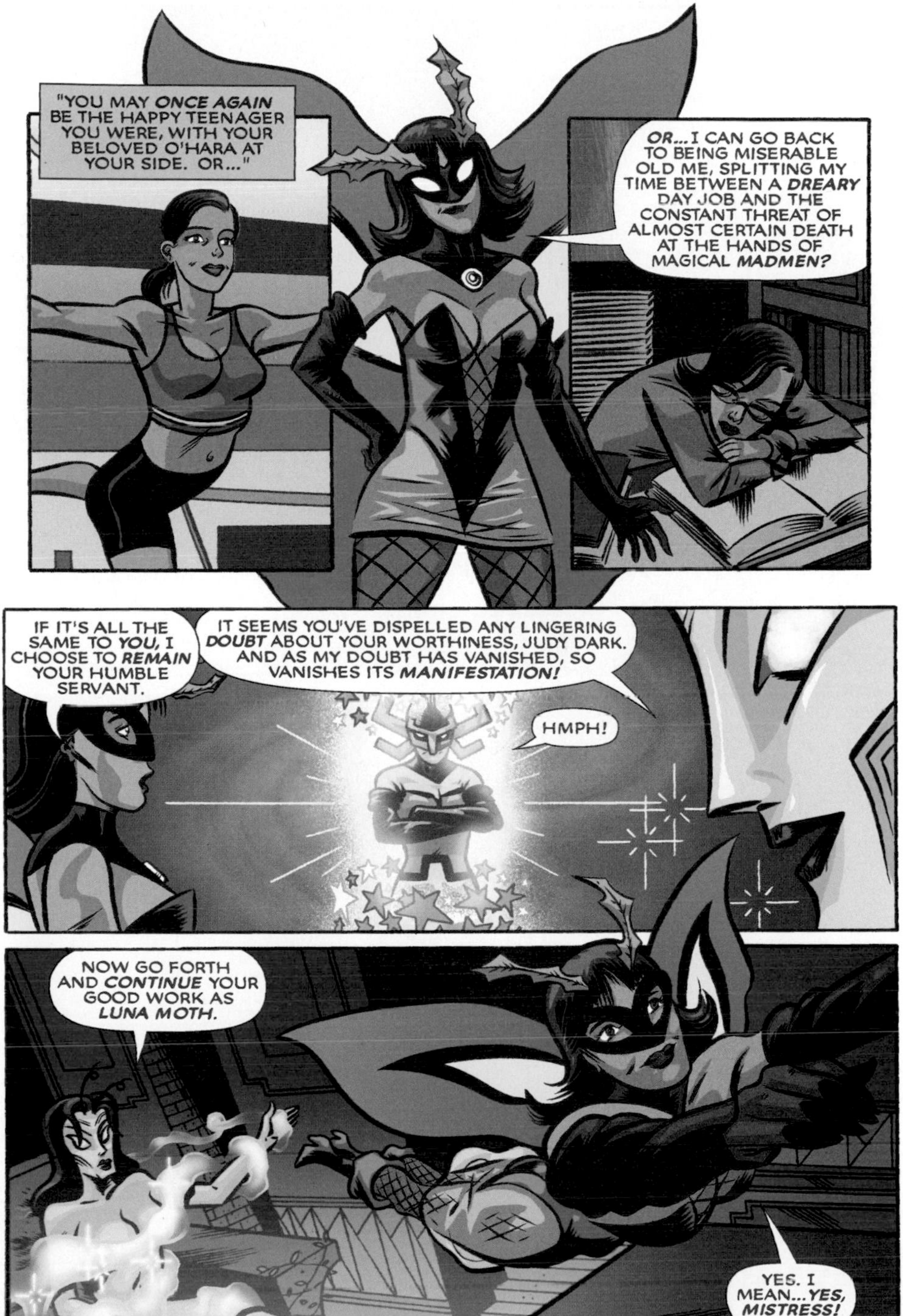

"YOU MAY ONCE AGAIN BE THE HAPPY TEENAGER YOU WERE, WITH YOUR BELOVED O'HARA AT YOUR SIDE. OR..."
OR...I CAN GO BACK TO BEING MISERABLE OLD ME, SPLITTING MY TIME BETWEEN A DREARY DAY JOB AND THE CONSTANT THREAT OF ALMOST CERTAIN DEATH AT THE HANDS OF MAGICAL MADMEN?
IF IT'S ALL THE SAME TO YOU, I CHOOSE TO REMAIN YOUR HUMBLE SERVANT.
IT SEEMS YOU'VE DISPELLED ANY LINGERING DOUBT ABOUT YOUR WORTHINESS, JUDY DARK. AND AS MY DOUBT HAS VANISHED, SO VANISHES ITS MANIFESTATION!
HMPH!
NOW GO FORTH AND CONTINUE YOUR GOOD WORK AS LUNA MOTH.
YES. I MEAN...YES, MISTRESS!

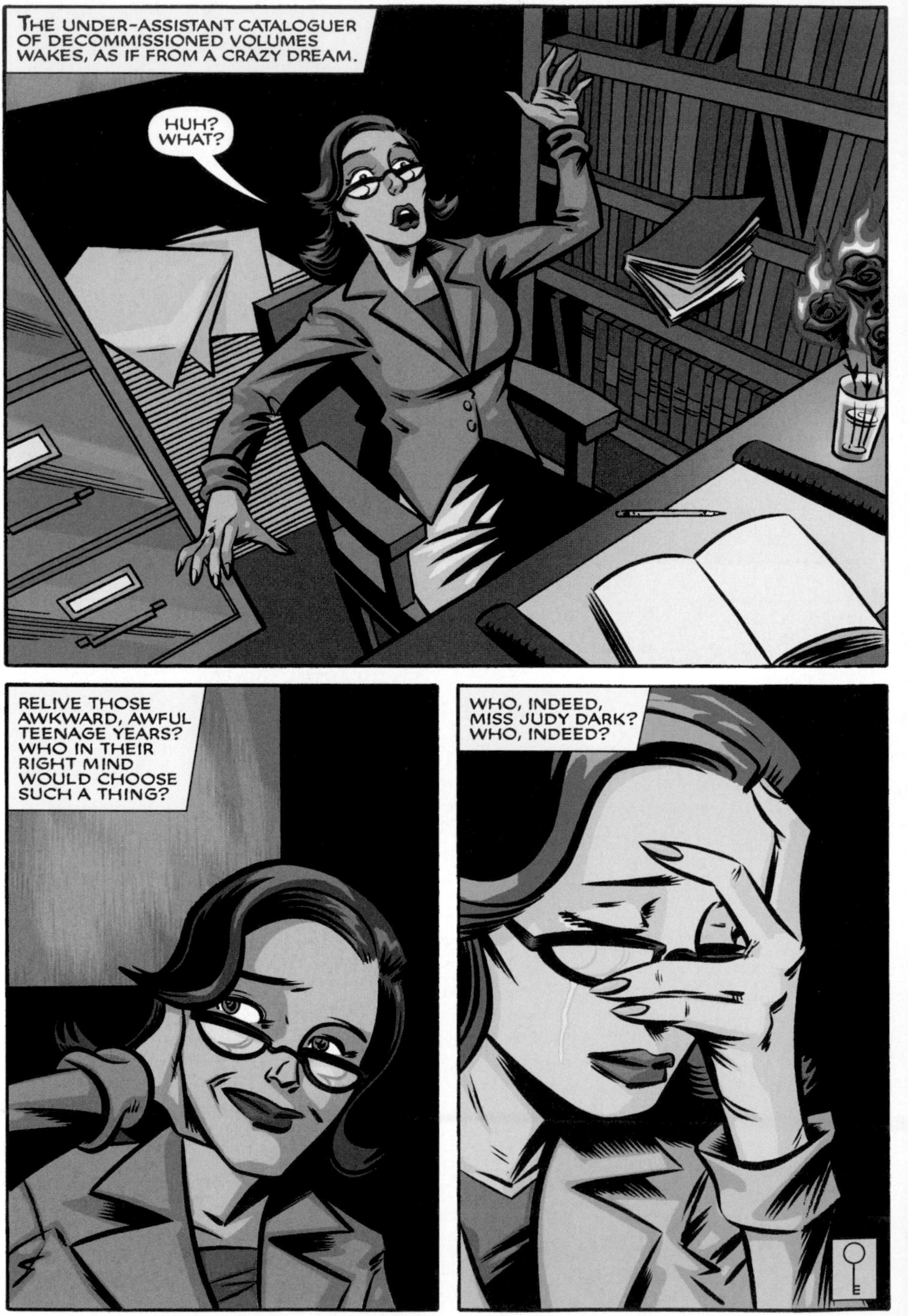
THE UNDER-ASSISTANT CATALOGUER OF DECOMMISSIONED VOLUMES WAKES, AS IF FROM A CRAZY DREAM.
HUH? WHAT?
RELIVE THOSE AWKWARD, AWFUL TEENAGE YEARS? WHO IN THEIR RIGHT MIND WOULD CHOOSE SUCH A THING?
WHO, INDEED, MISS JUDY DARK? WHO, INDEED?

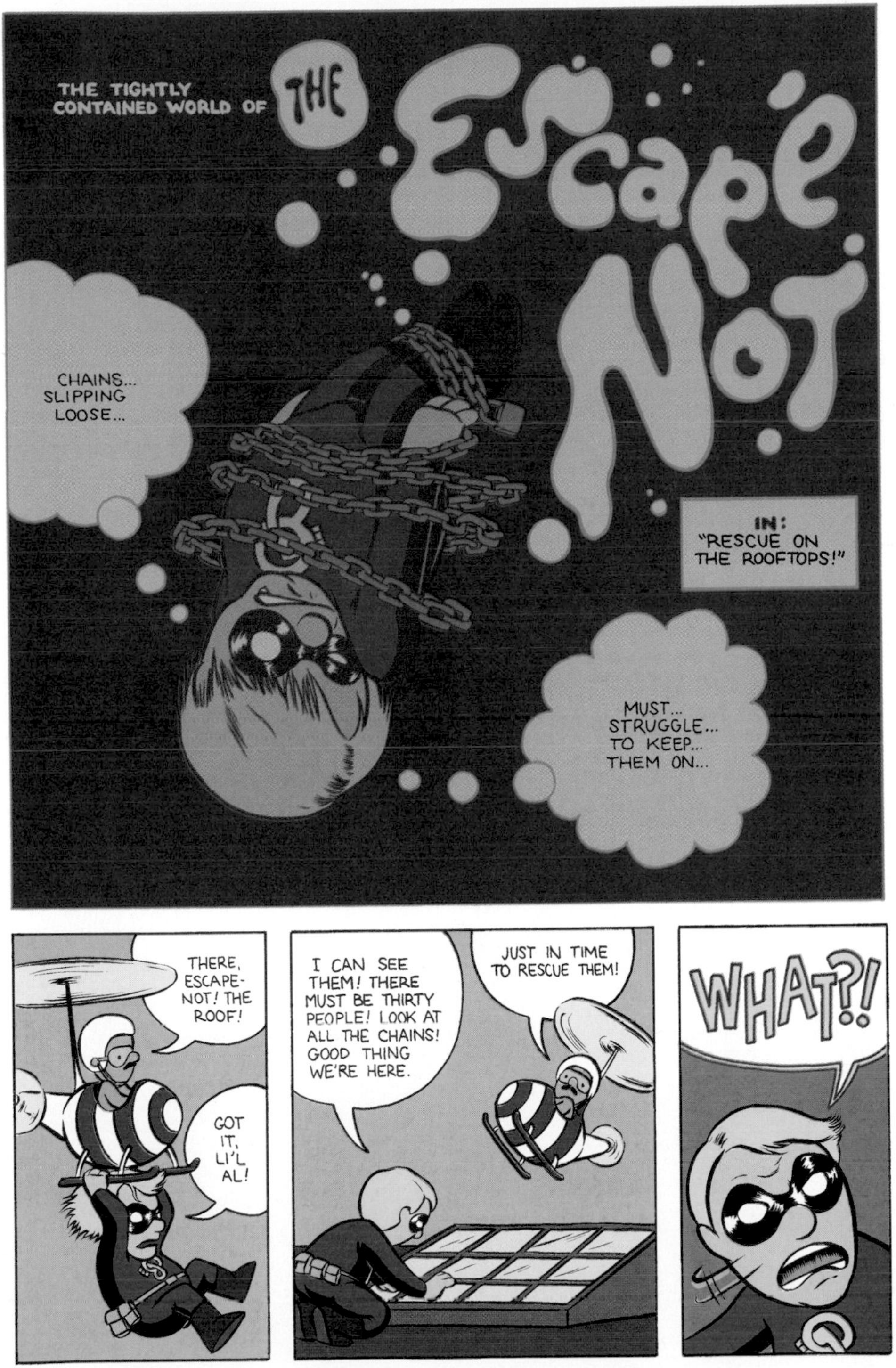
THE TIGHTLY CONTAINED WORLD OF
THE Escape Not
IN: "RESCUE ON THE ROOFTOPS!"
CHAINS... SLIPPING LOOSE...
MUST... STRUGGLE... TO KEEP... THEM ON...
THERE, ESCAPE-NOT! THE ROOF!
GOT IT, LI'L AL!
I CAN SEE THEM! THERE MUST BE THIRTY PEOPLE! LOOK AT ALL THE CHAINS! GOOD THING WE'RE HERE.
JUST IN TIME TO RESCUE THEM!
WHAT?!

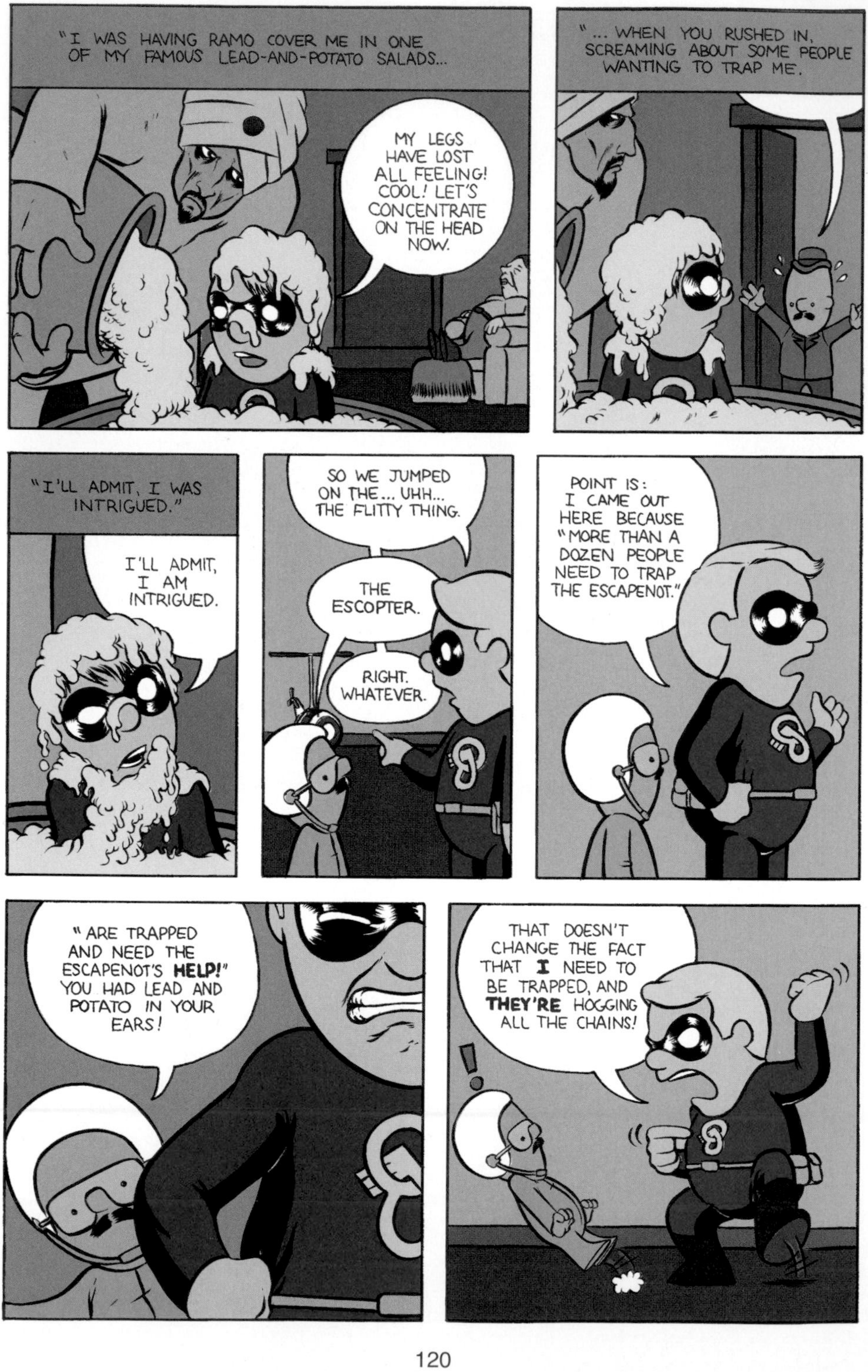
"I WAS HAVING RAMO COVER ME IN ONE OF MY FAMOUS LEAD-AND-POTATO SALADS...
MY LEGS HAVE LOST ALL FEELING! COOL! LET'S CONCENTRATE ON THE HEAD NOW.
"... WHEN YOU RUSHED IN, SCREAMING ABOUT SOME PEOPLE WANTING TO TRAP ME.
"I'LL ADMIT, I WAS INTRIGUED."
I'LL ADMIT, I AM INTRIGUED.
SO WE JUMPED ON THE... UHH... THE FLITTY THING.
THE ESCOPTER.
RIGHT. WHATEVER.
POINT IS: I CAME OUT HERE BECAUSE "MORE THAN A DOZEN PEOPLE NEED TO TRAP THE ESCAPENOT."
"ARE TRAPPED AND NEED THE ESCAPENOT'S **HELP!**" YOU HAD LEAD AND POTATO IN YOUR EARS!
THAT DOESN'T CHANGE THE FACT THAT **I** NEED TO BE TRAPPED, AND **THEY'RE** HOGGING ALL THE CHAINS!
!

COME TO YOUR **SENSES**, MAN! EVEN THE HUMAN CAVEFISH WOULD HELP THESE PEOPLE, AND **HE'S** LEGALLY BLIND!

SO? HE AND I DISAGREE ABOUT... WELL, ABOUT A LOT OF THINGS!

"I MEAN, HAVE YOU **SEEN** HIS COSTUME?"

Yeesh!

ESCAPENOT! THIS **ISN'T** A DEBATE! WE **HAVE** TO HELP THESE PEOPLE!

WAIT A MINUTE...

DID YOU EVEN ASK THESE PEOPLE IF THEY **WANT** TO BE FREE?

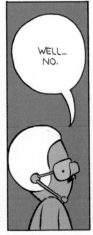

WELL... NO.

AND WHO'S TO SAY, EVEN IF YOU DID ASK, THAT THEY'D BE HONEST WITH YOU, OR THEMSELVES?

I'M OUTTA HERE.

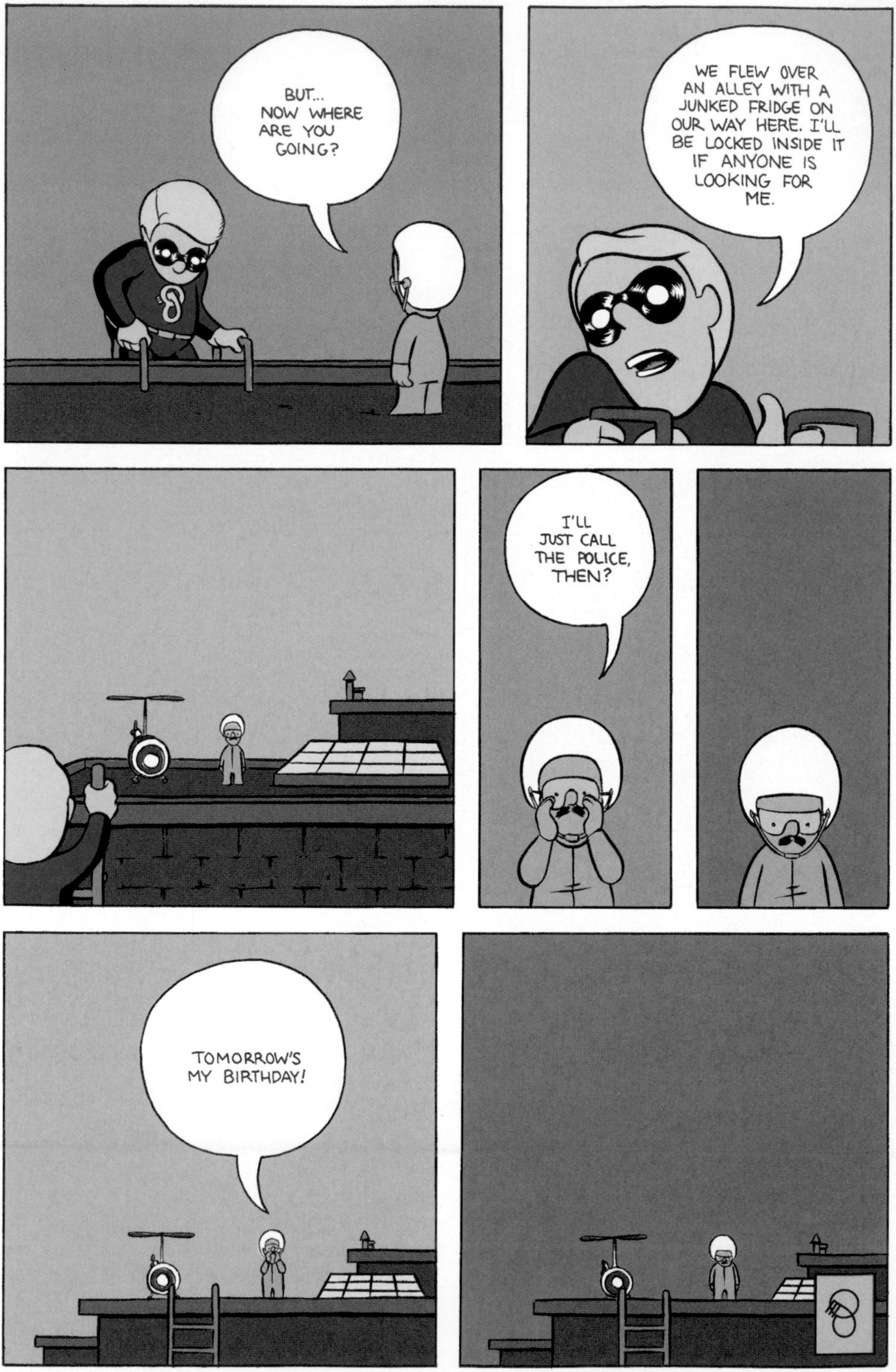
BUT... NOW WHERE ARE YOU GOING?
WE FLEW OVER AN ALLEY WITH A JUNKED FRIDGE ON OUR WAY HERE. I'LL BE LOCKED INSIDE IT IF ANYONE IS LOOKING FOR ME.
I'LL JUST CALL THE POLICE, THEN?
TOMORROW'S MY BIRTHDAY!

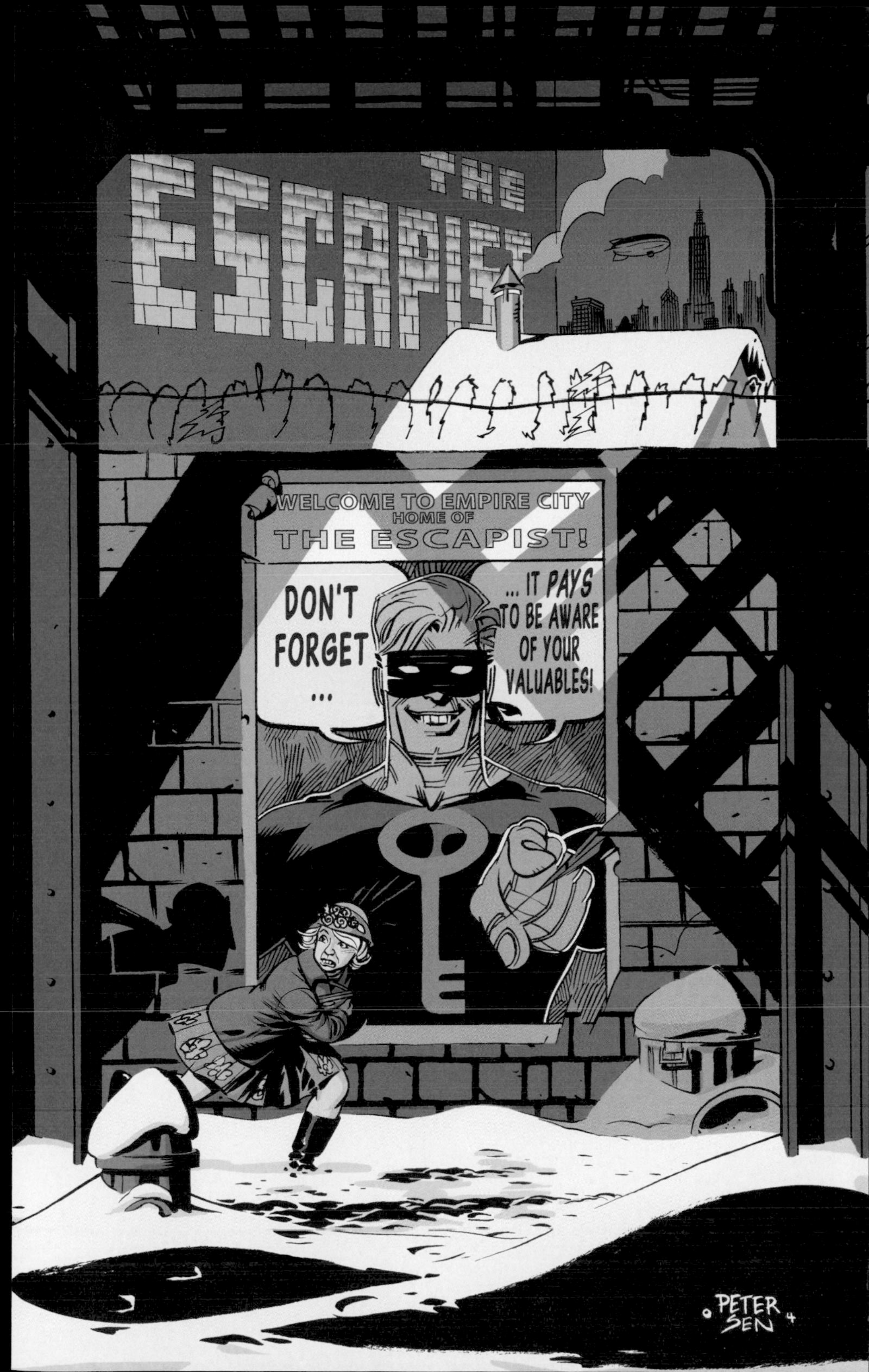
THE ESCAPIST
WELCOME TO EMPIRE CITY
HOME OF
THE ESCAPIST!
DON'T FORGET ...
... IT PAYS TO BE AWARE OF YOUR VALUABLES!
PETERSEN

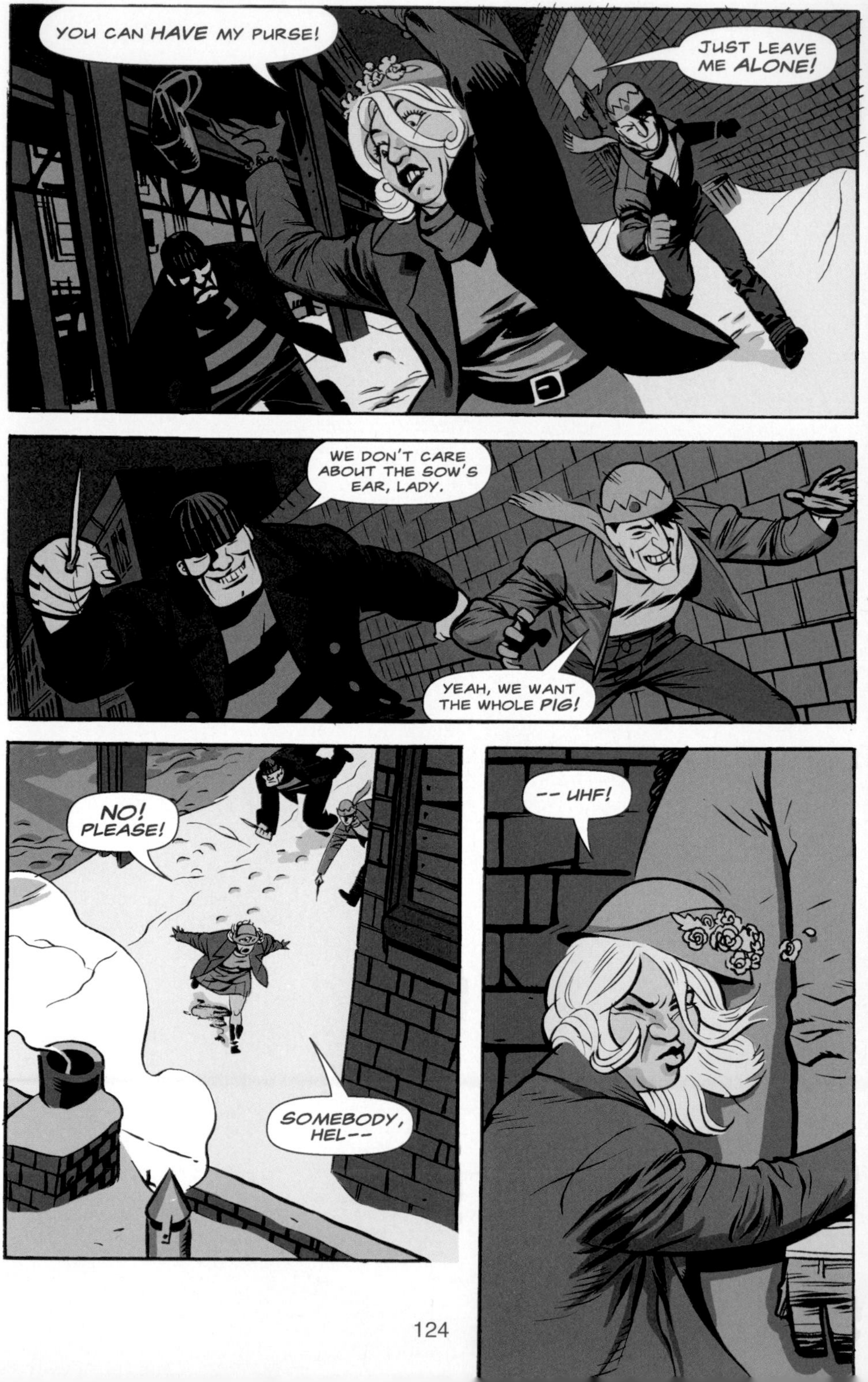
YOU CAN HAVE MY PURSE!
JUST LEAVE ME ALONE!
WE DON'T CARE ABOUT THE SOW'S EAR, LADY.
YEAH, WE WANT THE WHOLE PIG!
NO! PLEASE!
SOMEBODY, HEL--
-- UHF!

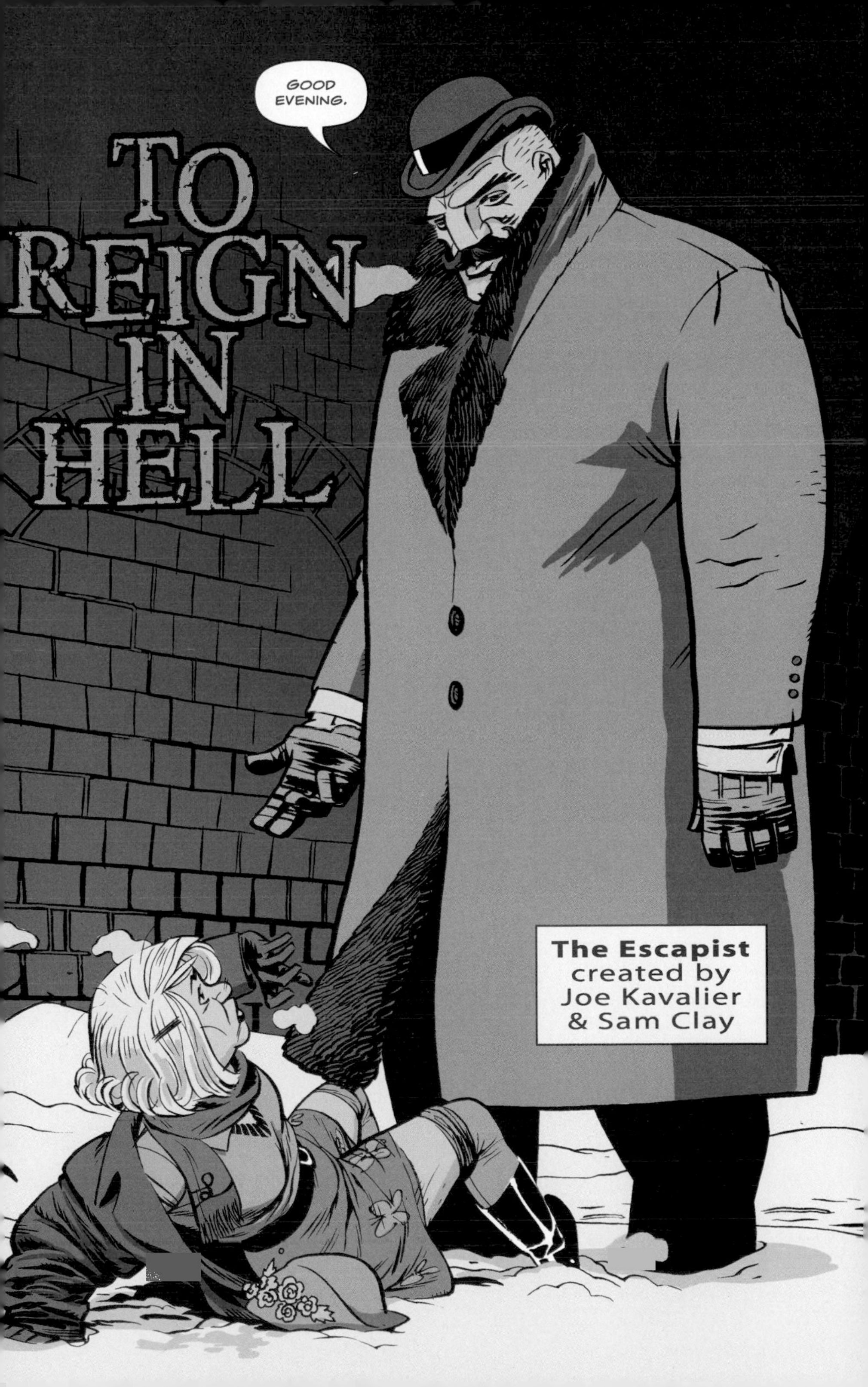
GOOD EVENING.
TO REIGN IN HELL
The Escapist created by Joe Kavalier & Sam Clay

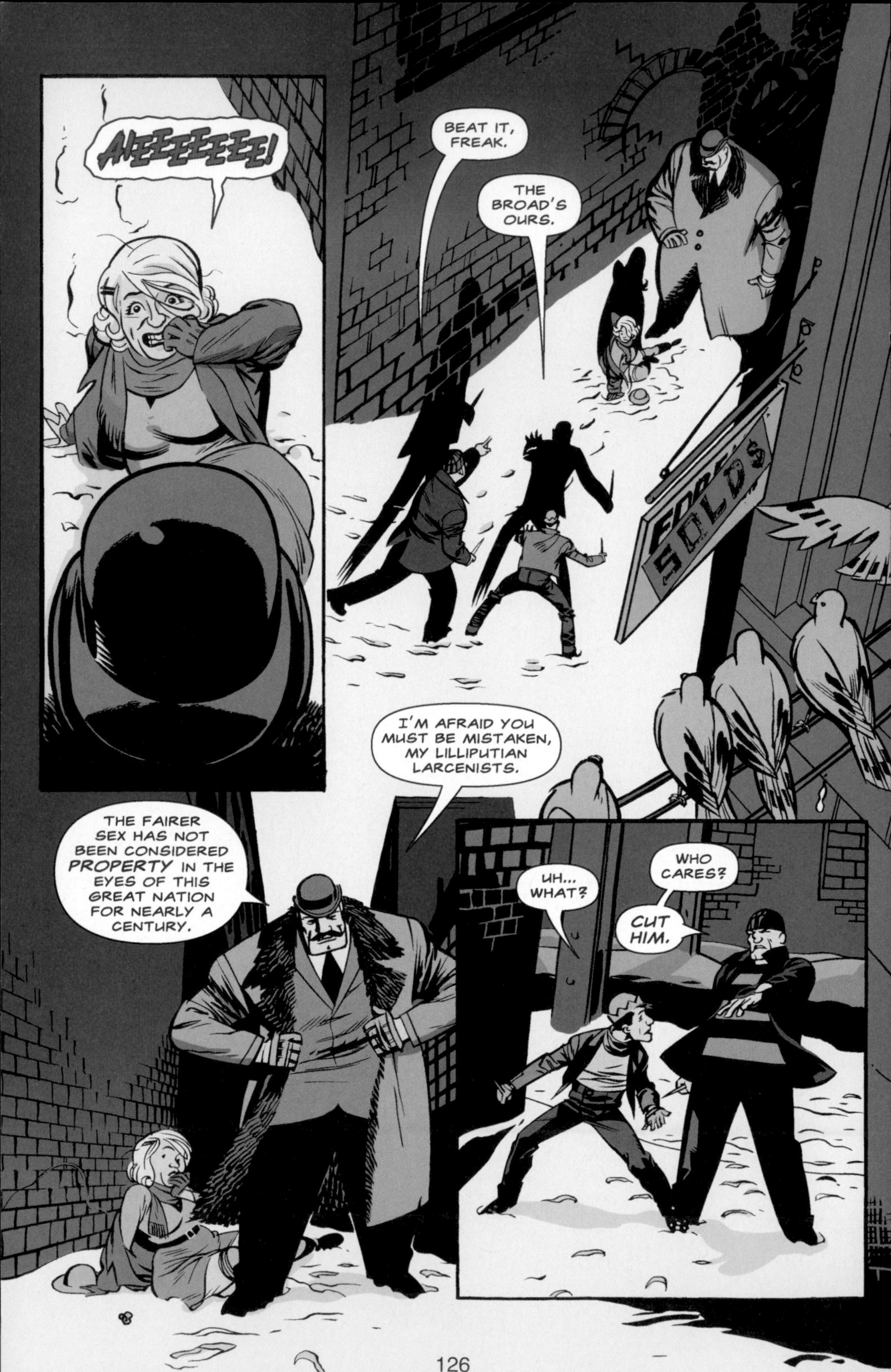
AIEEEEEEEE!
BEAT IT, FREAK.
THE BROAD'S OURS.
SOLDS
I'M AFRAID YOU MUST BE MISTAKEN, MY LILLIPUTIAN LARCENISTS.
THE FAIRER SEX HAS NOT BEEN CONSIDERED PROPERTY IN THE EYES OF THIS GREAT NATION FOR NEARLY A CENTURY.
UH... WHAT?
WHO CARES?
CUT HIM.

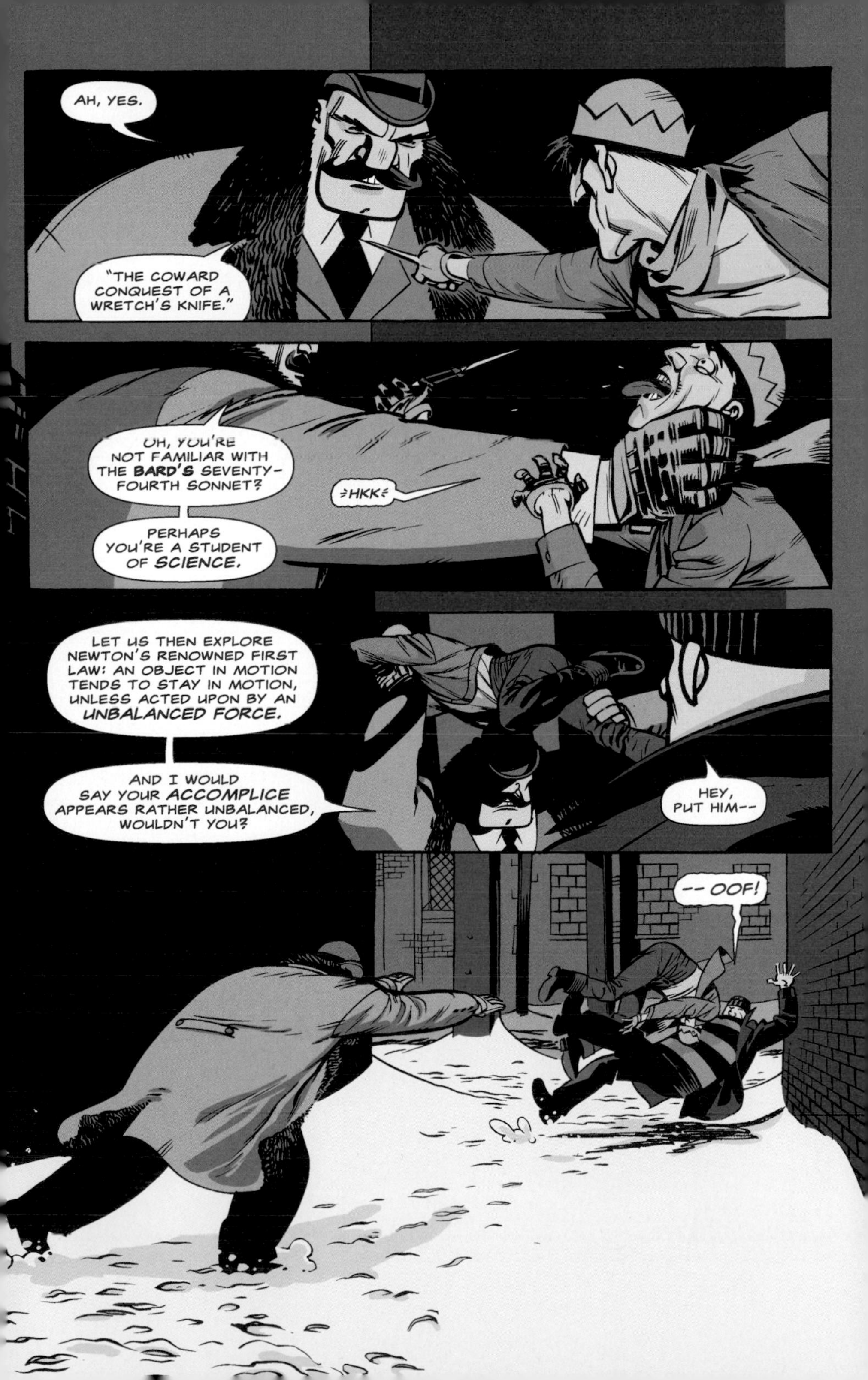
AH, YES.
"THE COWARD CONQUEST OF A WRETCH'S KNIFE."
OH, YOU'RE NOT FAMILIAR WITH THE BARD'S SEVENTY-FOURTH SONNET?
PERHAPS YOU'RE A STUDENT OF SCIENCE.
HKK
LET US THEN EXPLORE NEWTON'S RENOWNED FIRST LAW: AN OBJECT IN MOTION TENDS TO STAY IN MOTION, UNLESS ACTED UPON BY AN UNBALANCED FORCE.
AND I WOULD SAY YOUR ACCOMPLICE APPEARS RATHER UNBALANCED, WOULDN'T YOU?
HEY, PUT HIM--
-- OOF!

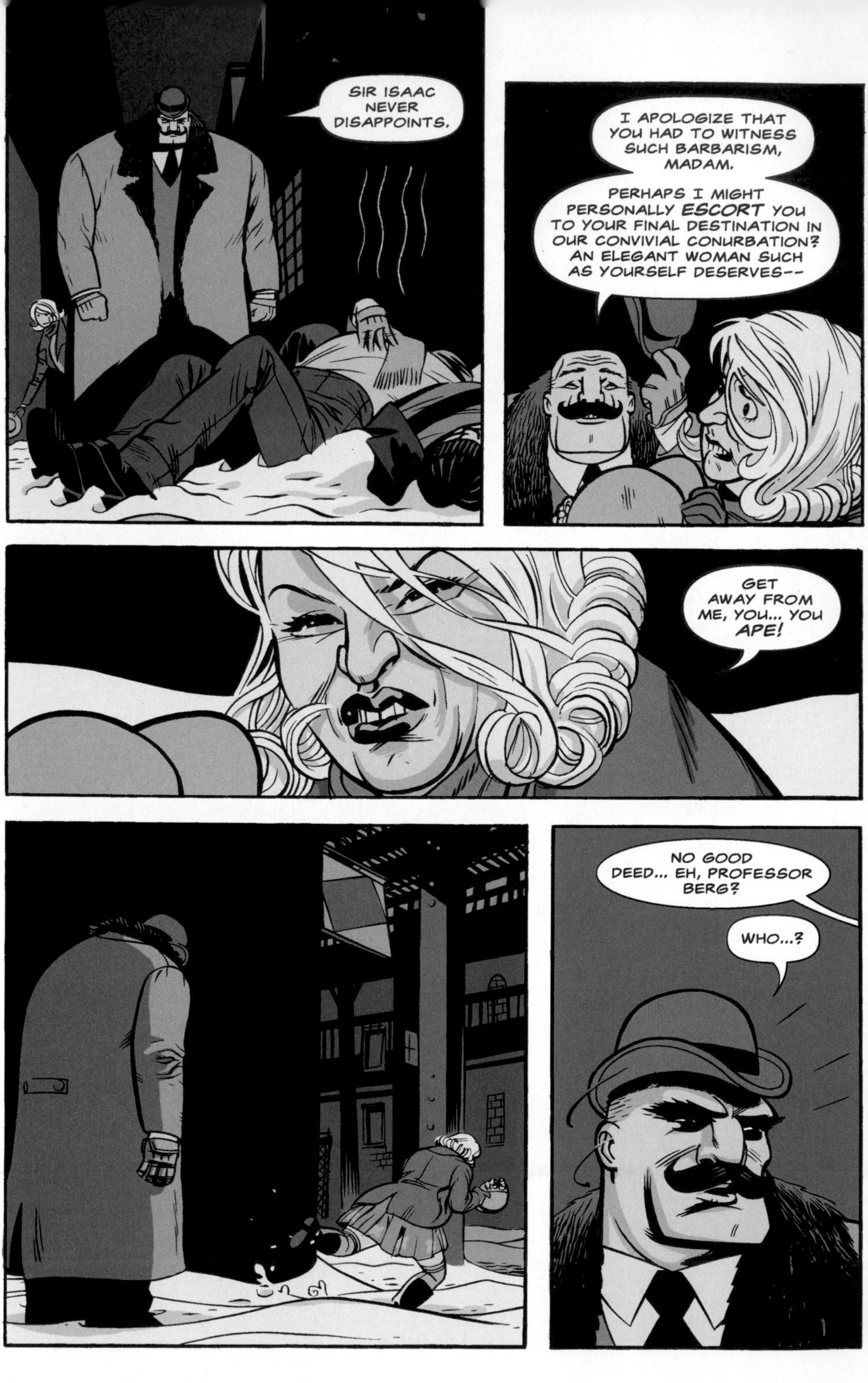
SIR ISAAC NEVER DISAPPOINTS.
I APOLOGIZE THAT YOU HAD TO WITNESS SUCH BARBARISM, MADAM.
PERHAPS I MIGHT PERSONALLY ESCORT YOU TO YOUR FINAL DESTINATION IN OUR CONVIVIAL CONURBATION? AN ELEGANT WOMAN SUCH AS YOURSELF DESERVES--
GET AWAY FROM ME, YOU... YOU APE!
NO GOOD DEED... EH, PROFESSOR BERG?
WHO...?

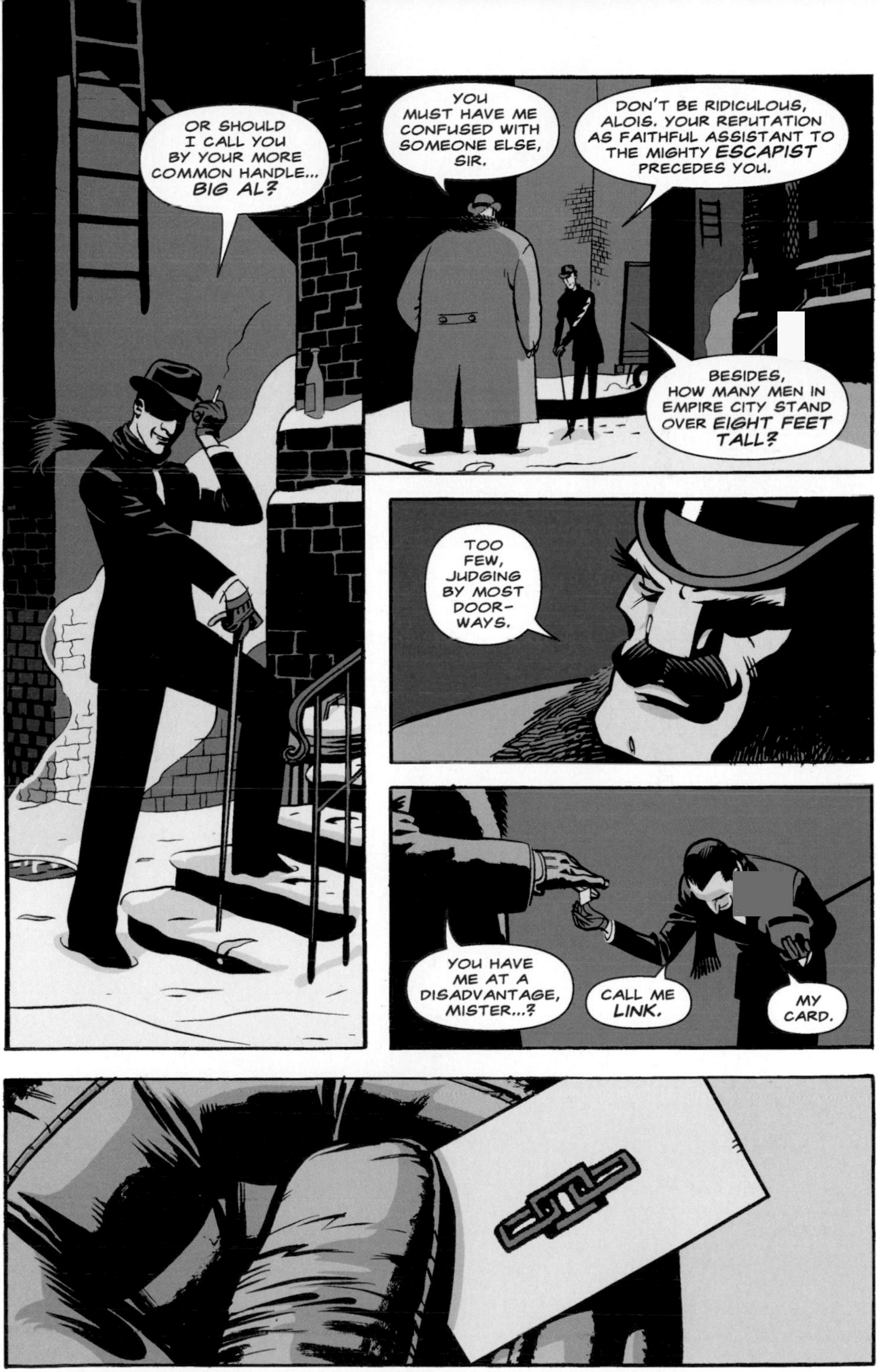
OR SHOULD I CALL YOU BY YOUR MORE COMMON HANDLE... BIG AL?
YOU MUST HAVE ME CONFUSED WITH SOMEONE ELSE, SIR.
DON'T BE RIDICULOUS, ALOIS. YOUR REPUTATION AS FAITHFUL ASSISTANT TO THE MIGHTY ESCAPIST PRECEDES YOU.
BESIDES, HOW MANY MEN IN EMPIRE CITY STAND OVER EIGHT FEET TALL?
TOO FEW, JUDGING BY MOST DOOR-WAYS.
YOU HAVE ME AT A DISADVANTAGE, MISTER...?
CALL ME LINK.
MY CARD.

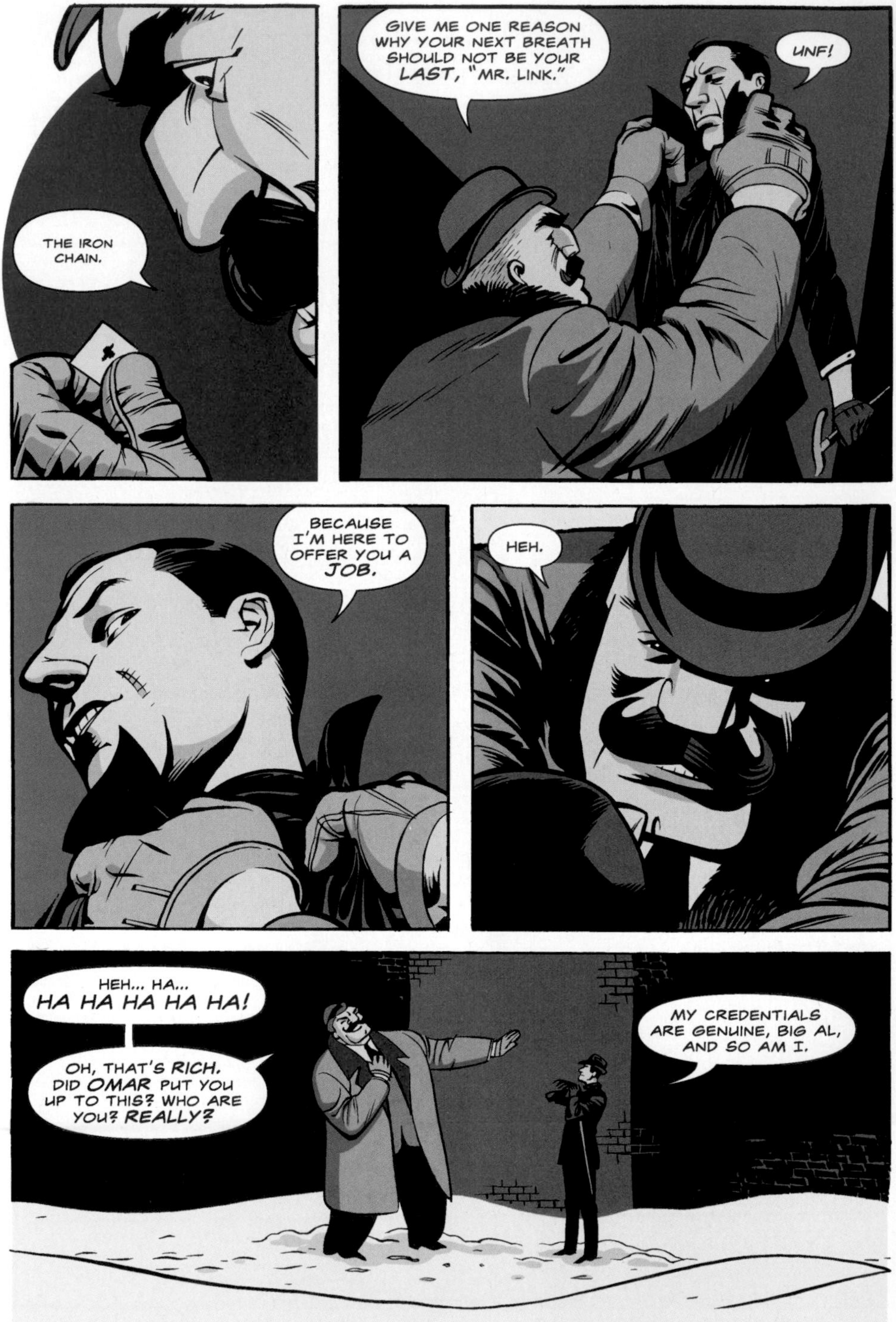
THE IRON CHAIN.
GIVE ME ONE REASON WHY YOUR NEXT BREATH SHOULD NOT BE YOUR LAST, "MR. LINK."
UNF!
BECAUSE I'M HERE TO OFFER YOU A JOB.
HEH.
HEH... HA... HA HA HA HA HA HA!
OH, THAT'S RICH. DID OMAR PUT YOU UP TO THIS? WHO ARE YOU? REALLY?
MY CREDENTIALS ARE GENUINE, BIG AL, AND SO AM I.

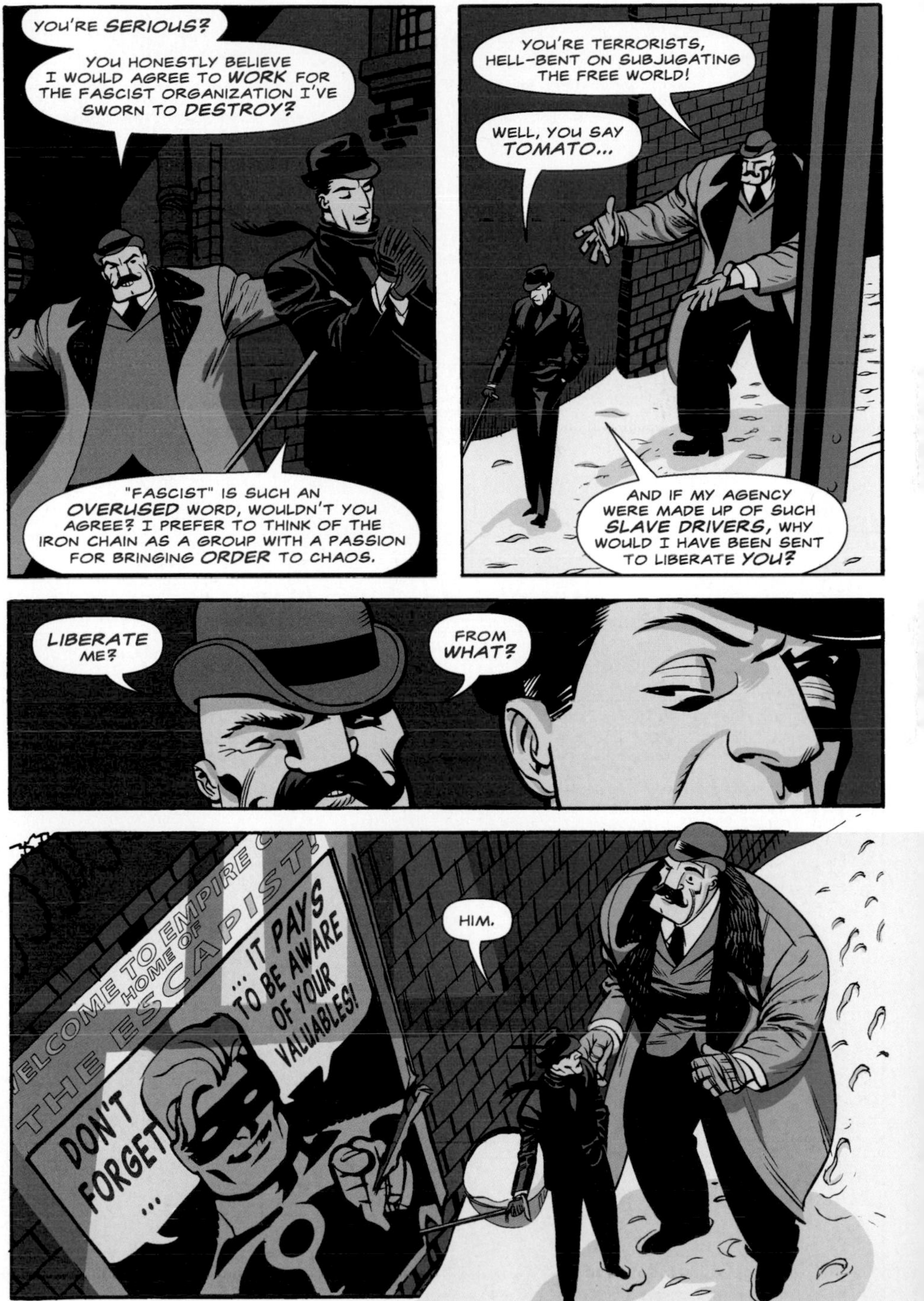
YOU'RE SERIOUS?
YOU HONESTLY BELIEVE I WOULD AGREE TO WORK FOR THE FASCIST ORGANIZATION I'VE SWORN TO DESTROY?
"FASCIST" IS SUCH AN OVERUSED WORD, WOULDN'T YOU AGREE? I PREFER TO THINK OF THE IRON CHAIN AS A GROUP WITH A PASSION FOR BRINGING ORDER TO CHAOS.
YOU'RE TERRORISTS, HELL-BENT ON SUBJUGATING THE FREE WORLD!
WELL, YOU SAY TOMATO...
AND IF MY AGENCY WERE MADE UP OF SUCH SLAVE DRIVERS, WHY WOULD I HAVE BEEN SENT TO LIBERATE YOU?
LIBERATE ME?
FROM WHAT?
WELCOME TO EMPIRE C
HOME OF
THE ESCAPIST!
DON'T FORGET ...
... IT PAYS TO BE AWARE OF YOUR VALUABLES!
HIM.

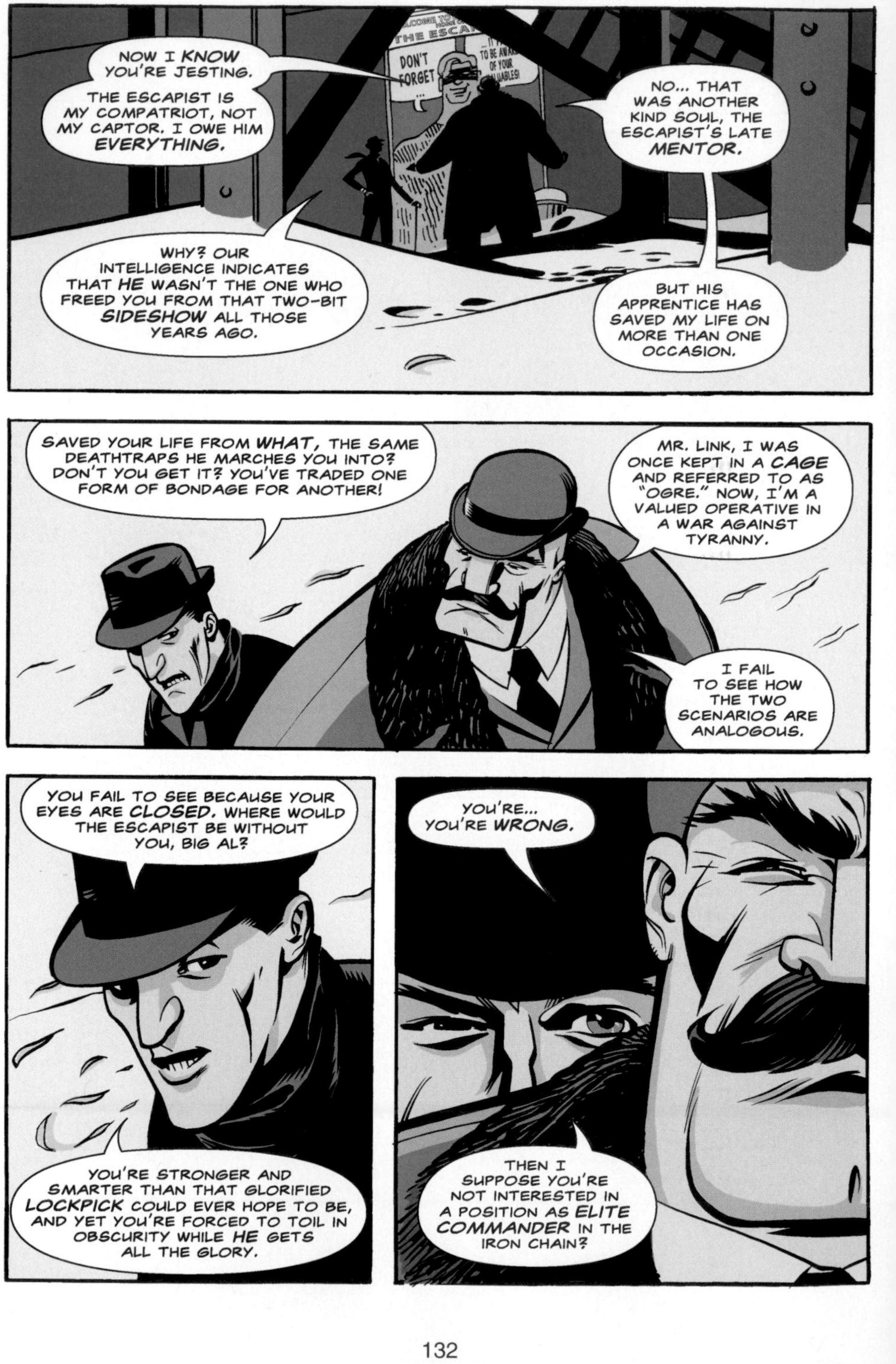
NOW I KNOW YOU'RE JESTING.
THE ESCAPIST IS MY COMPATRIOT, NOT MY CAPTOR. I OWE HIM EVERYTHING.
NO... THAT WAS ANOTHER KIND SOUL, THE ESCAPIST'S LATE MENTOR.
WHY? OUR INTELLIGENCE INDICATES THAT HE WASN'T THE ONE WHO FREED YOU FROM THAT TWO-BIT SIDESHOW ALL THOSE YEARS AGO.
BUT HIS APPRENTICE HAS SAVED MY LIFE ON MORE THAN ONE OCCASION.
SAVED YOUR LIFE FROM WHAT, THE SAME DEATHTRAPS HE MARCHES YOU INTO? DON'T YOU GET IT? YOU'VE TRADED ONE FORM OF BONDAGE FOR ANOTHER!
MR. LINK, I WAS ONCE KEPT IN A CAGE AND REFERRED TO AS "OGRE." NOW, I'M A VALUED OPERATIVE IN A WAR AGAINST TYRANNY.
I FAIL TO SEE HOW THE TWO SCENARIOS ARE ANALOGOUS.
YOU FAIL TO SEE BECAUSE YOUR EYES ARE CLOSED. WHERE WOULD THE ESCAPIST BE WITHOUT YOU, BIG AL?
YOU'RE STRONGER AND SMARTER THAN THAT GLORIFIED LOCKPICK COULD EVER HOPE TO BE, AND YET YOU'RE FORCED TO TOIL IN OBSCURITY WHILE HE GETS ALL THE GLORY.
YOU'RE... YOU'RE WRONG.
THEN I SUPPOSE YOU'RE NOT INTERESTED IN A POSITION AS ELITE COMMANDER IN THE IRON CHAIN?

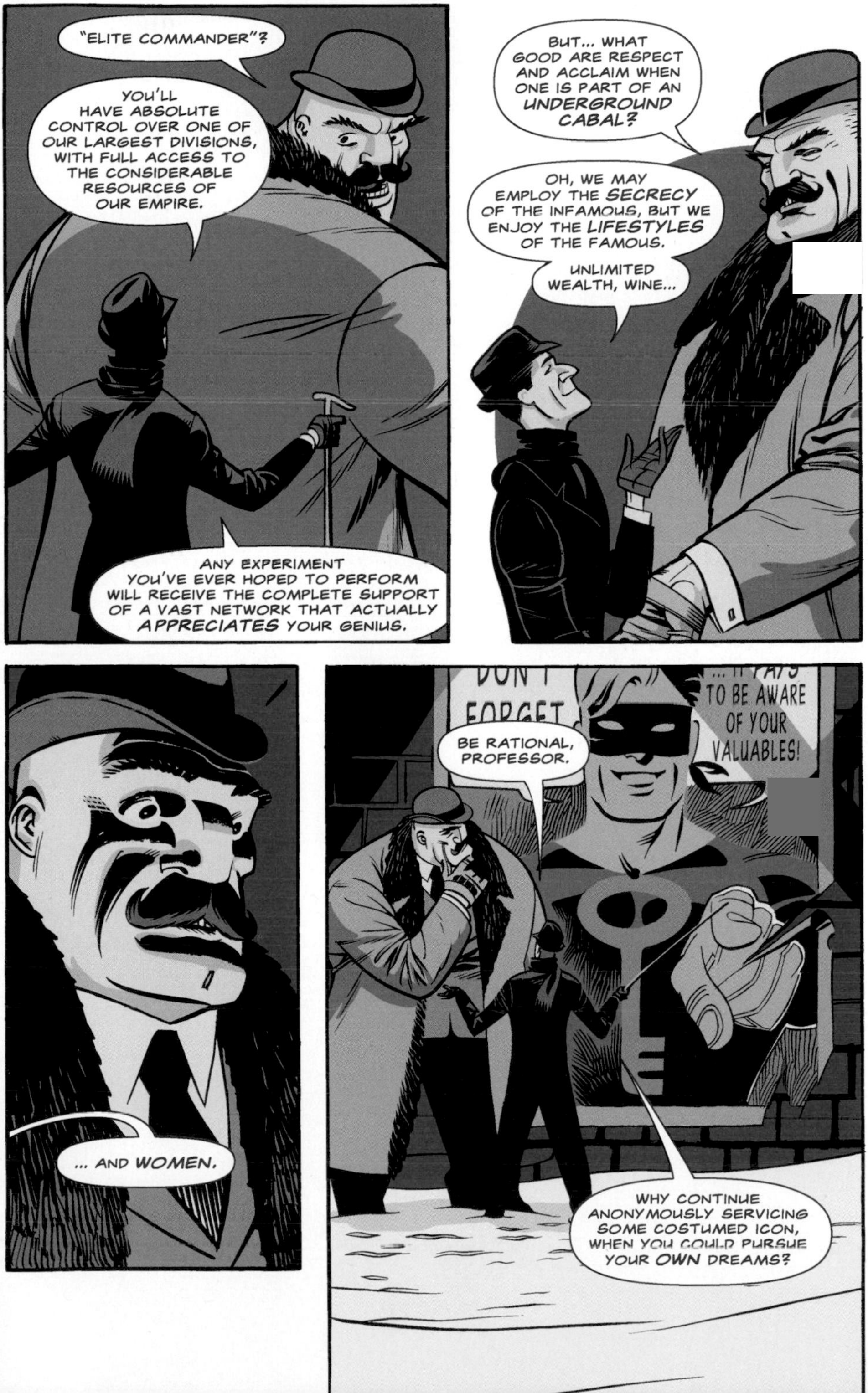
"ELITE COMMANDER"?
YOU'LL HAVE ABSOLUTE CONTROL OVER ONE OF OUR LARGEST DIVISIONS, WITH FULL ACCESS TO THE CONSIDERABLE RESOURCES OF OUR EMPIRE.
ANY EXPERIMENT YOU'VE EVER HOPED TO PERFORM WILL RECEIVE THE COMPLETE SUPPORT OF A VAST NETWORK THAT ACTUALLY APPRECIATES YOUR GENIUS.
BUT... WHAT GOOD ARE RESPECT AND ACCLAIM WHEN ONE IS PART OF AN UNDERGROUND CABAL?
OH, WE MAY EMPLOY THE SECRECY OF THE INFAMOUS, BUT WE ENJOY THE LIFESTYLES OF THE FAMOUS.
UNLIMITED WEALTH, WINE...
... AND WOMEN.
TO BE AWARE OF YOUR VALUABLES!
BE RATIONAL, PROFESSOR.
WHY CONTINUE ANONYMOUSLY SERVICING SOME COSTUMED ICON, WHEN YOU COULD PURSUE YOUR OWN DREAMS?

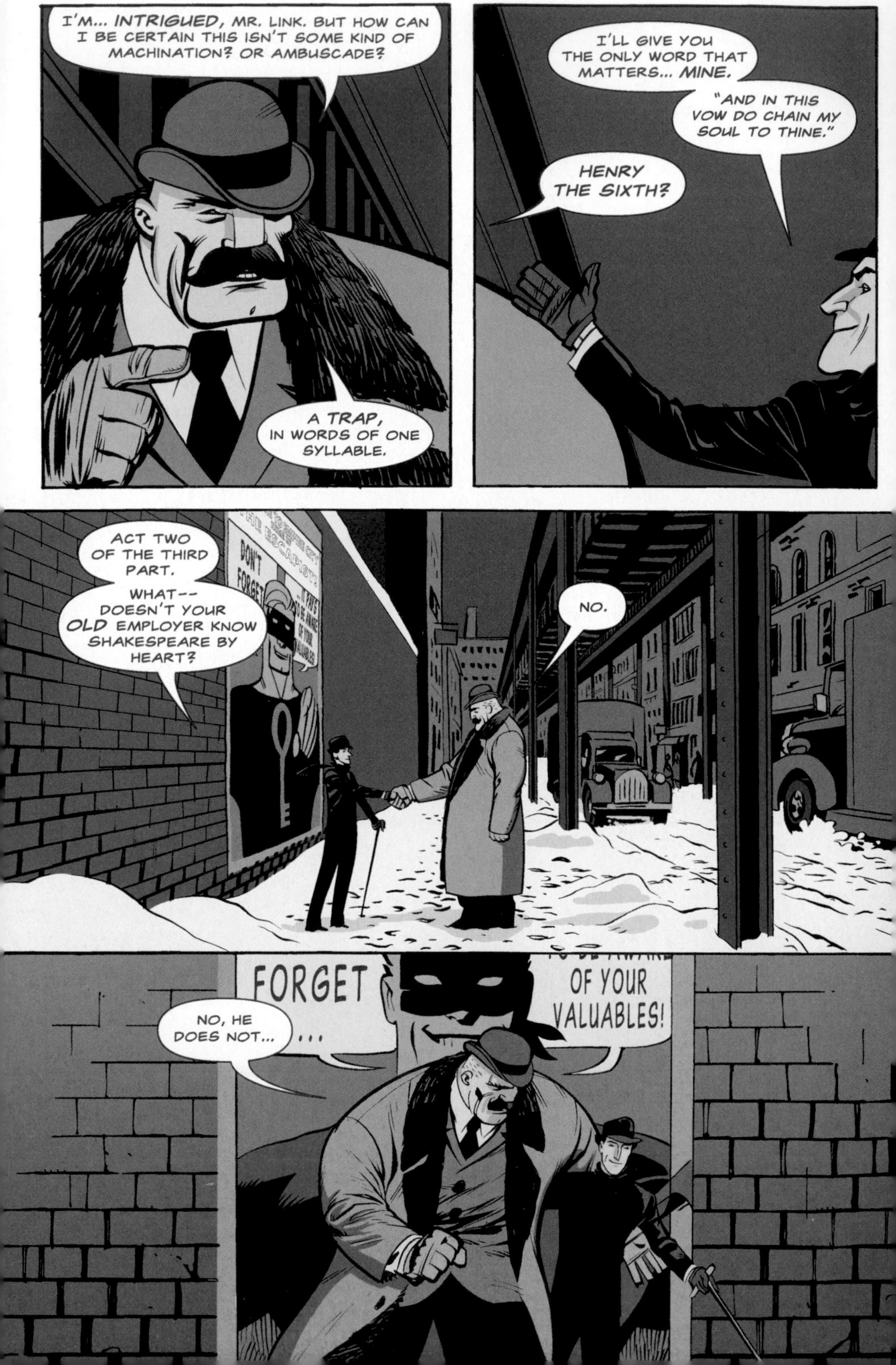
I'M... INTRIGUED, MR. LINK. BUT HOW CAN I BE CERTAIN THIS ISN'T SOME KIND OF MACHINATION? OR AMBUSCADE?
A TRAP, IN WORDS OF ONE SYLLABLE.
I'LL GIVE YOU THE ONLY WORD THAT MATTERS... MINE.
"AND IN THIS VOW DO CHAIN MY SOUL TO THINE."
HENRY THE SIXTH?
ACT TWO OF THE THIRD PART.
WHAT-- DOESN'T YOUR OLD EMPLOYER KNOW SHAKESPEARE BY HEART?
NO.
DON'T FORGET
FORGET
OF YOUR VALUABLES!
NO, HE DOES NOT...
...

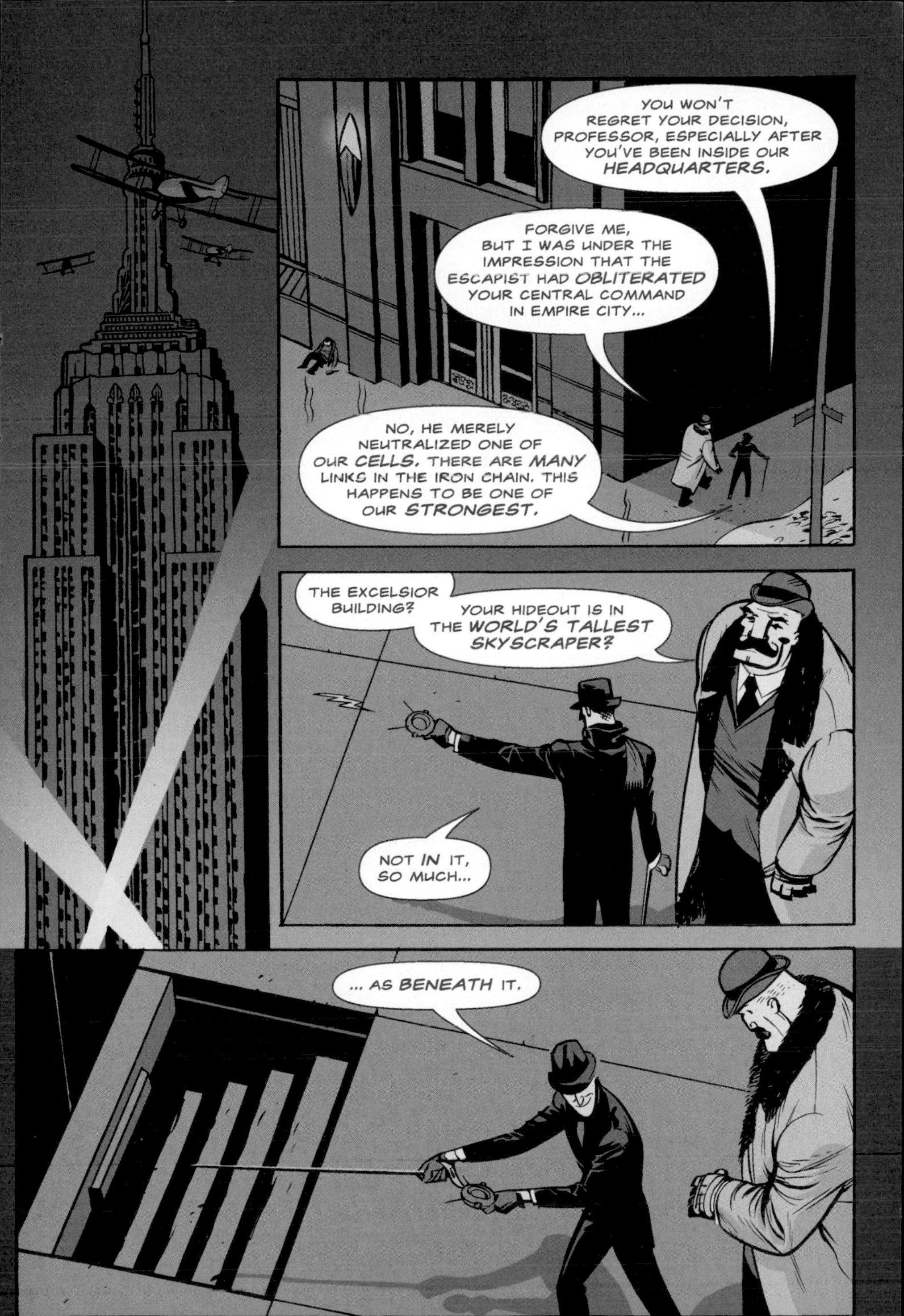
YOU WON'T REGRET YOUR DECISION, PROFESSOR, ESPECIALLY AFTER YOU'VE BEEN INSIDE OUR HEADQUARTERS.
FORGIVE ME, BUT I WAS UNDER THE IMPRESSION THAT THE ESCAPIST HAD OBLITERATED YOUR CENTRAL COMMAND IN EMPIRE CITY...
NO, HE MERELY NEUTRALIZED ONE OF OUR CELLS. THERE ARE MANY LINKS IN THE IRON CHAIN. THIS HAPPENS TO BE ONE OF OUR STRONGEST.
THE EXCELSIOR BUILDING?
YOUR HIDEOUT IS IN THE WORLD'S TALLEST SKYSCRAPER?
NOT IN IT, SO MUCH...
... AS BENEATH IT.

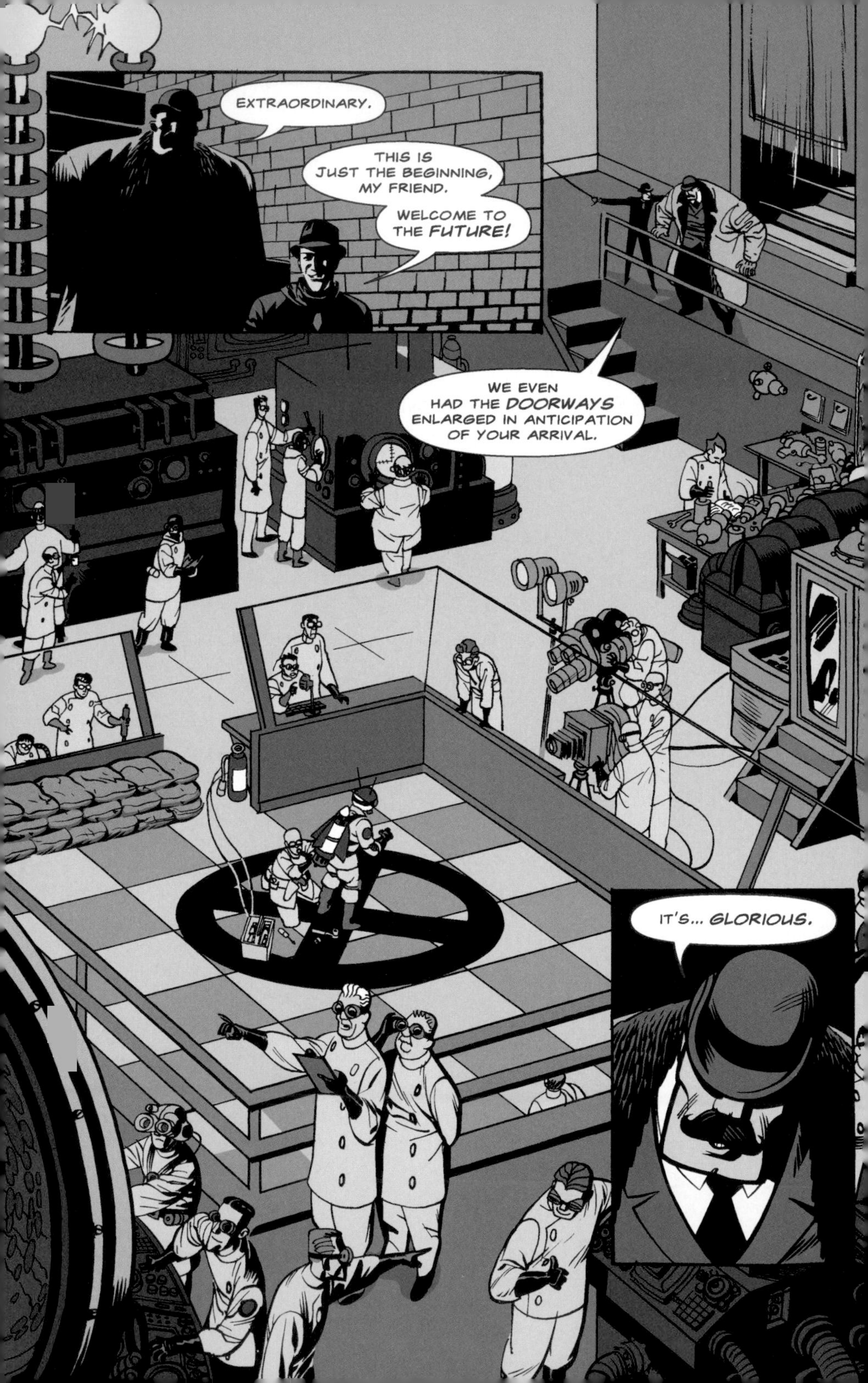
EXTRAORDINARY.
THIS IS JUST THE BEGINNING, MY FRIEND.
WELCOME TO THE FUTURE!
WE EVEN HAD THE DOORWAYS ENLARGED IN ANTICIPATION OF YOUR ARRIVAL.
IT'S... GLORIOUS.

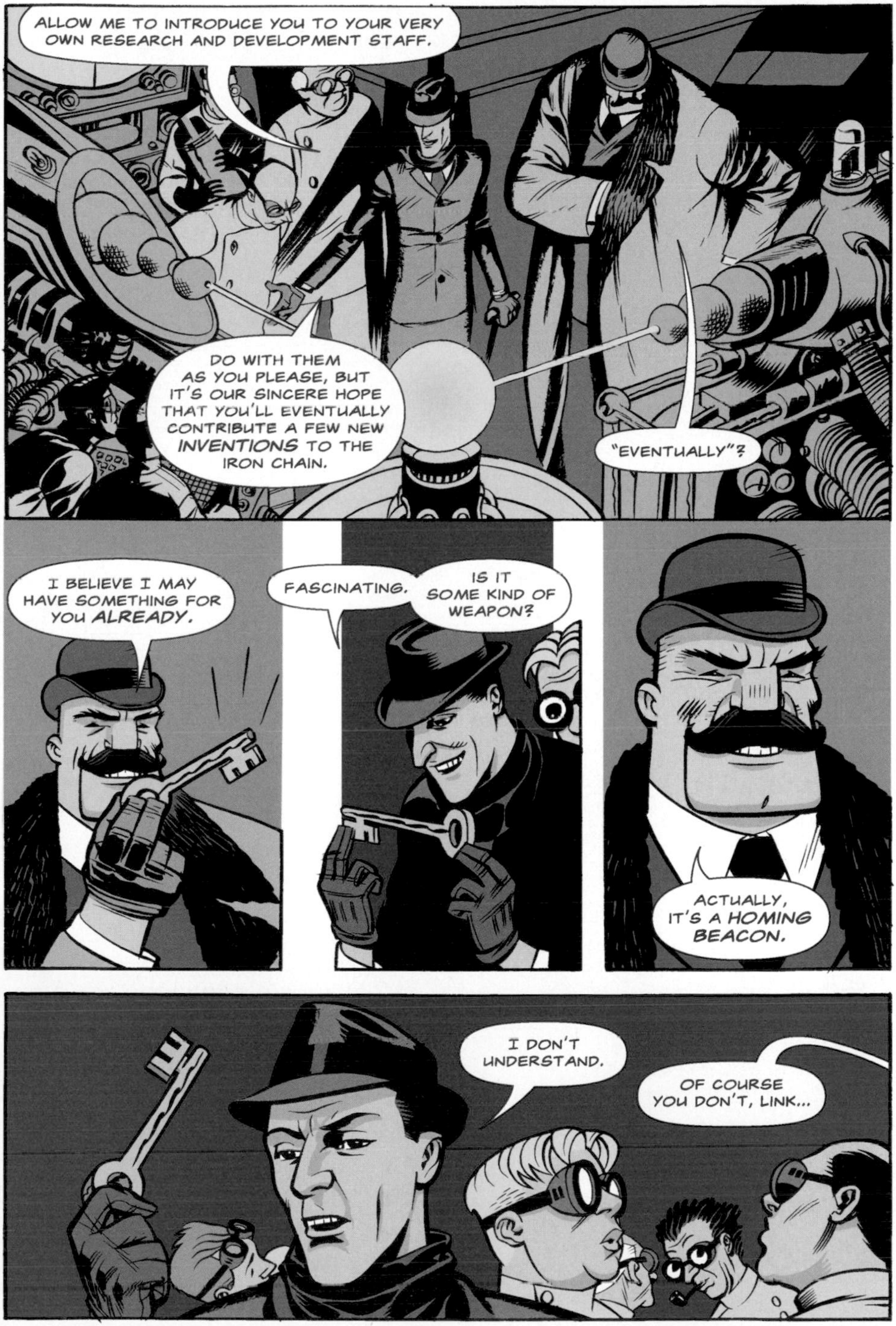
ALLOW ME TO INTRODUCE YOU TO YOUR VERY OWN RESEARCH AND DEVELOPMENT STAFF.
DO WITH THEM AS YOU PLEASE, BUT IT'S OUR SINCERE HOPE THAT YOU'LL EVENTUALLY CONTRIBUTE A FEW NEW *INVENTIONS* TO THE IRON CHAIN.
"EVENTUALLY"?
I BELIEVE I MAY HAVE SOMETHING FOR YOU *ALREADY.*
FASCINATING.
IS IT SOME KIND OF WEAPON?
ACTUALLY, IT'S A *HOMING BEACON.*
I DON'T UNDERSTAND.
OF COURSE YOU DON'T, LINK...

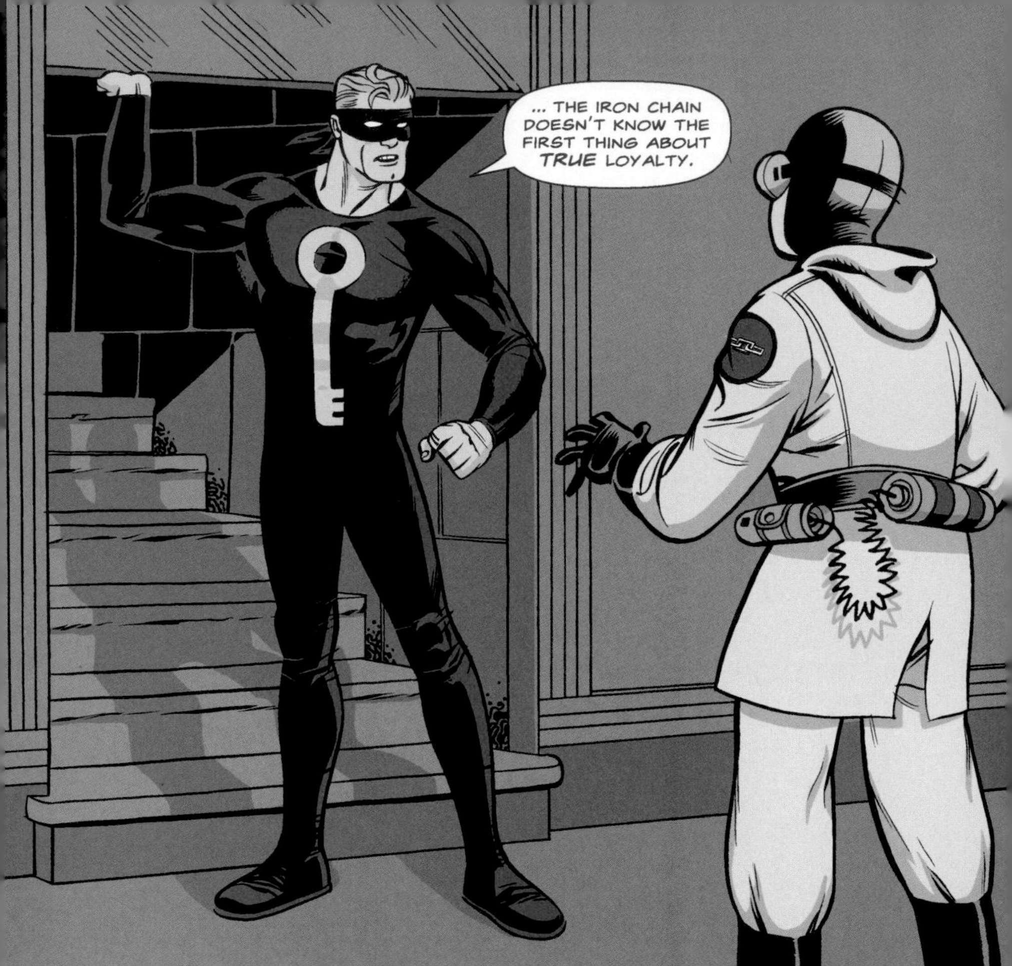
... THE IRON CHAIN DOESN'T KNOW THE FIRST THING ABOUT TRUE LOYALTY.

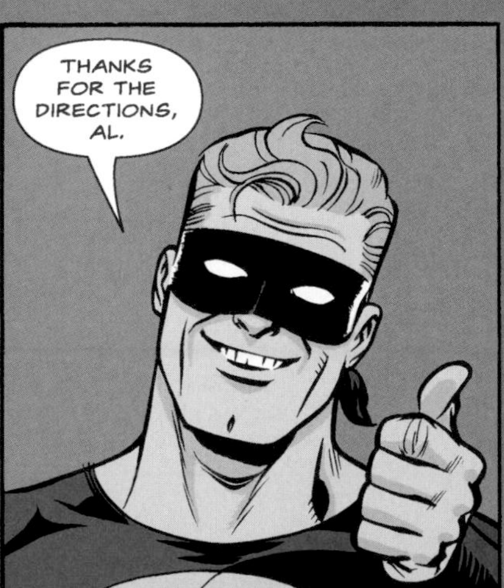
THANKS FOR THE DIRECTIONS, AL.

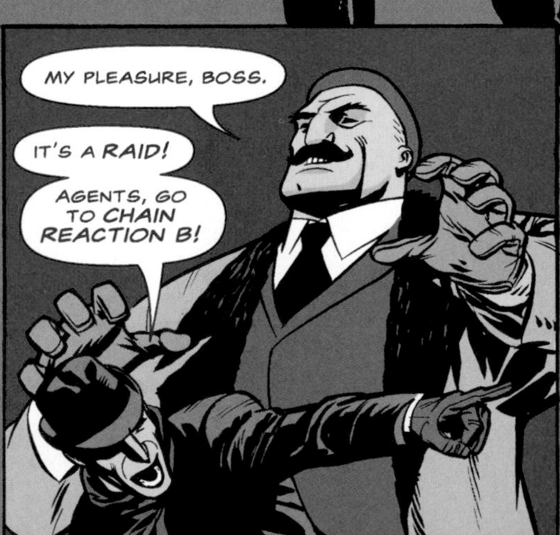
MY PLEASURE, BOSS.
IT'S A RAID!
AGENTS, GO TO CHAIN REACTION B!

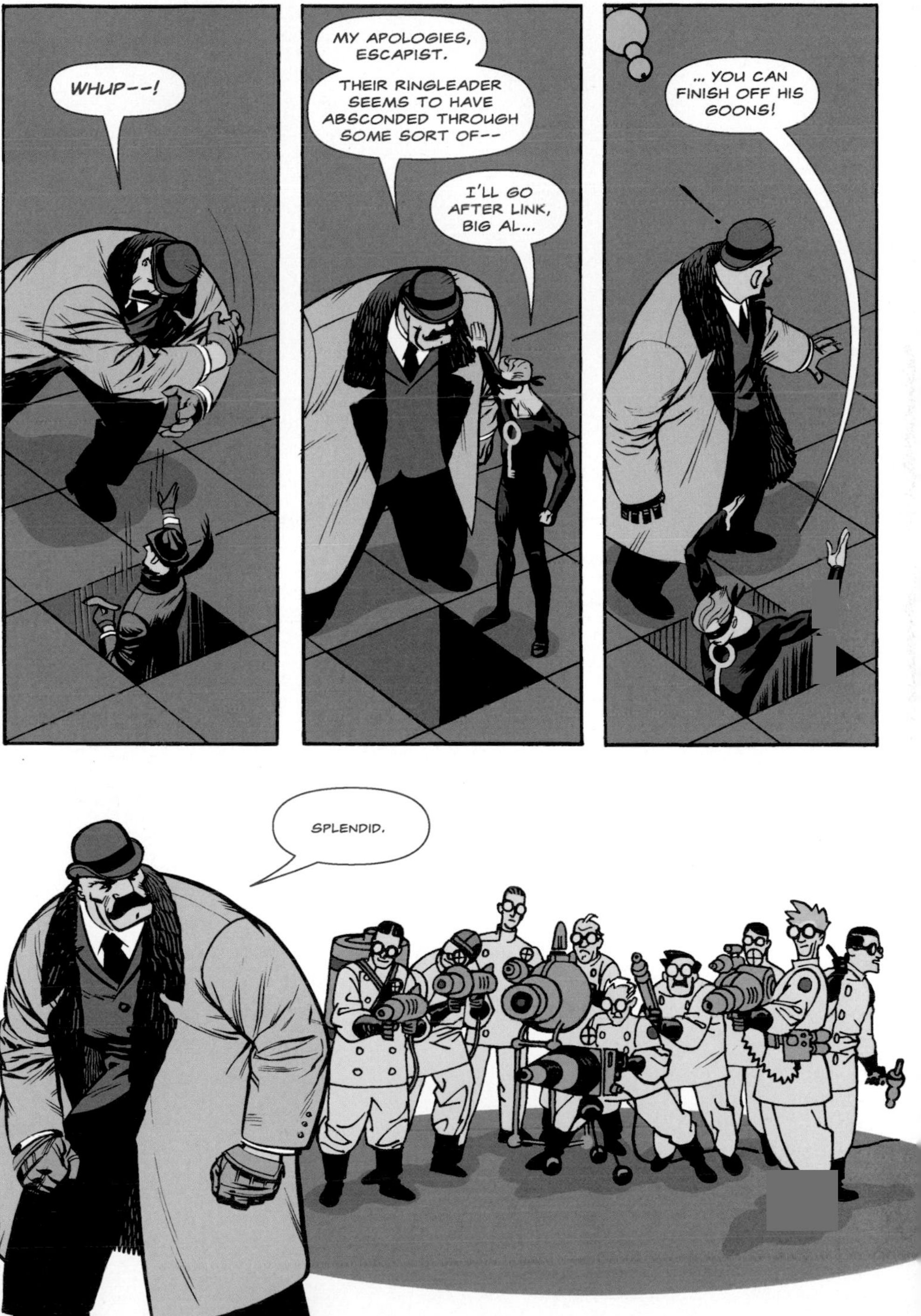
WHUP--!
MY APOLOGIES, ESCAPIST.
THEIR RINGLEADER SEEMS TO HAVE ABSCONDED THROUGH SOME SORT OF--
I'LL GO AFTER LINK, BIG AL...
... YOU CAN FINISH OFF HIS GOONS!
SPLENDID.

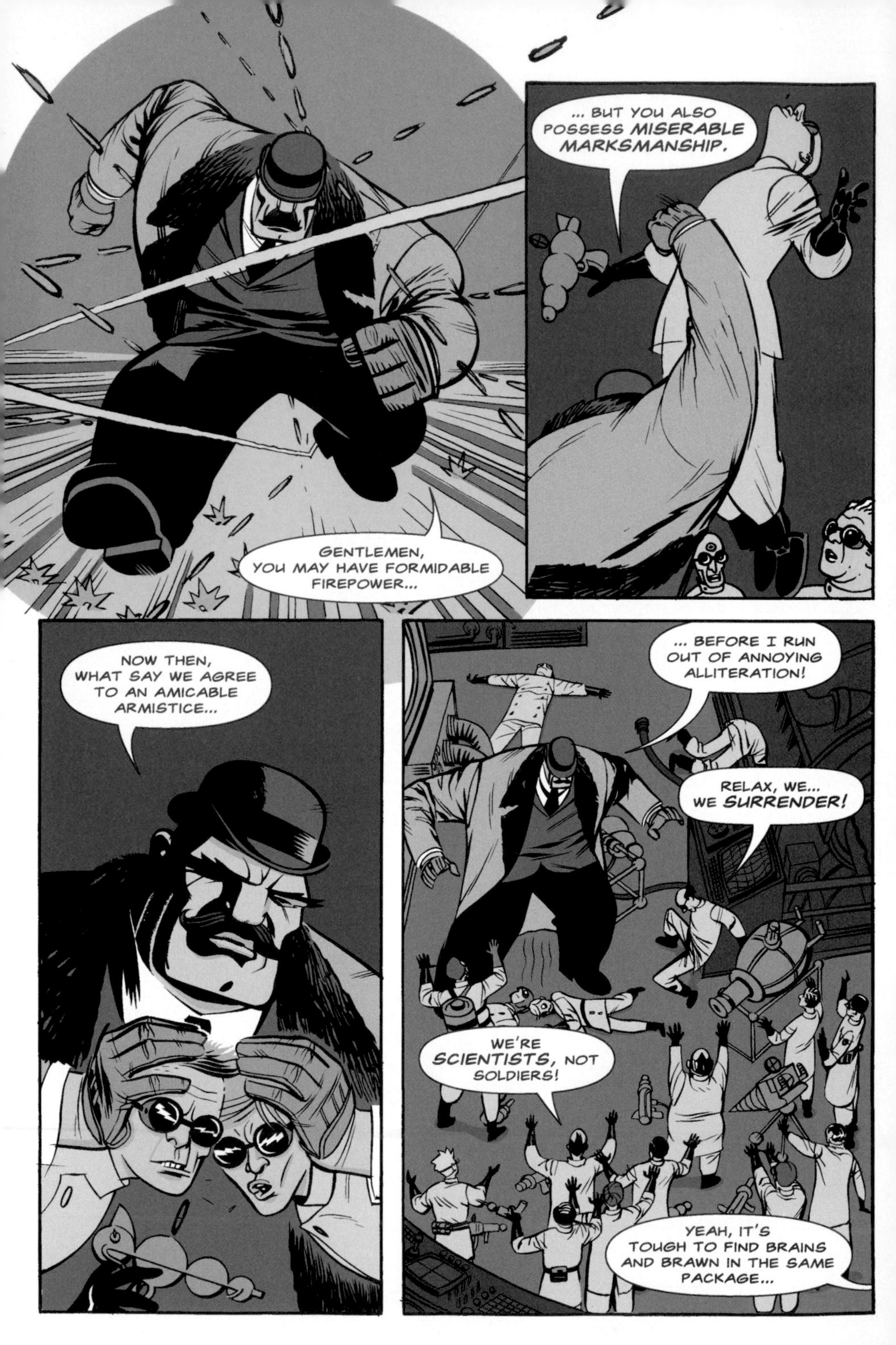
GENTLEMEN, YOU MAY HAVE FORMIDABLE FIREPOWER...
... BUT YOU ALSO POSSESS MISERABLE MARKSMANSHIP.
NOW THEN, WHAT SAY WE AGREE TO AN AMICABLE ARMISTICE...
... BEFORE I RUN OUT OF ANNOYING ALLITERATION!
RELAX, WE... WE SURRENDER!
WE'RE SCIENTISTS, NOT SOLDIERS!
YEAH, IT'S TOUGH TO FIND BRAINS AND BRAWN IN THE SAME PACKAGE...

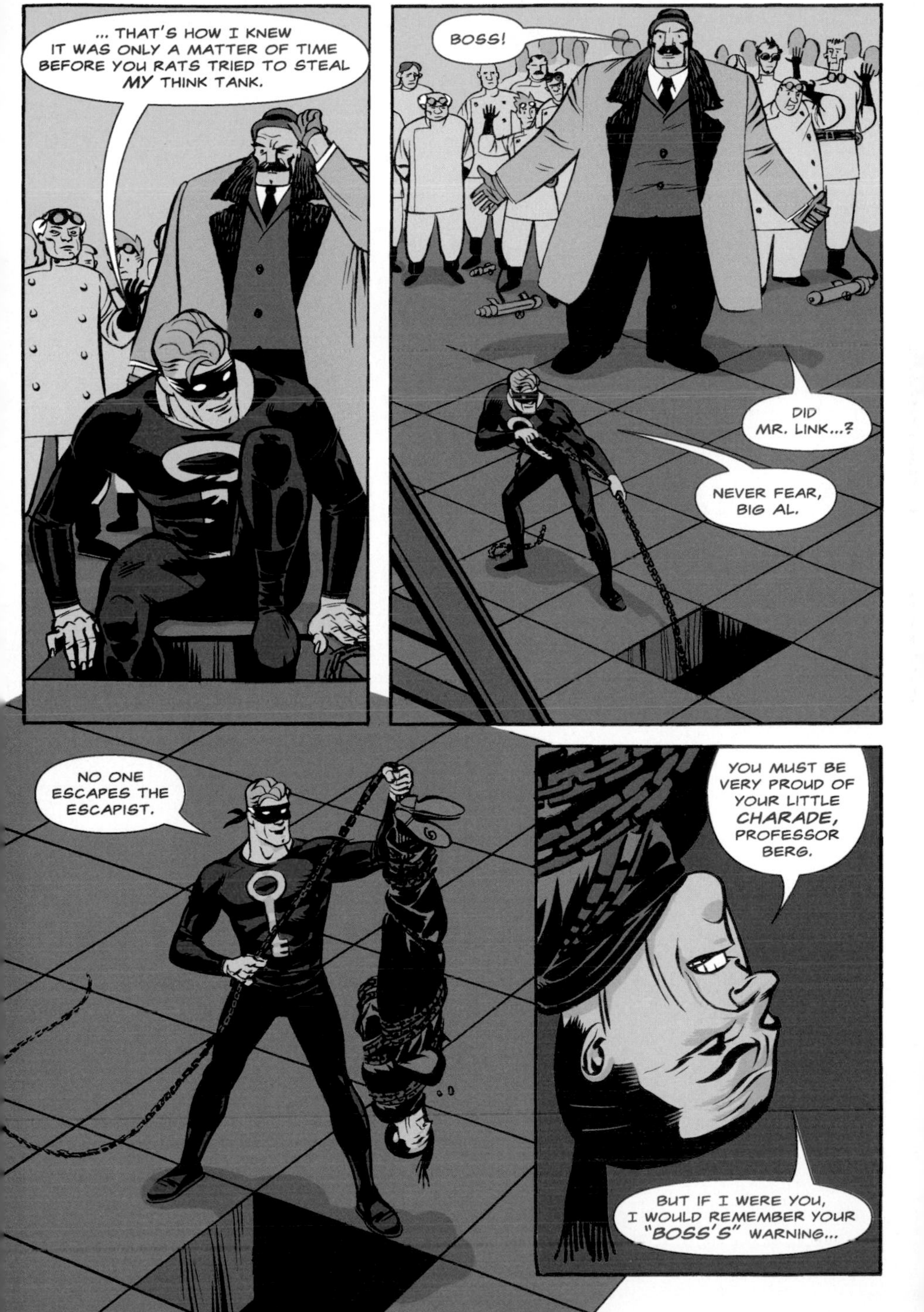
... THAT'S HOW I KNEW IT WAS ONLY A MATTER OF TIME BEFORE YOU RATS TRIED TO STEAL MY THINK TANK.
BOSS!
DID MR. LINK...?
NEVER FEAR, BIG AL.
NO ONE ESCAPES THE ESCAPIST.
YOU MUST BE VERY PROUD OF YOUR LITTLE CHARADE, PROFESSOR BERG.
BUT IF I WERE YOU, I WOULD REMEMBER YOUR "BOSS'S" WARNING...

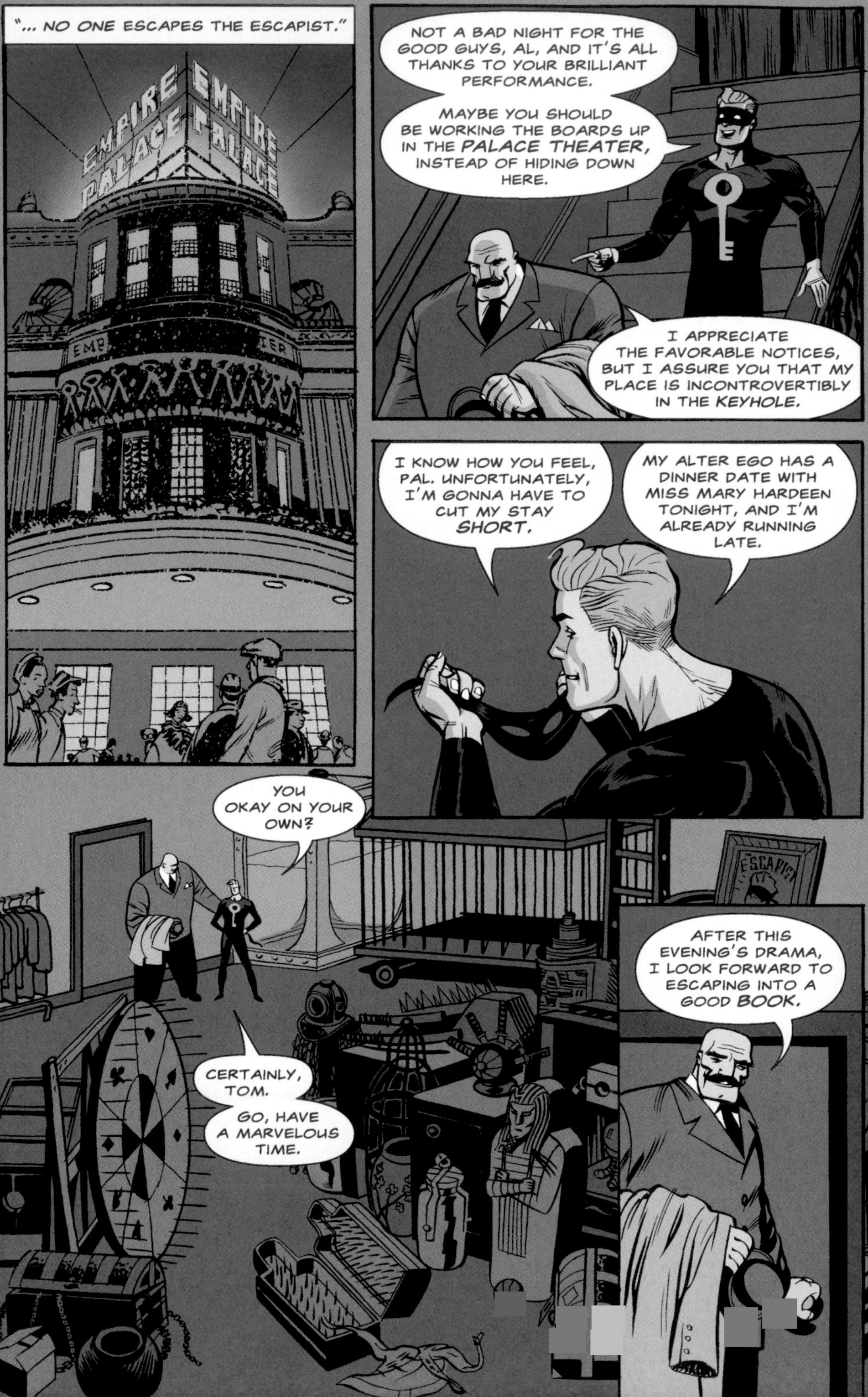
"... NO ONE ESCAPES THE ESCAPIST."
EMPIRE EMPIRE
PALACE PALACE
NOT A BAD NIGHT FOR THE GOOD GUYS, AL, AND IT'S ALL THANKS TO YOUR BRILLIANT PERFORMANCE.
MAYBE YOU SHOULD BE WORKING THE BOARDS UP IN THE *PALACE THEATER,* INSTEAD OF HIDING DOWN HERE.
I APPRECIATE THE FAVORABLE NOTICES, BUT I ASSURE YOU THAT MY PLACE IS INCONTROVERTIBLY IN THE *KEYHOLE.*
I KNOW HOW YOU FEEL, PAL. UNFORTUNATELY, I'M GONNA HAVE TO CUT MY STAY *SHORT.*
MY ALTER EGO HAS A DINNER DATE WITH MISS MARY HARDEEN TONIGHT, AND I'M ALREADY RUNNING LATE.
YOU OKAY ON YOUR OWN?
CERTAINLY, TOM.
GO, HAVE A MARVELOUS TIME.
ESCAPIST
AFTER THIS EVENING'S DRAMA, I LOOK FORWARD TO ESCAPING INTO A GOOD *BOOK.*

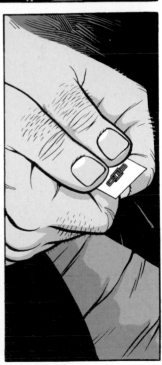

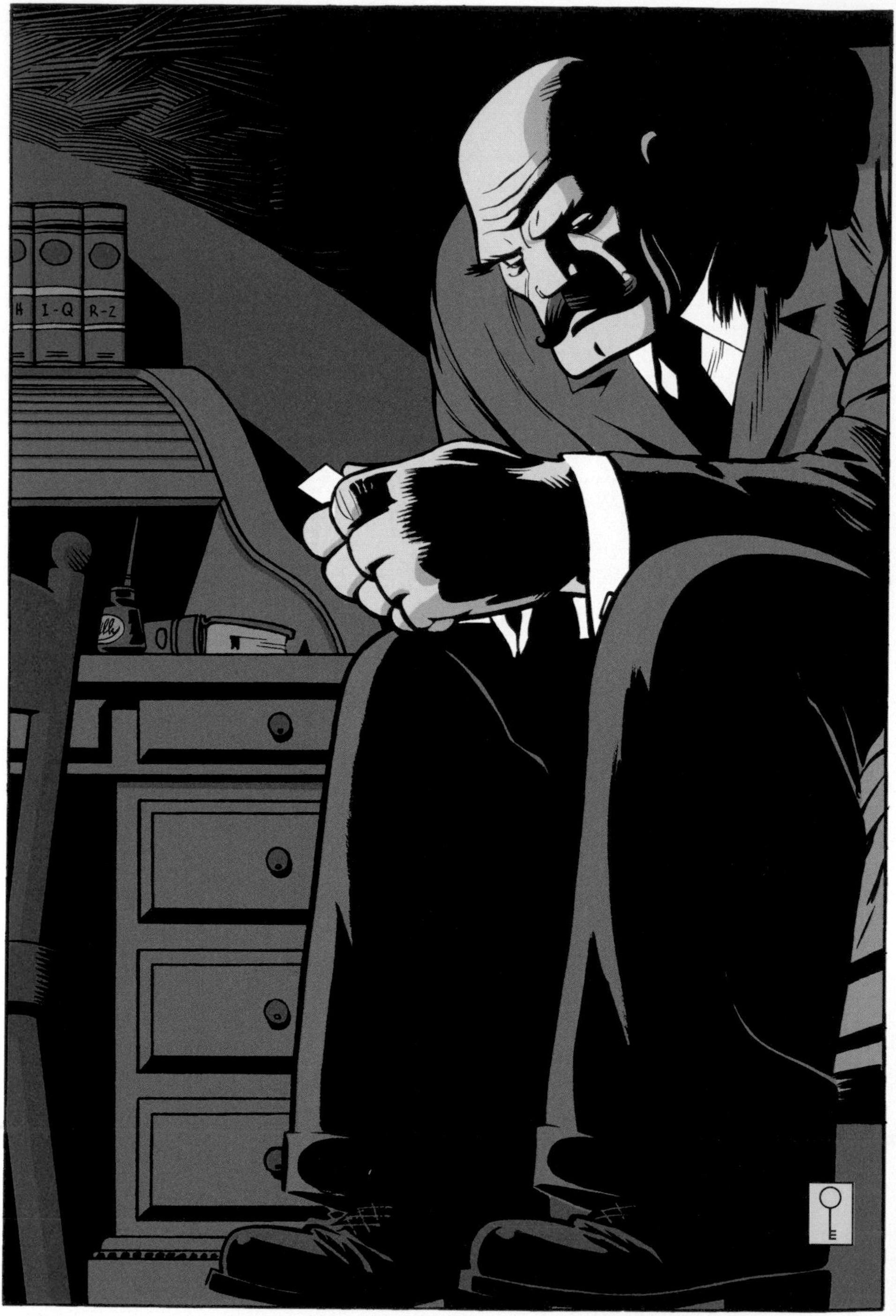
I-Q
R-Z

GALLERY

A Delectable Display of Daring Delineations
Fashioned with Flair & Flourish
by a Team of Titillating Talents

Jim Mahfood, with color by Jack Gray

Mike Mignola, with color by Dave Stewart

Farel Dalrymple

John Cassaday, with color by Nick Derington
and Dan Jackson

M.K. Perker

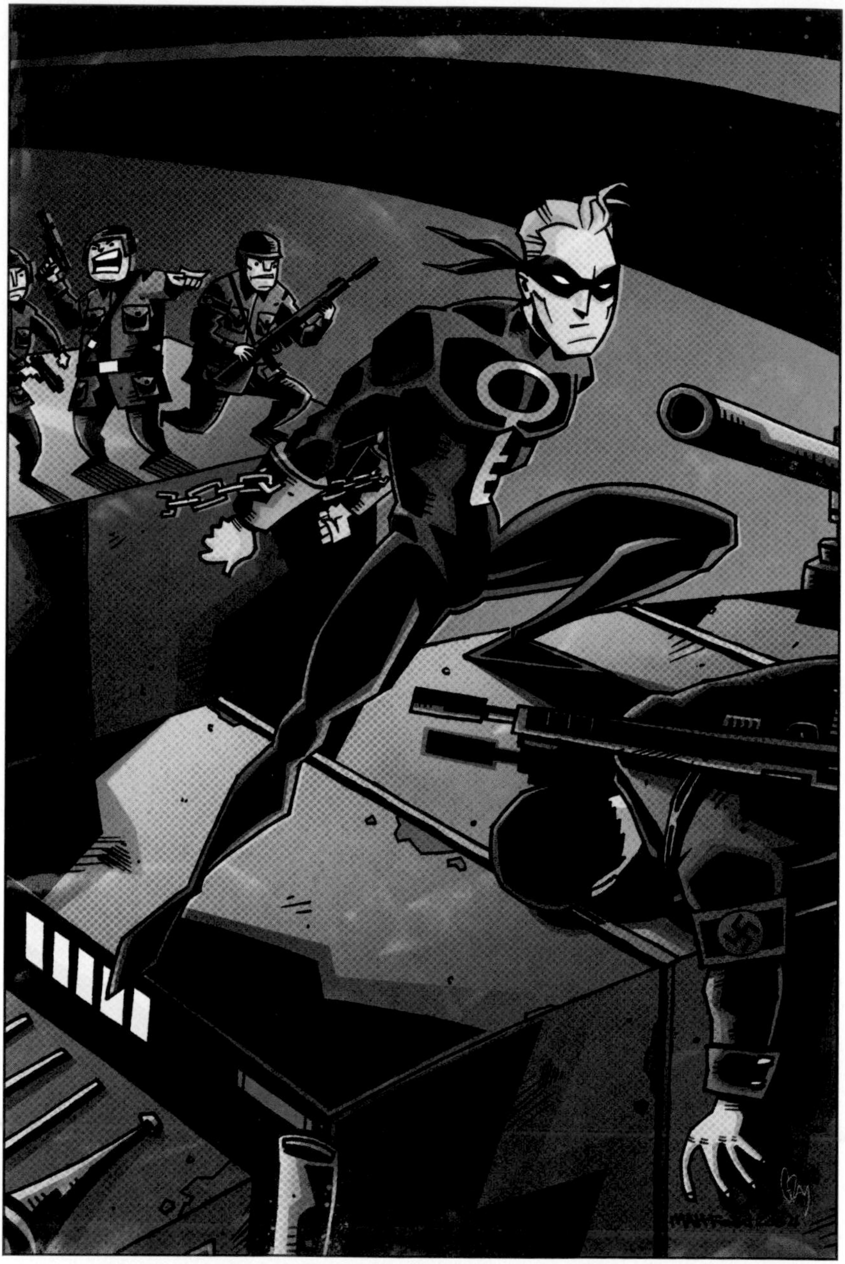

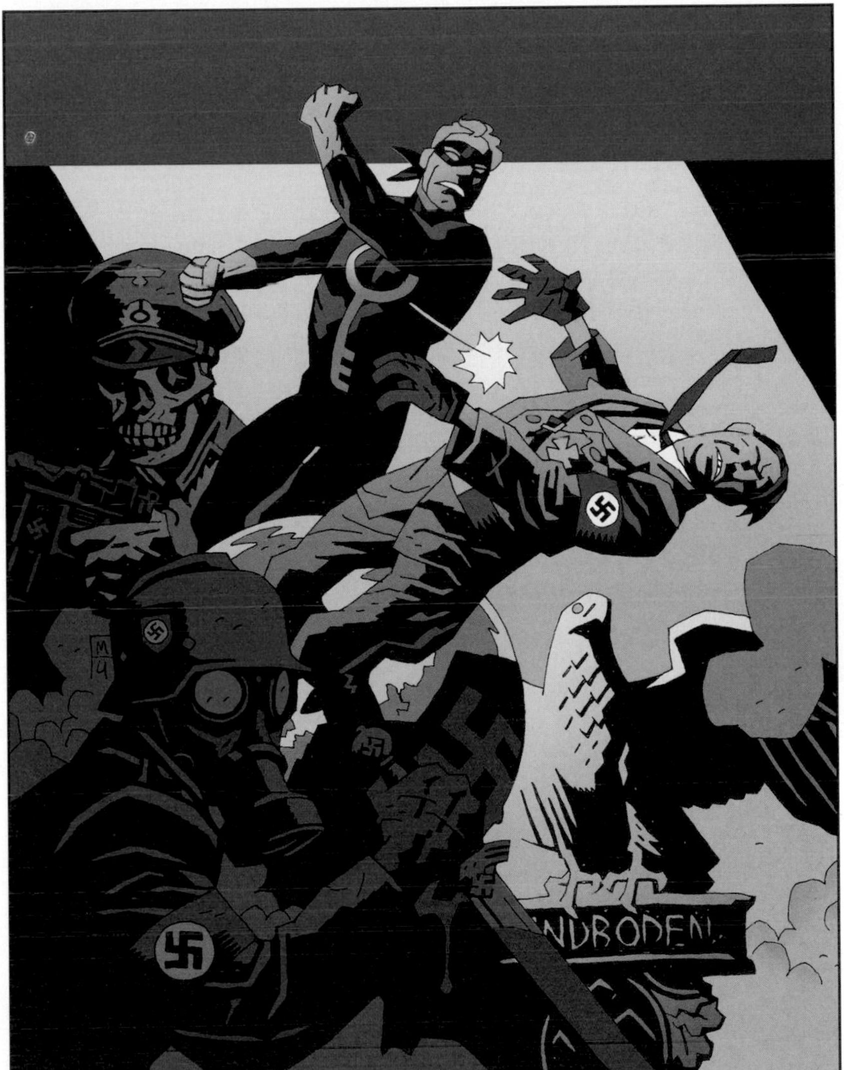
NDRODEN

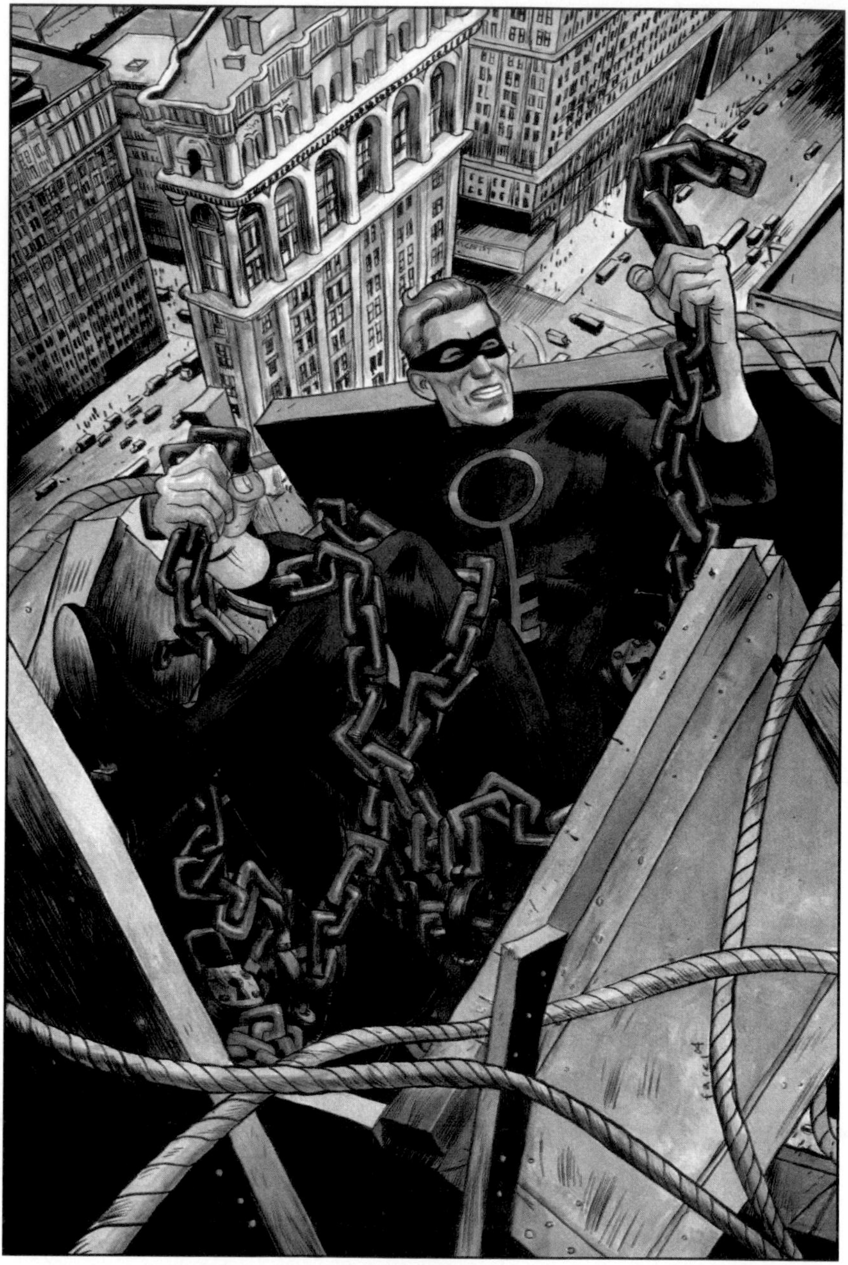

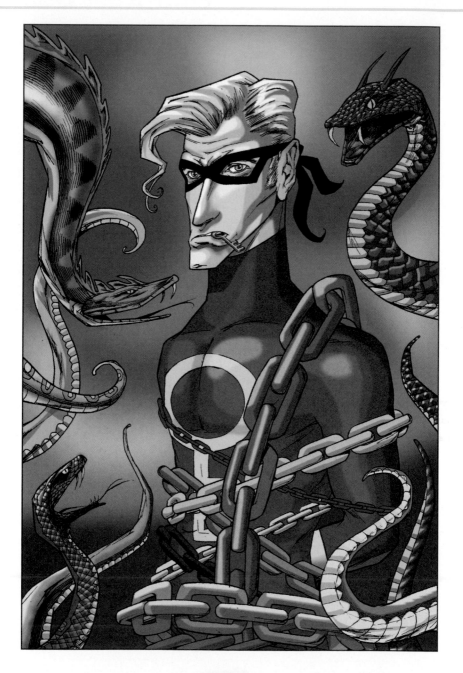

CREATOR BIOS

Eisner nominated and Eagle Award winner **STEVE CONLEY** is a cartoonist, self-publisher, and online pioneer. He has written and illustrated his online and printed comics series *Astounding Space Thrills* since 1998, and has run the award-winning design studio Conley Interactive since 1996. In addition to his co-creation <www.comicon.com>, Conley owns and manages such comics-related web sites as <www.iCOMICS.com>, <www.BLOOP.tv>, and The Pulse, a popular daily comics news site found at <www.comicon.com/pulse/>. He currently serves as Executive Director of SPX, the Small Press Expo.

Nominated for an Eisner Award for *Opposable Thumbs* and an Ignatz Award for *Aim to Dazzle*, **DEAN HASPIEL** is the author of super-psychedelic romances and semiautobiographical comics, and occasionally mangles franchise characters. A regular contributor to Harvey Pekar's *American Splendor*, his major credits include *Bizarro Comics*, *Batman Adventures*, *Justice League Adventures*, *Spider-Man's Tangled Web*, *The Thing: Night Falls on Yancy Street*, and *Captain America: Red, White, & Blue*. Haspiel can be found in Brooklyn or at <www.deanhaspiel.com>.

The Ignatz, Eisner, and Harvey Award nominated creator of *Forlorn Funnies*, **PAUL HORNSCHEMEIER** began working on comics while in college. In addition to *Mother, Come Home*, which collects the poignant *Forlorn Funnies* story arc, his most recently released work is *Return of the Elephant*, published by AdHouse Books. Hornschemeier presently lives in Chicago.

Co-creator of the critically celebrated series *Pistolwhip*, multiple Eisner and Harvey award nominee **MATT KINDT** is currently designing Alan Moore's long-awaited *Lost Girls*. He is also at work on short companion pieces to his latest creation, *2 Sisters: A Super-Spy Graphic Novel* from Top Shelf, in addition to a '60s-era science-fiction graphic novel. Kindt lives and works in Webster Groves, Missouri, with his wife and young daughter, and may be found at <www.supersecretspy.com>.

KEVIN McCARTHY began working as a comic book writer and artist in 1995 when he created *Casual Heroes*, which was subsequently published by Image under the Motown Animation imprint. Since then, he's written and/or drawn a few things here and there, including Marvel's *Spider-Man Team-Up*, DC's *Orion*, Top Cow's *Lara Croft: Tomb Raider*, and the creator-owned *ALIEN8* for Disney. He lives in St. Paul, Minnesota.

STUART MOORE has been a writer, a book editor, a kitchen worker, and an award-winning comics editor. His writing work includes *LONE* from Dark Horse, *Justice League Adventures* from DC, *PARA* from Penny-Farthing Press, stories for *Vampirella* and *Métal Hurlant*, projects with AiT/PlanetLar and Avatar, and an upcoming SciFi Channel original film. He lives in Brooklyn, New York, with his wife and two cats — the furry, non-robotic kind.

CREATOR BIOS

When not creating such comics as the Eisner and Ignatz Award nominated *Soulwind,* California native **SCOTT MORSE** dabbles in a variety of animation roles, currently art directing for Nickelodeon. His graphic novels include *Ancient Joe, Spaghetti Western, Southpaw, Visitations,* and *The Barefoot Serpent.*

The grandson of EC Comics great George Evans, baseball fan **ROGER PETERSEN** maintains that quiet understatement is coming back to comics, quietly. Raised on *Tintin, Johnny Hazard,* and Bob Hope movies, he has worked in advertising and illustration for all kinds of clients. In addition to the Escapist story in this issue, Petersen has drawn covers and cards for Marvel, *Swamp Thing* for DC, and *Predator: Kindred* and *SubHuman* for Dark Horse.

R. SIKORYAK is known for retelling classic literature through parodies of time-honored comic book styles, in *Drawn & Quarterly* and *RAW* magazine. In addition to his book, *The Seduction of Mike,* Sikoryak's illustrations have appeared in such publications as *The New Yorker, Nickelodeon Magazine, Esquire, Wired, TV Guide, Entertainment Weekly,* and the anthologies *Little Lit: It Was a Dark and Silly Night, Legal Action Comics, Rosetta 2,* and *SPX.* In his spare time, he assembles and hosts *Carousel:* a series of wildly eclectic comics slide shows for off-off-Broadway.

Eisner Award winner **JOE STATON** has been drawing comics and living in New York for over thirty years. The Tennessee native started working for Charlton Comics in 1971, creating *E-Man* and *Michael Mauser* with Nicola Cuti. Though the bulk of his work has been for DC, at last count Staton has worked for 30 publishers and 90 different editors. Among his profuse comics credits are *Action Comics, Green Lantern, The Legion, Scooby Doo, Classics Illustrated,* and various incarnations of *Batman.*

Harvey Award nominated writer **BRIAN K. VAUGHAN** is best known for penning the runaway hit *Y: The Last Man.* With professional credits including *Runaways, The Hood,* and the new superhero political thriller *Ex Machina,* Vaughan has also grappled with such characters as Batman, Spider-Man, and most recently, the X-Men. A former magician and president of his high school's "Circus Club," Brian used to perform a straitjacket routine that would make the Escapist cringe.

A former editor in chief at Marvel and senior editor at DC, award-winning scribe **MARV WOLFMAN** has written hundreds of comics since the early '70s. Possibly best known for creating the vampire-hunting character Blade, the New Teen Titans, and *Crisis on Infinite Earths,* he also composed scores of scripts for some of the most popular television cartoons of the '80s and '90s. His current projects include writing for the popular *Teen Titans* animated series, various comics, and a novel based on one of his more popular comics. Wolfman presently lives in Tarzana, California.